D1706783

THE TRANSFORMATION OF THE CLASSICAL HERITAGE

Peter Brown, General Editor

SYMEON THE HOLY FOOL

DEREK KRUEGER

SYMEON THE HOLY FOOL

Leontius's Life *and the Late Antique City*

UNIVERSITY OF CALIFORNIA PRESS

Berkeley • Los Angeles • London

University of California Press
Berkeley and Los Angeles, California

University of California Press, Ltd.
London, England

© 1996 by the Regents of the University of California

Parts of this book were published in earlier versions.
Chapter 5: "Diogenes the Cynic among the Fourth Century Fathers," *Vigiliae Christianae* 47
(1993). Reprinted by permission of E. J. Brill, Leiden, Netherlands.
Chapter 6: "The *Life of Symeon the Fool* and the Cynic Tradition," *Journal of Early Christian
Studies* 1 (1993). Reprinted by permission of Johns Hopkins University Press.

Library of Congress Cataloging-in-Publication Data

Krueger, Derek.
    Symeon the holy fool : Leontius's Life and the late antique city / Derek Krueger.
        p.   cm. — (Transformation of the classical heritage ; 25)
    Includes English translation of the Life.
    Includes bibliographical references and index.
    ISBN 0-520-08911-1 (alk. paper)
    1. Leontius, Bishop of Neapolis, 7th century.   Vita S. Symeonis Sali.   2. Simeon Salus,
Saint, ca. 522–ca. 588.   3. Christian hagiography.   4. Holy fools—Biography—History
and criticism.   5. Cyprus—History—Sources.   I. Leontius, Bishop of Neapolis, 7th century.   Vita S. Symeonis Sali.   English.   II. Title.   III. Series.
BR1720.S518K78   1996
270.2′092—dc20
[B]   94-41651
                                                                                                   CIP

Printed in the United States of America
9 8 7 6 5 4 3 2 1

The Cynic's habit was the same as a monk's and with the same virtue.

Diderot, *Rameau's Nephew*

CONTENTS

ACKNOWLEDGMENTS

I wish to express my appreciation for those friends, colleagues, and institutions which gave me assistance and support during the course of this project, only some of whom I cite here by name. My work on the *Life of Symeon the Fool* began as a doctoral dissertation in the Religions of Late Antiquity at Princeton University, directed by John Gager and Peter Brown, with sustained input from Martha Himmelfarb. I thank the three of them for fostering my scholarship with their particular talents as teachers, interlocutors, and friends. In a later stage of the project Peter again lent assistance in his role as series editor for the University of California Press.

The revision of the manuscript involved much reworking and rethinking. I am especially grateful to Georgia Frank, who read my draft chapter by chapter through the summer of 1993, ever patient both with me and with Priority Mail. Her careful combing of the manuscript and inspired suggestions for improvement have made this a much better book. A number of other colleagues read the entire manuscript at some point and made suggestions for its improvement, including Kathleen McVey, Susan Harvey, Robert Wilken, Robert Doran, and Vincent Déroche. These scholars spared me many errors of fact and helped me to hone my argument. Many of their suggestions I followed; others, for reasons of my own, I did not.

At key stages in the development of my work I had valuable conversations with and received helpful advice from Susan Harvey, Evelyne Patlagean, Claudia Rapp, Judith Herrin, Leslie MacCoull, Alexander Kazhdan, Eric Perl, Nancy Ševčenko, Susanna Elm, and fellow Cyprus enthusiast Annemarie Weyl Carr. Nick Trakakis kindly shared his translation of a section of the *Life of Symeon.*

I am indebted to Elizabeth Clark for her commitment to fostering the work of younger scholars and for her friendship and hospitality in the North Carolina Piedmont and to Henry Levinson, Head of the Religious Studies Department at the University of North Carolina at Greensboro, for his vision of the humanities and his sense of humor about the tensions inherent in the designation "teacher-scholar." Further afield I thank the Cyprus American Archaeological Research Institute (CAARI) in Nicosia and its director, Stuart Swiny, for hospitality and travel tips during my visit to Cyprus in the spring of 1993.

I also wish to thank my student Jeff Richey, who assisted diligently in the preparation of the manuscript, and Mary Lamprech, Rebecca Bauer, Tony Hicks, and Alice Falk of the University of California Press, who have offered expert guidance in readying this book for publication. Howard Rhodes produced the index.

I acknowledge financial support provided for my research and writing by a Junior Fellowship in Byzantine Studies at Dumbarton Oaks in 1990–91 and Summer Excellence Research Grants from the University of North Carolina at Greensboro in 1992 and 1994.

Finally I thank Gene Rogers, who contributed to this project in many ways, for his support, patience, and companionship.

ABBREVIATIONS

AB	*Analecta Bollandiana*
ACW	Ancient Christian Writers
ANF	Ante-Nicene Fathers
BZ	*Byzantinische Zeitschrift*
CSCO	Corpus Scriptorum Christianorum Orientalium
DOP	*Dumbarton Oaks Papers*
DS	*Dictionnaire de Spiritualité*
FOTC	Fathers of the Church
HTR	*Harvard Theological Review*
JAC	*Jahrbuch für Antike und Christentum*
JBL	*Journal of Biblical Literature*
JECS	*Journal of Early Christian Studies*
JÖB	*Jahrbuch der österreichischen Byzantinistik*
JRS	*Journal of Roman Studies*
JSJ	*Journal for the Study of Judaism*
JThS	*Journal of Theological Studies*
Lampe	*A Patristic Greek Lexicon,* edited by G. W. H. Lampe (Oxford: Oxford University Press, 1961)
LCL	Loeb Classical Library
LSJ	*A Greek-English Lexicon,* compiled by Henry George Liddell and Robert Scott, revised and augmented throughout by

	Sir Henry Stuart Jones, 9th ed., with supplement (Oxford: Oxford University Press, 1968)
NovTest	*Novum Testamentum*
NPNF	Nicene and Post-Nicene Fathers
NTSt	*New Testament Studies*
PG	*Patrologia Graeca*, ed. J. P. Migne
PL	*Patrologia Latina*, ed. J. P. Migne
PO	*Patrologia Orientalis*
RE	*Realencyclopädie der classischen Altertumswissenschaft*, ed. A. Pauly and G. Wissowa (Stuttgart, 1894–)
REB	*Revue des études byzantines*
RevThPh	*Revue de Théologie et de Philosophie*
SC	Sources chrétiennes
VC	*Vigiliae Christianae*
ZNTW	*Zeitschrift für die neutestamentliche Wissenschaft*

Titles of classical works follow abbreviations suggested by LSJ or Lampe, with occasional modification.

• ONE •

LEONTIUS OF NEAPOLIS AND
SEVENTH-CENTURY CYPRUS

Of the hagiographical writings which survive from Late Antiquity, perhaps none has more potential to amuse and scandalize the reader, ancient or modern, than the *Life and Conduct of Abba Symeon Called the Fool for the Sake of Christ*, written by Leontius, the bishop of Neapolis on Cyprus (modern Limassol) near the middle of the seventh century.[1] Pretending to be insane, Symeon the monk walks about naked, eats enormous quantities of beans, and defecates in the streets. Although Leontius was not the first to relate a tale of a Christian saint who pretended to be crazy, the *Life of Symeon* is the first full-length *vita* of a holy fool.

1. Bollandist Hippolyte Delehaye described the work as "une des plus curieuses productions de l'hagiographie ancienne"; "Saints de Chypre," *AB* 26 (1907): 246. A modern edition of the Greek text of the *Life of Symeon* was published by Lennart Rydén in 1963; he followed this edition with a commentary in 1970. A slightly revised version of Rydén's text was published with a French translation and commentary by A. J. Festugière in 1974, although it was available only in 1977. Leontius of Neapolis, *Das Leben des heiligen Narren Symeon von Leontios von Neapolis*, ed. Lennart Rydén (Uppsala: Almquist and Wiksell, 1963); Lennart Rydén, *Bemerkungen zum Leben des heiligen Narren Symeon von Leontios von Neapolis* (Uppsala: Almquist and Wiksell, 1970); *Vie de Syméon le Fou et Vie de Jean de Chypre*, trans. and commentary by A. J. Festugière (Greek text edited by Lennart Rydén) (Paris: Geuthner, 1974), pp. 1–222. A partial German translation appears in Hans Lietzmann, *Byzantinische Legenden* (Jena: Diederichs, 1911). For translations into other modern languages, see bibliography. The first edition of the text edited by Joannes Pinius appears in the *Acta Sanctorum* for the month of July, vol. 1 (Antwerp, 1719), cols. 136–69 (3rd ed., cols. 120–51). Pinius's text was reprinted by Migne, PG 93.1669–748.

Modern scholars considering the Christian saints of the Late Ancient world tend to think of holy people set apart from the rest of humanity by their outstanding virtue, mortifying their flesh in a constant fight against passion and desire. Paradigmatic cases include the legendary ascetic Antony, progressing ever farther into the Egyptian deserts to do battle with the demons, and the Syrian Symeon the Stylite, standing day and night upon a pillar, mediating between God above and humanity below. These figures, together with many other Late Antique saints, embody virtues highly valued in early Christian society. Showing the faithful how they too might achieve holiness, the narration of their extraordinary lives maps a journey away from quotidian cares toward communion with the divine. At the same time, the pursuit of the life of abstinence, of with-drawal from society—*anachōrēsis*—to live as a hermit in the desert, a solitary on the fringes of society, was not an option for most Late Ancient Christians. Thus, when most of the laity heard of saints, their life was not one to be pursued. Rather hagiography encapsulated the values of society as a whole, clarifying what was important, instructing implicitly how one was to live an ordinary life.

But suppose a saint was not an exemplar, was not a model to be emu-lated? Reading the lives of Late Ancient saints, we occasionally come across those who challenge our sometimes sanctimonious notions of early Christian piety. That such figures as holy fools were held in high regard by clergy and laity leaves us puzzled. These saints are clearly deviants—out-side the structures of society, and more importantly, outside the conven-tions for fleeing that society.

Reading such works as the *Life of Symeon the Fool* one wonders whether some Late Ancient Christians sanctified deviance. But why? Moreover, an unmistakable feature of these tales of holy fools is the comedy. Is it possi-ble that early Christians had a sense of humor? And to what use did they put this humor? These stories surely challenge our unexamined concep-tion of Late Ancient Christians as a dour lot.

Ironically the legacy of Leontius's holy fool has received more atten-tion than the *Life* itself. For the most part, scholars have seen the signifi-cance of the *Life of Symeon the Fool* in retrospect; its value for understand-ing Orthodox piety is established by what came later. The *Life of Symeon the Fool* has received attention in studies of holy folly in the Greek Ortho-dox, and especially the Russian Orthodox traditions, as well as in Western traditions.[2] The holy fool tradition can be traced from Symeon to the pa-

2. See for example Ernst Benz, "Heilige Narrheit," *Kyrios* 3 (1938): 1–55; Peter Haupt-mann, "Die 'Narren um Christi Willen' in der Ostkirche," *Kirche im Osten* 2 (1959): 27–49, with extensive bibliography p. 27 n. 1; George P. Fedotov, *The Russian Religious Mind II: The*

tron of St. Basil's Cathedral in Red Square in Moscow and in literary form to the protagonist of Dostoevsky's *The Idiot*.[3] In the West an interest in holy folly can be seen to thrive among the French Jesuits of the seventeenth century.[4]

Leontius, of course, did not intend to initiate such a trajectory; his work only became part of a "tradition" about three hundred years later when, sometime in the tenth century, the second author of a full-length fool's *vita* decided to make extensive use of Leontius's work in composing the *Life of Andrew the Fool*.[5] In fact, it was the *Life of Andrew*, not the *Life of Symeon*, which would be so important for Russian culture. Thus, those elements of the *Life of Symeon the Fool* which are found to have analogues in later sources have received attention while aspects of the work which do not have an afterlife in later Byzantine and Russian sources have been largely ignored. This study corrects this imbalance, seeing the *Life of Symeon the Fool* not as the beginning of a long, later tradition, but as the product of a Late Antique world, understanding the traditions on which it draws, and interpreting its relationship to texts which had come before.

At the same time, I have not undertaken an exhaustive study of the *Life*. I have chosen instead to highlight the more distinctive aspects of the *Life of Symeon*, emphasizing Symeon's shamelessness, and therefore focus-

---

Middle Ages, the 13th to 15th Centuries, ed. with a foreword by John Meyendorff (Belmont, Mass.: Nordland, 1975), pp. 316–43 (the chapter is entitled "The Holy Fools"); Natalie Challis and Horace W. Dewey, "Byzantine Models for Russia's Literature of Divine Folly (*Jurodstvo*)," *Papers in Slavic Philology in Honor of James Ferrell*, vol. 1, ed. Benjamin Stolz (Ann Arbor: University of Michigan, Department of Slavic Languages and Literatures, 1977), pp. 36–48; Irina Goraïnoff, *Les fols en Christ dans la tradition orthodoxe* ([Paris]: Desclée de Brouwer, 1983), with a good bibliography; Rydén, "The Holy Fool," in *The Byzantine Saint*, ed. Sergei Hackel (San Bernardino, Calif.: Borgo, 1983), pp. 106–13; Ewa Thompson, *Understanding Russia: The Holy Fool in Russian Culture* (Lanham, Md.: University Press of America, 1987). On Western traditions see John Saward's very readable *Perfect Fools: Folly for Christ's Sake in Catholic and Orthodox Spirituality* (Oxford: Oxford University Press, 1980).

    3. Thompson, *Understanding Russia*, pp. ix–x.

    4. Saward, *Perfect Fools*, pp. 104–84.

    5. The dating of the *Life of Andrew the Fool* is a typically vexed problem in the study of Byzantine hagiography. John Wortley ("The Political Significance of the Andreas-Salos Apocalypse," *Byzantion* 43 [1973]: 248–63) dates the work to the late ninth or early tenth century. Cyril Mango ("The Life of Saint Andrew the Fool Reconsidered," *Rivista di studi bizantini e slavi* 2 [1982]: 297–313) has argued for a late-seventh-century date of composition, which most other scholars have regarded as unlikely (but see most recently John F. Haldon, *Byzantium in the Seventh Century* [Cambridge: Cambridge University Press, 1990], pp. xxii, 116, 336 n. 33). Rydén ("The Date of the *Life of Andreas Salos*," *DOP* 32 [1978]: 127–56) dates the work to the 950s. His new edition, nearing publication, will no doubt attempt to settle the issue. On the literary relationship between the *Life of Symeon* and the *Life of Andrew* see José Grosdidier de Matons, "Les Thèmes d'édification dans la Vie d'André Salos," *Travaux et mémoires* 4 (1970): 277–329.

ing on the second half of the *Life,* in which Symeon behaves as a fool, rather than on the first half of the *Life,* which presents a more conventional portrait of Symeon's ascetic preparations. Moreover, I have chosen to emphasize the literary and intellectual aspects of the *Life.* In recent years, much scholarship has been produced on ascetic traditions and practice, while little attention has been paid to the literary models which shaped these traditions.

The approach of this study depends on the idea that the meaning of a particular literary text depends on its context, on its situation in time and space. For this reason I have chosen to flesh out a broad picture of the religious, intellectual, and social environment in which a single work was created. Since the focus of this investigation is Leontius of Neapolis's *Life of Symeon the Fool,* a text which we know to have been composed at the end of Late Antiquity on the island of Cyprus, this chapter presents a portrait of Leontius's Cyprus. The next chapter will take up a number of problems posed by the text, especially the question of which, if any, sources Leontius might have used in his composition of the *Life of Symeon.* I will suggest that Leontius's text is loosely based on a brief description of a certain Symeon of Emesa in Evagrius Scholasticus's *Ecclesiastical History,* but that the *Life of Symeon* should be treated as the work of Leontius. Chapters 3 and 4 consider literature with similar themes written before the *Life* in order to gain a sense of Leontius's literary environment. The study would be incomplete unless it takes into account its non-Christian precursors. While Leontius's text can be seen to have precursors in Christian hagiography, it also betrays a strong debt to traditions about Diogenes the Cynic philosopher; chapter 5 therefore traces the reception of traditions about Cynicism in Late Antique Christianity. Chapters 6 and 7 return to the *Life of Symeon* to establish Leontius's allusion to Cynicism and his use of biblical types in order to assess their significance for a reading of the text. The appendix to this volume contains the first English translation of Leontius's *Life of Symeon the Fool.*

The *Life of Symeon* and Seventh-century Cyprus

Scholars have reasonably assumed that the *Life of Symeon* was written after Leontius's other extant hagiographical work, the *Life of John the Almsgiver,* which can be dated with some certainty to 641/2.[6] Moreover, noth-

6. In the *Life of John* 5, Leontius mentions the death of Heraclius (which occurred either in April or May 641). Therefore the text must have been composed after this date. Two scholia published by Festugière in his apparatus to the *Life of John* (*Vie de Syméon le Fou et Vie de Jean de Chypre,* pp. 2–3, 411 *ad* 71 and 88) establish that the work was commissioned by Ar-

ing in the *Life of Symeon* betrays knowledge of Muʿawiya's devastating attack on Cyprus in 649 or its effects. On the contrary, Leontius's relatively sanguine portrayal of urban life assumes prosperity, not crisis. Therefore we can date the *Life of Symeon* to the period between 642 and 649.[7]

The fact of the Cypriot provenance of the text in itself justifies a consideration of the world in which it was produced. While the evidence for life on Cyprus in the first half of the seventh century is admittedly limited, the portrait which emerges is of an environment of relative prosperity, cultural diversity, and religious conflict. Despite Leontius's explanation in the prologue of his *Life of John the Almsgiver* that he has written in a "prosaic, unadorned, and humble style so that even the unlearned and illiterate will be able to take profit from these words," both the *Life of John* and the *Life of Symeon* betray Leontius's rhetorical training.[8] Chapter 6 will show that in the *Life of Symeon*, Leontius makes sustained allusion to anecdotes about Diogenes of Sinope, a figure prominent in the school exercises

---

cadius, archbishop of Constantia, who died in the second half of 641 or early in 642. See Mango, "A Byzantine Hagiographer at Work: Leontios of Neapolis," in *Byzanz und der Westen: Studien zur Kunst des europäischen Mittelalters*, ed. Irmgard Hutter (Vienna: Österreichischen Akademie der Wissenschaften, 1984), p. 33. The *Life of Symeon* can be assumed to postdate the *Life of John* since in the introduction to the *Life of John*, Leontius refers to an earlier work, a *Life of Spyridon* (now lost) as if it was his only earlier saint's life. Leontius of Neapolis, *Leben des heiligen Iohannes des Barmherzigen* (Freiburg: Mohr, 1893), ed. H. Gelzer, p. xiii. Cf. Rydén, *Das Leben des heiligen Narren Symeon*, p. 25; Mango, "A Byzantine Hagiographer," p. 29. (The *Life of Spyridon* edited by P. van den Ven [*La légende de S. Spyridon, évêque de Trimithonte* (Louvain: Publications universitaires, 1953), pp. 104–28] is not to be identified with the work by Leontius.)

7. Cf. Gelzer, "Ein griechischer Volksschriftsteller des 7. Jahrhunderts," in *Ausgewählte kleine Schriften* (Leipzig: Teubner, 1907), p. 2. On the conquest of Cyprus, see A. I. Dikigoropoulos, "The Political Status of Cyprus A.D. 648–965," in *Report of the Department of Antiquities, Cyprus, 1940–1948* (Nicosia: Government Printing Office, 1958), pp. 94–114; Andreas N. Stratos, *Byzantium in the Seventh Century*, vol. 3 (642–668), trans. Harry T. Hionides (Amsterdam: Hakkert, 1968–80), p. 39; Robert Browning, "Byzantium and Islam in Cyprus in the Early Middle Ages," *Epeteris tou Kentrou Epistemonikon Spoudon* 9 (1977/79): 101–16; Walter Kaegi, "The Disputed Muslim Negotiations with Cyprus in 649," *Fourteenth Annual Byzantine Studies Conference (1988): Abstracts of Papers* (Houston: Byzantine Studies Conference, 1988), pp. 5–6, and *Byzantium and the Early Islamic Conquests* (Cambridge: Cambridge University Press, 1992), pp. 253–54. The publication of two inscriptions from Soloi now confirm that the first Arab invasion of Cyprus took place in 649, not in 647 or 648. See Jean des Gagniers and Tran Tam Tinh, *Soloi: Dix campagnes de fouilles (1964–1974)*, vol. 1 (Sainte Foy, Québec: Université Laval, 1985), pp. 115–25; cf. *Supplementum Epigraphicum Graecum* 35 (1985): no. 1471. On two successive invasions of Cyprus cf. al-Balâdhuri, abu'l Abbâs Ahmad ibn-Jâbir [Ahmad ibn Yahya], *Kitâb futûh al-buldân*, 152–158, trans. Philip K. Hitti, *The Origins of the Islamic State* (New York: Columbia University Press, 1916), pp. 235–43.

8. *Life of John*, prologue, ed. Festugière, p. 344. On Leontius's style, see Festugière, *Vie de Symeon*, pp. 9–13. Averil Cameron ("Cyprus at the Time of the Arab Conquests," *Epeteris tis Kypriakis Etaireias Istorikon Spoudon 1989* [Nicosia, 1992], p. 39) has written, "The claim to write for the general public is often an affectation . . . and on closer inspection Leontius's actual style often turns out not to be simple at all."

common in Late Antiquity and Byzantium. This evidence points toward the availability of formal grammatical and rhetorical schooling on Cyprus and the likelihood that Leontius had received such a formation. As for the separate though related issue of audience, economic conditions were such that Cyprus could indeed have provided an educated readership. At the same time, we should not expect that Leontius wrote with only local readers in mind.

This study treats the *Life of Symeon* as an integral whole; this is an approach which I feel is not merely expedient, but appropriate. The next chapter addresses questions of earlier versions of the text and hypothesized sources for the narrative. As I shall discuss, Leontius reports that the text we possess is his second edition and that he had wanted to revise his first version of the text. While we can posit some reasons why Leontius might have felt compelled to revise the narrative, it is unlikely that we can distinguish newer material from earlier material with certainty. Furthermore, some scholars have attempted to see a major literary source standing behind the work, a collection of anecdotes about the holy man deriving from Syria in the 560s or so. While we cannot rule out this possibility, I will argue that this solution to various textual problems is not likely. Moreover, even if Leontius did rely on an extensive written source, we must agree that Leontius's final product represents his choices regarding the presentation of the narrative as a unified text. In a parallel case, New Testament scholars regard the integrity of the Gospel of Matthew while at the same time acknowledging its author's reliance on at least two extant written sources; these scholars have fruitfully studied the author's intent, point of view, theological concerns, and literary merit. Thus whether Leontius relied on sources or not, his work merits attention in the form in which he crafted it.

From the outset, this inquiry jettisons the notion that one can gain access to a historical figure named Symeon, a "real" person in Emesa who pretended to be a fool. Such an endeavor confuses the modern purposes of biography and history with those of hagiography in the early Byzantine world. This is not to deny the existence of a man who appeared to be crazy but was regarded in retrospect as a saint; it is merely to stress that the study of the *Life of Symeon* cannot establish reliable information about him. In ways that will become clear, Leontius constructed his own portrait of such a man when he composed the *Life of Symeon*, motivated by literary, pedagogical, and ultimately theological concerns. Modern readers must remind themselves that Leontius's purpose in creating the *Life* was not to relate "historical truth" as we might now think of it, but rather, in his own words, to "unveil . . . a nourishment which does not perish but which leads our souls to life everlasting" (p. 121).[9] In creating his narration, Leontius intended not to deceive, but to edify. Ultimately Leontius, like the Symeon about whom he writes, was trying to save souls.

The richly constructed, heavily allusive character of the *Life of Symeon* makes it impossible to reach a "real" figure behind this powerful text. As a literary work the *Life* is a *fictio*, in the sense of "something fashioned." By remaining agnostic regarding a "historical person," this study is able to open a window onto the religious imagination of the seventh century. But bracketing claims for historical reference in the account of this holy fool does not diminish the value of the work for the student of history. Recent assessments of the historical value of saints' lives have pointed this out. In the introduction to their recent volume of translations of Syriac lives of women saints, Sebastian Brock and Susan Ashbrook Harvey have written that "variation in historicity does not detract from the worth of these texts as social documents for their period of composition, offering us insight and information on the world from which they come."[10] When such works are considered as the literary output of given individuals, produced in a specific time and place, they reveal something of their authors' hopes and concerns.

Although set in the Syrian city of Emesa during the sixth century, the "Emesa" in the *Life of Symeon* reveals much about seventh-century Cyprus. Leontius wrote the *Life* on Cyprus in the 640s, a period for which we have little other information, although a portrait of Cyprus in the preceding decades can be drawn with the help of surviving literary, archeological, and art-historical evidence. The seventh century was a period of tremendous change in the Byzantine empire, and the decades of the 630s and 640s saw much of Byzantium fall into Arab hands. Leontius's *Life of Symeon* was composed on the eve of the Arab invasion of Cyprus, after the fall of Symeon's Emesa (in 635/6) and John the Almsgiver's Alexandria (641).[11] The composite image of Cyprus which emerges from the evidence may account for why Cyprus sustained such a level of literary production

9. Citations in the text are to the pagination in Rydén's 1963 edition of the *Life of Symeon*, which is retained in the inner margins of Rydén's 1974 revised edition printed in Festugière and Rydén (*Vie de Syméon le Fou*). This method of citing the text has become the rule among scholars. I have retained this pagination in square brackets in the translation of the *Life of Symeon* appended to this volume. Throughout this study translations of the *Life of Symeon* are from the 1974 text, now the standard edition. All translations from the *Life of Symeon* are my own, as are all translations from other ancient texts unless I have specified otherwise in the notes.

10. Sebastian Brock and Susan Ashbrook Harvey, introduction, *Holy Women of the Syrian Orient* (Berkeley: University of California Press, 1987), p. 3.

11. For details of these events, see Stratos, *Byzantium in the Seventh Century*, vol. 2 (634–641), pp. 62, 111; cf. Kaegi, *Byzantium and the Early Islamic Conquests*, p. 67.

in an era proverbial for its upheaval, denigrated for its cultural decline, and bemoaned for its paucity of literary sources. The *Life* in turn reflects certain aspects of social and cultural life on Cyprus at the end of Late Antiquity, particularly the economy of the city and the preservation of Greco-Roman secular culture through traditional systems of education. The *Life of Symeon* suggests that in many ways, regardless of the state of the rest of Byzantium, seventh-century Cyprus continued to preserve the markers of a Late Antique society.

The seventh century was a decisive period in the slow transformation which, for scholars, marks the vague boundary between Late Antiquity and the early Middle Ages. The first half of the century was a time of military upheaval in Byzantium, under threat first from the Persians and then from the Arabs. By the midpoint of the century, Syria, Egypt, and Cyprus were forever severed from the empire. Imperial ideology held that loyalty to the Orthodox Church meant loyalty to the emperor. The Emperor Heraclius's attempts to forge a unity between Chalcedonians, who held that Christ was of two natures, divine and human, and Monophysites, who held that Christ was of a single nature which was both divine and human, were also attempts to hold together an ethnically and linguistically diverse empire in the face of external threats.[12] The desire for religious conformity is also reflected in Heraclius's decree of 634 demanding the baptism of Jews.[13] The *Life of Symeon* reflects several of these tensions.

The Urban Context

Unlike much of the classic hagiography of the preceding centuries which celebrates withdrawal to the desert, the *Life of Symeon* is above all an urban saint's life, exploring the potential for sanctity within the city. Debate continues over the fortunes of cities in the course of the seventh century. However, it is generally agreed that, on the whole, the cities and towns of the Byzantine empire experienced a decline beginning in the second half of the sixth century and continuing through the seventh. Many factors contributed, including natural disasters, famines, plagues, and war. Despite regional variation, the overall trend was toward the eclipse of the

---

12. Haldon, *Byzantium in the Seventh Century*, pp. 48–49, 283.

13. F. Dölger, *Regesten der Kaiserurkunden der oströmischen Reiches von 565–1453* (Munich: Oldenbourg, 1924–65), no. 206; Cf. Haldon, *Byzantium in the Seventh Century*, pp. 303–4, 346. The study of conflict between Jews and Christians in the period is now greatly aided by Gilbert Dagron and Vincent Déroche, "Juifs et Chrétiens dans l'orient du viiᵉ siècle," *Travaux et mémoires* 11 (1991): 17–273, and Déroche, "La polémique anti-judaïque au viᵉ et au viiᵉ siècle: un mémento inédit, les Képhalaia," *Travaux et mémoires* 11 (1991): 275–311.

Late Roman *polis*. During the late sixth century structures of taxation and government gradually evolved, with administrative power taken increasingly away from local authorities and concentrated in a centralized imperial government. Moreover, beginning with the Persian wars during the reign of Heraclius, towns lost their role as economic centers and tended to function more as military fortifications.[14] Literary evidence from the period suggests that the Byzantines themselves perceived that their society was in crisis.[15]

Did this general decline interrupt Late Roman modes of life on Cyprus? Apparently not. During the 640s, Leontius, the bishop of Neapolis on Cyprus, composed two saints' lives which stand among the greatest literary achievements of Early Byzantium. That these works were produced in a period known for its military, political, theological, and economic upheaval should give the historian pause. Seventh-century Cyprus cannot be dismissed as a backwater.[16] Its situation on vital shipping routes provided a constant influx of goods and visitors from Syria and Egypt. Given the economic difficulties experienced throughout the Eastern Mediterranean in this period, Cyprus appears to have been relatively prosperous. The lavish objects of the Cyprus treasures discovered near Lambousa, which include nine silver plates depicting scenes from the life of David, bear stamps dating from the late sixth century and first half of the seventh and attest to the tremendous wealth of at least one Cypriot family during Leontius's life.[17] Cyprus enjoyed imperial favors due to its great copper reserves, which presumably helped finance the Emperor Heraclius's mili-

14. Indispensable is the extended discussion in Haldon, *Byzantium in the Seventh Century*, pp. 92–124. For broad perspective on the problem of urban history in the period, see Averil Cameron, *The Mediterranean World in Late Antiquity, AD 395–600* (London: Routledge, 1993), pp. 152–75.

15. On Byzantine awareness of decline see Haldon, *Byzantium in the Seventh Century*, pp. 39–40; Kaegi, *Byzantium and the Early Islamic Conquests*, pp. 109, 207–13. Some regions suffered more heavily than others; to date there has been no attempt to correlate the Cypriot evidence with the larger picture.

16. On seventh-century Cyprus generally see Costas Kyrris, *History of Cyprus: With an Introduction to the Geography of Cyprus* (Nicosia: Nicocles, 1985), pp. 160–80; Kyrris, "Cypriot Ascetics and the Christian Orient," *Vyzantinos Domos* 1 (1987): 95–108; and Averil Cameron, "Cyprus at the Time of the Arab Conquests."

17. Some pieces in the treasure may have been commissioned by the Emperor Heraclius in 626–30 as a gift for a wealthy Cypriot whose silver trove had earlier been confiscated to help finance the war of 621. On the Cyprus treasures, see O. M. Dalton, "A Byzantine Silver Treasure from the District of Kerynia, Cyprus, Now Preserved in the British Museum," *Archaeologia* 57 (1900): 159–74; Dalton, "A Second Silver Treasure from Cyprus," *Archaeologia* 60 (1906): 1–24; A. and J. Stylianou, *The Treasures of Lambousa* (Vasilia, Cyprus, 1969); cf. Kyrris, *History of Cyprus*, p. 173. For the alienation of church plate to finance military campaigns, cf. Nicephorus, *Short History* 11; Theophanes, *Chronicle* 303.

tary efforts against Persia.[18] The victorious emperor seems to have understood his debt to Cyprus. In exchange, in the late 620s, Cyprus received a massive (thirty-five-mile) aqueduct carrying water from the Kyrenia range across the Mesaorian plain to Constantia (Salamis, near modern Famagusta). This building project was overseen, at least in part, by Archbishop Arcadius, who later commissioned Leontius's *Life of John the Almsgiver.*[19]

While the *Life of Symeon* reflects larger political and social changes, it is particularly rich with evidence of daily life. Although set in Syria in the late sixth century, the small-town life which Leontius recreates in the *Life of Symeon* would have been quite familiar to his Cypriot audience.[20] The town includes an agora with food stalls, a bath complex, a glass workshop, and a tavern, and it is peopled with rich and poor, with merchants, artisans, a sorceress, a schoolmaster, and with monks. The portrait in the text is one of economic well-being, not decline. Moreover, there is no trace of wistfulness in the text for such prosperity. While there are references to earthquake and plague—natural realities of life in this era—there are no references to famine or economic collapse. That Leontius presented such an ordinary portrait of urban life to his audience contradicts the notion of general economic decline in early-seventh-century Byzantium illustrated by many economic and social historians and contributes to the general sense that in this period Cyprus remained relatively more prosperous.

The *Life of Symeon* is not the only witness to this unexpected prosperity. A brief and curious text from the period, the *Vision of Kaioumos*, tells of a wealthy shipowner, merchant, and landowner of Constantia, a certain Philentolos son of Olympus. Philentolos supported the poor and orphans and built a hospital (νοσοκομεῖον). He was, however, prone to fornication. After he died, debate arose among the bishops of the various sees on Cyprus as to whether Philentolos had been saved. Since no agreement could be reached, Arcadius consulted the monks in monasteries, the

18. From 615 to 618 and again in 626/7 copper coins were minted at Constantia. On coins 615–18: Michael Hendy, *Studies in the Byzantine Monetary Economy, 300–1450* (Cambridge: Cambridge University Press, 1985), pp. 415–17; Haldon, *Byzantium in the Seventh Century,* pp. 176, 224. On copper folles 626/7: Philip Grierson, *Byzantine Coins* (London: Methuen, 1982), pp. 121, 359. Cyprus also minted a limited number of coins in 608–10; see Grierson, *Byzantine Coins,* pp. 46, 73.

19. T. B. Mitford, "Some New Inscriptions from Early Christian Cyprus," *Byzantion* 20 (1950): 105–75, esp. pp. 118–25.

20. My point is not that the *Life of Symeon* contains an accurate portrait of Cyprus, only that the city which Leontius creates in the text can reasonably be expected to reflect the city in which he created it. My informal survey of Late Roman cities on Cyprus conducted in the spring of 1993 confirmed that Cypriot town planning conformed in a general way to patterns familiar from other regions.

stylites, and the hermits. Eventually God revealed in a vision to the hermit Kaioumos that Philentolos was neither in heaven nor hell, but was standing between the two, with the souls of unbaptized children, saved from the fires of Gehenna by his generosity.[21] Apparently this vision guaranteed that there was nothing preventing the use of Philentolos's generous legacy. Besides indicating the substantial wealth of some Cypriots in the period, the *Vision of Kaioumos* shares a major theme with the hagiographical works of Leontius of Neapolis, namely concern for donations to the poor and needy and most especially the role of the Church in engineering this effort.

Religious Life

The history of religious life in Cyprus provides a context for understanding many of Leontius's concerns in the *Life of Symeon*. After the reign of Archbishop Epiphanius of Salamis-Constantia (died 402) in the late fourth century, the Church of Cyprus was able to establish itself as autonomous, independent of the patriarch of Antioch. From then on, the archbishop of Constantia was the head of the island's bishops.[22] In the early seventh century the island's Christian population included Chalcedonians and Monophysites (Akephaloi and others). In addition to indigenous speakers of Greek, recent unrest in Syria had brought communities of Syriac-speaking refugees to the island. John of Ephesus reports that during the Persian invasion of 577, the Emperor Maurice relocated a group of Syrian Monophysites to Cyprus, granting them lands throughout the island.[23]

21. F. Halkin, "La Vision de Kaioumos et le sort éternel de Philentolos Olympiou," *AB* 63 (1945): 56–64; cf. Kyrris, "The Admission of the Souls of Immoral but Humane People into the *'Limbus Puerorum,'* according to the Cypriot Abbot Kaioumos (VIIth Century A.D.) Compared to the Quran's *al 'Araf* (Suras 7:44–46, 57:13ff.)," *Revue des études sud-est européennes* 9 (1971): 461–77.

22. On the church in Cyprus in this period see George Hill, *A History of Cyprus,* vol. 1 (Cambridge: Cambridge University Press, 1940), pp. 248–51, 273–82; Kyrris, *History of Cyprus,* pp. 164–68; Kyrris, "Cypriot Ascetics and the Christian Orient." The development of autocephaly is discussed in detail in J. Hackett, *A History of the Orthodox Church of Cyprus* (London: Methuen, 1901), pp. 13–33.

23. John of Ephesus, *Historia ecclesiastica* (hereafter John of Ephesus, *HE*) 6.15. Cf. Mango, "Chypre: Carrefour du monde byzantin," *XVᵉ Congrès international d'études byzantines: rapports et co-rapports* 5.5 (Athens, 1976). Mango writes that it is "abundantly clear that there were many Syrians and other Orientals living on the island [i.e., Cyprus] as evidenced, *inter alia,* by the prevalence there of the Monophysite heresy" (pp. 3–4). See also Marina Sacopoulo, *La Theotokos à la mandorle de Lythrankomi* (Paris: Maisonneuve et Larose, 1975), pp. 80–87.

Another group of Syrian refugees arrived in 610.[24] The Persian invasions also brought refugees from Alexandria.[25] Because of its proximity to the mainland and its separation from it, Cyprus absorbed refugees of military conflicts throughout the Levant, a role which it has played also in recent times. Despite the decline of urban populations elsewhere in the empire over the course of the late sixth and early seventh centuries, the influx of people to the island may have contributed to the sustenance of urban life on Cyprus in this period. This immigration also maintained the island's religious diversity.

The island also appears to have had a sizable Jewish population.[26] Eutychius, patriarch of Alexandria during the first half of the tenth century, basing his accounts on earlier sources, reports that Jews from Cyprus were among those who mounted an attack on the Christian population of Tyre during the Persian invasions of 610.[27] The tales attributed to Anastasius the Sinaite, himself a native Cypriot, composed late in the seventh century, include an account of a Jew named Daniel who was burned at the stake in Constantia in 637 for practicing magic and a Jew who sought baptism from the bishop of Amathus during the Arab invasion of 649.[28]

24. On Paul the Syrian, see below. John Moschus (*Spiritual Meadow* 30) tells of a certain Isidore of Melitene, formerly a Severan Monophysite who had once desecrated the host in a catholic (Chalcedonian) church; later he became a monk on Cyprus, constantly weeping in repentance.

25. This fact is reported in a text concerning a posthumous miracle of Epiphanius (BHG 601m) soon to be published by Claudia Rapp. The passage in manuscript Paris gr. 1596, pp. 550–51, is discussed briefly by F. Nau and L. Clugnet, "Vies et récits d'anachorètes (IVᵉ–VIIᵉ siècles)," *Rèvue de L'Orient Chrétien* 8 (1903): 92. Many thanks to Dr. Rapp for the reference and for permission to mention this text. John the Almsgiver's return to Cyprus prior to 619 was prompted by these invasions (*Life of John* 52).

26. The inscriptional evidence, while attesting to the presence of a sizable Jewish community in the preceding centuries, yields nothing datable with certainty to our period. Mitford dated the inscription from the Synagogue at Constantia to the sixth century ("New Inscriptions," pp. 110–16), but Baruch Lifshitz preferred to date it to the third century. Lifshitz however argued that an inscription from Lapethos which Mitford had dated to the sixth century and described as Christian (pp. 141–43) was in fact a Jewish inscription of the fifth century. Lifshitz, *Donateurs et fondateurs dans les synagogues juives* (Paris: Gabalda, 1967), pp. 73–76. On Jewish inscriptions from Late Antique Cyprus, see also R. P. Jean-Baptiste Frey, *Corpus inscriptionum judaicarum*, vol. 2 (Vatican: Pontificio instituto di archeologia christiana, 1952), pp. 6, 7. The fourth-century bishop and heresiarch Epiphanius of Salamis-Constantia was a convert from Judaism (*Life of Epiphanius* 2).

27. Eutychius, *Annals* 1.218ff., PG 111.1084–85. Cf. *Gli Annali*, trans. Bartolomeo Pirone (Cairo: Franciscan Centre, 1987), pp. 308–9; Michael Breydy, *Das Annalenwerk des Eutychios von Alexandrien* (Louvain: Peeters, 1985), pp. 101–3. See also Joshua Starr, "Byzantine Jewry on the Eve of the Arab Conquest (565–638)," *Journal of the Palestine Oriental Society* 15 (1935): 285.

28. "Le texte grec des récits utile à l'âme d'Anastase (le Sinaïte)," ed. F. Nau, *Oriens Christianus* 3 (1903): 70–71; Starr, *The Jews of the Byzantine Empire (641–1204)* (Athens: Verlag der "Byzantinisch-Neugriechischen Jahrbucher," 1939), pp. 85–86. The attribution and historicity of these accounts is uncertain.

Cyprus's varied religious life is reflected in the population of Leontius's "Emesa" which included Monophysites and Jews.

Cyprus was important in the theological debates that shook Christianity in the seventh century. It was to Archbishop Arcadius that the Emperor Heraclius addressed an edict *circa* 625 or 626 proposing, as a sort of "experiment," the doctrine of Monotheletism in an effort to unite the island's Chalcedonians and Monophysites.[29] This edict was a precursor to Heraclius's Ekthesis of 638 by which he tried to use the formula of a "single will" to bring about religious unity throughout the empire.[30]

During the first half of the seventh century many of the major figures of the Chalcedonian church visited Cyprus. John the Almsgiver, patriarch of Alexandria *circa* 610–17, was a native of Cyprus and returned to the city of Amathus, not far from Neapolis, before his death.[31] John Moschus, the author of the *Spiritual Meadow,* and his friend Sophronius, later patriarch of Jerusalem, were part of John the Almsgiver's circle in Alexandria, and from Moschus's own testimony are both known to have visited Cyprus between 614 and 619.[32] Together Moschus and Sophronius composed a *Life of John the Almsgiver* which was available to Leontius on Cyprus. After 633 Sophronius became one of the major opponents of the Monothelete doctrine. Another great opponent of Monotheletism was Maximus the Confessor, perhaps the greatest theologian of the seventh century. It can be inferred from his correspondence with Marinus, a Cypriot monk, that Maximus visited Cyprus, probably between 626 and 630.[33]

29. G. D. Mansi, *Sacrorum conciliorum nova et amplissima collectio* (Paris: Weller, 1901–27), 11, col. 561ab; cf. col. 525b. See V. Grumel, "Recherches sur l'histoire du monothélisme," *Echos d'Orient* 27 (1928): 6.

30. See P. Verghese, "The Monothelite Controversy—A Historical Survey," *Greek Orthodox Theological Review* 13 (1968): 196–211. Shortly after 631 Sergius, the patriarch of Constantinople, and Cyrus, the Chalcedonian archbishop of Alexandria, proposed that Christ's two natures should be understood to function as a single energy. After this solution proved unsuccessful, Heraclius issued the Ekthesis of 638 in which the doctrine of the single energy was abandoned in favor of a doctrine of a single will (monotheletism). These efforts too largely failed, and the issue became irrelevant as Egypt and Syria, the regions with the largest Monophysite populations, fell out of Byzantine hands. Cf. George Ostrogorsky, *History of the Byzantine State,* trans. Joan Hussey (New Brunswick, N.J.: Rutgers University Press, 1969), pp. 107–9; Judith Herrin, *The Formation of Christendom* (Princeton: Princeton University Press, 1987), pp. 206–11; Haldon, *Byzantium in the Seventh Century,* pp. 48–49.

31. Leontius, *Life of John* 52.

32. Leontius, *Life of John* 23; John Moschus, *Spiritual Meadow* 30. This accords with the information given in the biographical prologue found in some manuscripts of the *Meadow* (ed. Hermann Usener, *Der Heilige Tychon* [Leipzig: Teubner, 1907], pp. 91–93), which relates that Moschus and Sophronius traveled from Alexandria to Rome (some time after 614 and before Moschus's death in 619) by way of the islands (p. 92 l. 29); cf. Henry Chadwick, "John Moschus and His Friend Sophronius the Sophist," *JThS* 25 (1974): 58.

33. Maximus the Confessor, *Ep.* 20; Polycarp Sherwood, *An Annotated Date-List of the Works of Maximus the Confessor* (Rome: Pontifical Institute, 1952), pp. 5–6, 34.

A polemical early Syriac *Life of Maximus* describes a synod on Cyprus convened to discuss the Monothelete doctrine. The meeting was suggested by Maximus and Sophronius to the Archbishop Arcadius, who summoned a number of bishops. The synod was attended by Cyrus, patriarch of Alexandria, by representatives of Pope Honorius and of Sergius, patriarch of Constantinople, as well as by Sophronius and others. The biographer claims that Maximus did not attend because he was afraid.[34] While the date of such a meeting cannot be established, and some aspects of the narration do not conform to what is known from other sources, it is quite possible that such a meeting did take place; and thus this *Life of Maximus* would be further evidence not only for the presence of major intellectual figures in Cyprus during the first half of the seventh century, but also for the centrality of Cyprus in the Monothelete controversy, as doctrinal reconciliation was viewed by Arcadius and others as crucial to the political unity of the eastern provinces and the security of the island.[35] This concern is also reflected in the *Life of Symeon* where Symeon converts all religious nonconformists. If Leontius was already bishop of Neapolis when the synod was held, he may well have attended.

Further evidence of religious and intellectual activity on Cyprus is found in the work of the Syrian Paul, once Monophysite bishop of Edessa, who had escaped to Cyprus during the Persian invasion in 619. Connected to the monastery at Qenneŝrin, renowned for its scholars, Paul devoted himself to the massive project of preparing a Syriac translation of the sermons of Gregory of Nazianzus, which he completed in 624 while on Cyprus.[36]

Leontius of Neapolis

Despite his important role in the Cypriot church, little is known about the life of Leontius of Neapolis. Given his literary activity in the 640s it is reasonable to assume he was born in the early decades of the century. He probably died sometime during the reign of Constans II (d. 668). In addition to the lives of John the Almsgiver and Symeon the Fool, and a no

---

34. Sebastian Brock, "An Early Syriac Life of Maximus the Confessor," *AB* 91 (1973): 299–346.

35. Herrin, *Formation of Christendom*, p. 251.

36. He also translated works by Severus of Antioch and Jacob of Edessa. Ignatius Ortiz de Urbina, *Patrologia Syriaca* (Rome: Pontifical Institute, 1958), pp. 161–62; William Wright, *A Short History of Syriac Literature* (London: Black, 1894), p. 135. Manuscripts of these texts are described in Wright, *Catalogue of Syriac Manuscripts in the British Museum* (London, 1871), pp. 423–36.

longer extant *Life of Spyridon*, he is probably the author of a treatise entitled *Against the Jews* which includes a defense of the veneration of images,
perhaps the earliest defense of icons in the Byzantine world.[37]

The circumstances surrounding the composition of the *Life of John the
Almsgiver* shed light on Leontius's role in Cypriot affairs of his own time.
Commissioned by the prominent archbishop of Constantia, Arcadius, a
benefactor of Cyprus, the *Life of John* was specifically designed to celebrate
Cypriot pride and to honor the aristocratic Cypriot family of which John
had been a member. The work attests to the continuing importance of cultural ties between Egypt and Cyprus. While it is impossible to say with
certainty that the commissioning of the work postdates the conquest of
Alexandria by the Arabs in 641, this seems most likely since refugees
came from Alexandria to Cyprus in the aftermath of this event. The work
may have served as a rallying cry for the reversal of affairs.[38]

External evidence also provides clues. Leontius should probably be
identified with the Leontius of Neapolis recorded to have been present at
the Lateran council held in Rome in October 649. While a coincidence is
possible, it seems unlikely that in 649 both Neapolis, Cyprus, and Naples,
Italy, would have bishops with identical names. The dating fits nicely, so
soon after the Arab invasion of Cyprus, and would make Leontius one of
the numerous eastern clerics in attendance at the council who were
refugees of the military upheaval in the Levant. Pope Martin hosted the
council to condemn the Ekthesis and the teaching of Monotheletism; the
drafting of the *Acts* themselves was carefully engineered by Maximus
the Confessor, and they were quickly circulated, much to the displeasure
of the Emperor Constans.[39] No other Cypriot see was represented at the

37. The document survives only through fragments quoted by John of Damascus in his
treatise *On the Divine Images* and in the *Acta* of the Second Nicene Council in 787 CE. If the-
work is authentic, perhaps it dates from the period of Heraclius's anti-Jewish legislation in
634. In John of Damascus: PG 94.1272A–76B, 1313A, 1381D–88D. An English translation is
available in *On the Divine Images: Three Apologies against Those Who Attack the Divine Images*,
trans. David Anderson (Crestwood, N.Y.: St. Vladimir's Seminary, 1980). In Nicaea II: PG
93.1597B–610A; cf. Mansi, *Sacrorum conciliorum* 13, cols. 44–54. Vincent Déroche ("L'Authenticité de l' 'Apologie contre les Juifs' de Léontios de Néapolis," *Bulletin de correspondance
hellénique* 110 [1986]: 655–69) has argued strongly for the authenticity of the work. Paul
Speck ("Zu dem Dialog mit einem Juden des Leontios von Neapolis," *Poikila Byzantina* 4
[1984]: 242–49), however, believes it to be a work of the eighth century.

38. In fact, the Byzantines retook Alexandria in 645, only to lose it for good in 646, although at the time this could hardly have appeared permanent. Haldon, *Byzantium in the
Seventh Century*, p. 55; cf. Stratos, *Byzantium in the Seventh Century* 3:35–38.

39. For the council see Rudolf Riedinger, ed., *Concilium Lateranense a. 649 celebratum*
(Berlin: de Gruyter, 1984). Leontius of Neapolis is #87 in the Synodal lists. See also Riedinger,
"Die Lateransynode von 649 und Maximos der Bekenner," in *Maximus Confessor: Actes du
Symposium pour Maxime le confesseur (Fribourg, 2–5 Sept. 1980)*, ed. F. Heinzer and C. Schön-

council, but a letter from Sergius, archbishop of Constantia, to Pope
Theodore, written in 643 affirming the orthodoxy of the island and ex-
pressing his opposition to Monotheletism, was read out in the course of
the meetings. It is likely that Leontius would have followed his superior
in opposing the doctrine and would have found the proceedings of the
council acceptable. Whether Leontius later returned to Cyprus, we do not
know. In 649, Mu'awiya and his troops raided the island of Cyprus, in the
words of one chronographer "sacking Constantia and the whole island,"[40] and with a second raid in 653 decisively removed Cyprus from
Byzantine control. According to some Arab sources, the Cypriots negoti-
ated a peace with the Arabs by which they were to pay tribute to their
new overlords,[41] but archeological evidence suggests that life along the
coasts of Cyprus was disrupted and that Cypriots turned to the construction of numerous fortifications both along the coast and further inland.[42]
By 692, the archbishop of Constantia and a group of Cypriot refugees
were living in exile in Cyzicus in the province of Hellespont near the sea
of Marmara.[43] Leontius may have died in exile.

It is reasonable to assume that Leontius had firsthand knowledge of
many of the theological disputes of his day and may have known personally such "international" figures as Sophronius. Distances on Cyprus are
short, and travel by sea was easily accomplished. The journey from Neapolis (modern Limassol) to Constantia (Famagusta) took about twenty-four
hours by sea.[44] Leontius's inclusion of Jews (pp. 145, 154, 163, 168), Mo-

born (Fribourg: Éditions universitaires, 1982), pp. 111–21; cf. Haldon, *Byzantium in the Seventh Century*, p. 57. On Eastern religious in Rome in this era see Jean-Marie Sansterre, *Les
moines grecs et orientaux à Rome aux époques byzantine et carolingienne (milieu du vi^e s.–fin du ix^e
s.)*, 2 vols. (Brussels: Palais des académies, 1980). Sansterre does not mention Leontius of
Neapolis in this context. J. R. Martindale (*The Prosopography of the Later Roman Empire*, vol. 3:
A.D. 527–641, bk. 2 [Cambridge: Cambridge University Press, 1992], pp. 773–82) reveals that
Leontius was a fairly common name (forty-one instances) attested over a wide geographical
range, including twice in Italy and once in Sicily in the late sixth century.

    40. Theophanes, *Chronicle* 344.
    41. Kyrris, *History of Cyprus*, pp. 176–77; Kaegi, *Byzantium and the Early Islamic Con-
quests*, pp. 253–54, esp. n. 47 on the debate among scholars on the question of the authenticity of the Muslim accounts of the peace treaty. Theophanes (*Chronicle* 344) refers to a treaty
between Mu'awiya and the residents of Castellus in the raids of 649.
    42. Kyrris, *History of Cyprus*, p. 176.
    43. Cf. the Acts of the Council *in Trullo* 39; NPNF 2.14, pp. 383–84.
    44. See Claude Delaval Cobham, *Excerpta Cypria: Materials for a History of Cyprus* (Cam-
bridge: Cambridge University Press, 1908), for a number of accounts of sailing from one
place to another in Cyprus; e.g., Le Huen, *circa* 1486 (p. 52): "Friday, September 7, we left
Salines [Salamis/Famagusta]. . . . Saturday, the feast of the Nativity of our Lady, it was calm,
and we stayed at Lymesson [Limassol]." Cf. Fürer, 1621 (p. 77): "On the last day of March we
left Larnica at night, for the intolerable heat made travelling by day impossible, and the fol-

nophysites (pp. 146, 154), and even the debate over the status of Origen (pp. 152–53) in the *Life of Symeon* reflects the diverse religious world with which he was familiar. His interest in pilgrimage to Jerusalem and the veneration of the True Cross on the Feast of the Exaltation of the Cross reflect the enthusiasm felt throughout the empire for Heraclius's military successes, symbolized most effectively in his "recovery" of the Cross while on campaign to liberate Jerusalem from the Persians in 622. Heraclius personally restored the Cross to Jerusalem in 630 while on the first pilgrimage ever made to the city by a reigning Christian emperor.[45] In Leontius's narrative, composed while Jerusalem was in Arab hands, Symeon travels twice to the holy city to visit the sites connected to the life of Jesus. Whether Leontius's information about the Holy Land came from his own experience or from travelers' accounts, we do not know.

Leontius's work not only reflects the Christian environment in which it was composed, it remains a witness to the survival of Greco-Roman literary and intellectual culture into the seventh century. The first half of the seventh century saw the composition of the last great hexameter epic, George of Pisidia's *Heracliad*.[46] And Theophylact Simocatta's *Ethical Epistles* display a great concern with the texts traditionally studied in the educational curriculum. Similarly, the descriptions of Symeon's shameless behavior, his defecation in public, his consumption of lupines (legumes which cause gas), his ingestion of raw meat, and his dragging a dead dog into the city are references to the anecdotes about Diogenes of Sinope, the Cynic philosopher, preserved in large part in the rhetorical curriculum of Hellenistic and Late Antique schools, where they served to illustrate grammatical points and were utilized as building blocks for composing practice speeches. Allusion to these in Leontius's text together with the rhetorical character of the introduction to the *Life* suggests not only that

---

lowing morning we entered Famagusta." The journey to Rhodes took 4 days (Benjamin of Tudela, in the 1160s; p. 5), and Fra. Noe (earliest edition 1500) describes leaving Egypt and arriving "in no long time at the island of Cyprus, at the city of Famagosta, a seaport" (p. 53). I thank Annemarie Carr for bringing these accounts to my attention.

45. Nicephorus, *Short History* 18. A. Frolow, "La Vraie Croix et les expéditions d'Héraclius en Perse," *REB* 11 (1953): 88–105; cf. J. Moorhead, "Iconoclasm, the Cross, and the Imperial Image," *Byzantion* 55 (1985): 174–75. On the date (630, not 631) see Kaegi, *Byzantium and the Early Islamic Conquests*, p. 74, and also p. 210; cf. Haldon, *Byzantium in the Seventh Century*, p. 46; Mango, *Short History by Nicephorus* (Washington, D.C.: Dumbarton Oaks, 1990), p. 185. While the ritual of the Exaltation of the Cross in Jerusalem may be dated to the sixth century, the rite was popularized elsewhere in the early seventh century, being initiated in Constantinople in 614.

46. George of Pisidia, *Heraclias*, in *Poemi, I: Panegirici epici*, ed. A. Pertusi (Ettal: Buch-Kunst Verlag, 1960); D. F. Frendo, "Classical and Christian Influences in the *Heracliad* of George of Pisidia," *Classical Bulletin* 64.2 (1986): 53–62.

he had received a traditional education, but that he could assume such a level of education among at least a sector of his audience. Thus the *Life of Symeon* is evidence for the persistence of the Late Ancient educational curriculum and therefore a Christianized version of Greco-Roman secular culture on Cyprus into the mid-seventh century.

The text's literary aspects as well as various theological concerns to be uncovered in the course of this study raise questions about Leontius's intended audience. The use of tools derived from the educational tradition shows Leontius to have been a part of a broader Eastern Mediterranean intellectual culture. As we shall see, Leontius utilized literary skill deliberately and effectively. His art points not only toward a local Cypriot audience, but toward a more international readership as well. At the same time, the literary content of the text lies side-by-side with slapstick and bawdy. This diglossic character of Leontius's work indicates that a text which aimed to manipulate the high cultural tradition also sought to please the common people.

On the eve of the Arab invasion of Cyprus, Late Roman culture was flourishing. Against this background of vibrant social, economic, and religious life, Leontius undertook to make his peculiar literary contribution, a saint's life which challenged the conventional notions of sanctity and recast the problem of finding holiness in everyday life. To appreciate the significance of Leontius's achievement, we turn next to the problem of his literary sources.

TWO

LEONTIUS AND HIS SOURCES

The *Life of Symeon the Fool* begins with a complex prologue in which Leontius suggests some of his motives in writing (pp. 121–23) and concludes with an epilogue in which Leontius reflects on the parenetic significance of the saint's life he has just related (pp. 169–70). The main body of the text divides into two sections, vastly differing in style. The first section (pp. 124–45) is written in a style often syntactically complex and heavily rhetorical, including long speeches which reflect the language of church sermons and the formulae of prayer.[1] In it, Leontius provides a chronology of Symeon's career before his arrival in Emesa in Syria. He narrates how Symeon left his native Edessa to go on pilgrimage to Jerusalem, how he and his friend John first entered a monastery in the Jordan and later lived as hermits, grazing in the desert like sheep. Twenty-nine years later, after achieving a state of spiritual perfection, Symeon left the desert for Emesa, in order to devote himself to saving the souls of the urban laity.

The second half of the *Life* (pp. 145–69) is a collection of anecdotes, written in a colloquial style with a marvelously rich vocabulary which probably reflects the spoken language of Leontius's seventh-century Cyprus.[2] Here Leontius gives an account of Symeon's conduct in Emesa in a series

---

1. See Festugière's comments on this section in *Vie de Syméon le Fou*, pp. 9–11.

2. For studies of the linguistic character of this section see Rydén, "Style and Historical Fiction in the Life of St. Andreas Salos," *JÖB* 32 (1982): 175–83; Willem Aerts, "Leontios of Neapolis and Cypriot Dialect Genesis," *Praktika B' diethnous Kypriologikou Synedriou*, vol. 2 (Nicosia: Etaireia Kypriakōn Spoudōn, 1986), pp. 379–89; and the many discussions of individual words in Lennart Rydén, *Bemerkungen zum Leben des heiligen Narren Symeon von Leontios von Neapolis* (Uppsala: Almquist and Wiksell, 1970), *passim*, and in Festugière's edi-

of thirty-one brief episodes. From the moment he entered the city, dragging a dead dog behind him, Symeon pretended to be crazy. He disrupted
a church service by throwing nuts at the women parishioners. He walked
naked through the streets on the way to the public baths, and he used the
women's bathhouse. Yet through his insane ravings he was able to convert
heretics, Jews, prostitutes, and actors to Chalcedonian Christianity and improve the moral life of the city as a whole. As Leontius writes, "Through his
inventiveness, he nearly put an end to sinning in the whole city" (p. 162).

The *Life of Symeon the Fool* is the product of a single author, Leontius of
Neapolis. Nevertheless, scholars have put forth differing theories concerning Leontius's sources for Symeon and his use of these sources, attempting to determine how he assembled them or redacted them. There
are also problems concerning a possible earlier version of the text. Cyril
Mango has argued that Leontius is responsible only for the first half of the
Life of Symeon, and that he merely copied the second half of the *Life* from a
preexistent text supposedly composed in Emesa in the 560s, based on oral
traditions about the saint.[3] This chapter seeks to sort out the evidence concerning Leontius's possible direct literary sources and earlier versions of
the text. We cannot deny that Leontius had access to a variety of oral traditions about Symeon, or that in composing his work he drew heavily on
folkloric forms. These borrowings, however, cannot be documented, since
such traditions are not preserved.

    The central issue for those scholars who have considered Leontius's
relationship to and use of possible sources is the "sudden change [in style]
in the midst of the narrative" which Mango declared was "unparalleled,"
leading him to argue that in compiling his narrative, Leontius had done
"a pretty careless job."[4] Festugière, on the other hand, attempted to re-

---

tion. As a side note, Cyril Mango ("A Byzantine Hagiographer at Work: Leontios of Neapolis," in *Byzanz und der Westen: Studien zur Kunst des europäischen Mittelalters*, ed. Irmgard
Hutter [Vienna: Österreichischen Akademie der Wissenschaften, 1984], p. 27) suggests that a
change in style can be detected again at p. 166, just preceding the narration of Symeon's
death, where the style is more like the rhetorical style of the first half of the text. This return
to a more eloquent style is commonplace at the end of saints' lives.
    3. Mango, "A Byzantine Hagiographer," pp. 30ff. Mango's evidence for Leontius's re-
liance on a written source is, first, the contrasting styles of the first and second halves of the
Life; second, possible dates of the earthquake and the plague described in the text; and third,
inconsistency or "carelessness" regarding chronological details. Mango further attempts to
demonstrate that the second half of the *Life* reflects the concerns of the mid-sixth century.
These arguments will be raised again in a forthcoming study by Vincent Déroche.
    4. Mango, "A Byzantine Hagiographer," pp. 30, 33.

solve the discrepancy in styles by asserting that Leontius had composed the entire work himself and had conceived of the work as a unified entity.[5] Shifts in level of language are quite common in Byzantine saints' lives, as in Byzantine literature generally.[6] Moreover, attempts to correlate "high levels" of language with educated audiences and "low levels" of language with less-educated audiences are generally unconvincing. The differing character of the two halves of the *Life of Symeon* deserves to be reexamined; I shall here review previous discussions on the composition of the *Life of Symeon* and propose some solutions which I believe will assist us in understanding the author and his text.

As I have suggested, we should regard the historical Symeon as elusive. In a similar manner, we should not expect the Emesa which Leontius creates in the text to resemble a given historical city. Emesa's archeological record preserves little from Late Antiquity, and thus it is difficult to assess the degree to which details of the topography represented in the *Life of Symeon* conform to a specific town plan.[7] Leontius's native Neapolis presents a similar problem. The *Life of Symeon* is full of details about economic and social life, as has been recognized by social historians. Leontius's "Emesa" has a main gate, a church, a bathhouse, a theater, a few taverns and workshops, a colonnade, and an agora, but these features suggest little more than a generic Late Antique city. The city which Leontius invents may bear greatest resemblance to the city with which he and his audience were most familiar, and townsfolk represented in the text may even be local types. In any case, we should not be tempted to use the *Life of Symeon* as reliable evidence for urban conditions in sixth-century Syria.[8] The *Life*'s portrait of vibrant urban life is commensurate with the relative prosperity of Cyprus in the first half of the seventh century dis-

---

5. Festugière, *Vie de Syméon le Fou,* p. 13; "Il n'est donc pas douteux que l'ouvrage entier ne soit de Léontios et qu'il l'ait conçu comme formant un même ensemble." J. Hofstra ("Leontius van Neapolis als Hagiograaf," in *De heiligenverering in de eerste eeuwen van het christendom,* ed. A. Hilhorst [Nijmegen: Dekker en van de Vegt, 1988], pp. 186–92) has attempted to understand the shift in style as part of a critique of monasticism.

6. Festugière, *Vie de Syméon le Fou,* p. 15.

7. On Emesa see N. Elisséeff, "Ḥimṣ," *Encyclopedia of Islam,* new ed., 3.397–402, which includes a diagram and an aerial photograph.

8. As has recently been done by Mark Whittow, "Ruling the Late Roman and Early Byzantine City: A Continuous History," *Past and Present* 129 (November 1990): 3–29, esp. pp. 24–25. Dorothy Zani de Ferranti Abrahamse ("Hagiographic Sources for Byzantine Cities, 500–900 A.D." [Ph.D. diss., University of Michigan, 1967], p. 280) took the character of the Jewish glassblower as evidence for the role of Jews in the Syrian economy. But there is no reason to assume that this Jew is presented either in a stereotyped profession or in a profession restricted to Jews in Syria. Leontius may well have known Jewish glassblowers in Cyprus.

cussed above.[9] The burden of proof, it seems, rests with those who would argue that this text reflects life in an era and a place other than that in which it was produced.[10]

A "historical" Symeon should probably be dated, as Festugière and Mango have dated him, to the reign of Justinian. The only account of Symeon other than Leontius's *Life of Symeon the Fool* which we possess is found in Evagrius Scholasticus's *Ecclesiastical History*, written at Antioch during the last decade of the sixth century. Evagrius presents Symeon in his discussion of events during the reign of Justinian. Dating Symeon to this period necessarily creates problems for those seeking historical accuracy in the *Life of Symeon*. The earthquake which Symeon predicts in Evagrius's account can apparently be identified as the quake which struck Phoenice Maritima in 551.[11] Leontius, however, claims that Symeon predicted an earthquake during the reign of Maurice (p. 150), perhaps the earthquake of 588. Thus it has appeared to some that Leontius has shifted Symeon's activity forward about forty years. This discrepancy, among others, led Mango to be sharply critical of Leontius's credibility and prompted him to inquire "why Leontius felt impelled to falsify the facts."[12] Evagrius, it should be noted, had no written sources for Symeon. After sketching a few details about Symeon's behavior and relating three anecdotes about him, Evagrius remarks, "Many other things he also did which require a separate treatise [πραγματείας ἰδιαζούσης δεῖται]."[13] It seems that Evagrius had no knowledge of such a treatise. One scholar has suggested that Evagrius received his information from his employer, the Patriarch Gregory of Antioch, or from his monastic circle.[14] Even if Evagrius faithfully recorded his oral sources, and despite his proximity to the supposed events of Symeon's life, his account may be of no greater historicity than the material in the *Life of Symeon*. Evagrius should be taken not as evidence for the historical Symeon, but rather as the earliest account of a tradition about Symeon. We return to the details of Evagrius's account at the end of this chapter.

9. This issue is addressed more fully in chapter 5.

10. As we shall see, these warnings apply directly to Mango's arguments concerning Leontius and his sources.

11. Cf. Evagrius Scholasticus, *The Ecclesiastical History of Evagrius with the Scholia*, ed. J. Bidez and C. Parmentier (1898; rpt. New York: AMS, 1979) (hereafter Evagrius, *HE*) 4.34; John Malalas, *Chronicle* 18.112. Festugière, introduction, *Vie de Syméon le Fou*, pp. 3–8; Mango, "A Byzantine Hagiographer," pp. 27–28.

12. Mango, "A Byzantine Hagiographer," p. 28.

13. Evagrius, *HE*, 4.34; trans. *A History of the Church from A.D. 322 to the Death of Theodore of Mopsuestia, A.D. 427 by Theodoret, Bishop of Cyrus, and from A.D. 431 to A.D. 594 by Evagrius . . .* (London: Bohn, 1854), p. 416.

14. Pauline Allen, *Evagrius Scholasticus the Church Historian* (Louvain: Spicilegium Sacrum Lovaniense, 1981), pp. 199–200.

Leontius's Claims Concerning Sources

Leontius does not pretend to have had firsthand knowledge of Symeon, but he does claim to have had access to an eyewitness account (p. 125). There is consensus among scholars that Leontius's claim is a fabrication, an example of a convention of hagiography in this period which the Bollandist Hippolyte Delehaye described as "the fiction of the well-informed witness."[15] In the *Life of John the Almsgiver,* Leontius claims to have functioned as a stenographer, taking down the testimony of a certain Menas concerning the patriarch. Otto Kresten has shown this assertion to be "pure fancy."[16] While the *Life of Symeon* employs a similar narrative device, the text appears to create some confusion about whether Leontius is claiming that his information from the Deacon John came to him in oral or written form.

Of course, it is a historical impossibility that an eyewitness to events in Emesa in the mid-sixth century could have lived long enough to relate his account directly to Leontius almost one hundred years later (or perhaps sixty years later if we follow Leontius himself and date Symeon's activity in Emesa to the reign of Maurice).[17] On this point there is consensus. Nevertheless, most scholars have taken Leontius to be appealing (albeit falsely) to an oral source. Leontius writes,

> All this Symeon narrated in Emesa, where he pretended to be a fool, to a certain deacon of the holy cathedral church of the same city of Emesa, an excellent and virtuous man, who, by the divine grace which had come to him, understood the monk's work. . . . The aforementioned John, beloved of God, a virtuous deacon, narrated [διηγήσατο] for us almost the entire life of that most wise one, calling on the Lord as witness to his story, that he had written [ἐπέγραψεν] nothing to add to the narrative [διηγήματι], but rather that since that time he had forgotten most things. (p. 125)

15. "La fiction du témoin bien informé"; H. Delehaye, *Les passions des martyrs et les genres littéraires* (Brussels: Société des Bollandistes, 1966), pp. 182–83. Cf. Rydén, *Bemerkungen,* pp. 43–47; Festugière, *Vie de Syméon le Fou,* pp. 14–15; Otto Kresten, "Leontios von Neapolis als Tachygraph? Hagiographische Texte als Quellen zu Schriftlichkeit und Buchkultur im 6. und 7. Jahrhundert," *Scrittura e civiltà* 1 (1977): 157–58, esp. n. 10; Mango, "Byzantine Hagiographer," pp. 29–30 (although Mango's solution to this problem creates other difficulties, which I shall discuss below). Wolfgang Speyer includes Leontius of Neapolis in his general treatment of the convention of the fictitious witness in his *Die Literarische Fälschung im heidnischen und christlichen Altertum: Ein Versuch ihrer Deutung* (Munich: Beck, 1971), pp. 71–74.

16. Kresten, "Leontius von Neapolis als Tachygraph," pp. 158–59. The passage in question is Leontius, *Life of John,* prologue, pt. 2, ed. Festugière, p. 346.

17. Cf. Mango, "A Byzantine Hagiographer," pp. 29–30.

Festugière believes Leontius's claim that the testimony he received was oral.[18] By this reasoning, the word ἐπέγραψεν, "he had written," in the passage quoted above must be seen as a lapse on Leontius's part. For Festugière it is merely a mistake; Leontius accidentally confuses the convention of claiming a nonexistent oral source for claiming a nonexistent written one. But a careful consideration of this passage reveals that there is nothing here to suggest that Leontius is claiming to have received John the deacon's account in oral form.

Leontius fully intends to convey here that his source is a written document. The words διήγημα and διηγέομαι, "narrative" and "narrate," do not necessarily refer to oral testimony, and in this context should be taken to refer to a written text.[19] By this understanding, *pace* Festugière,[20] ἐπέγραψεν is not a lapse. This observation prompts an examination of the other two passages where Leontius describes his relationship to the testimony of John the deacon. Twice in the anecdotal section he refers to John who "narrated this life for us" (p. 148, l. 22: ἡμῖν ὑφηγησάμενος; p. 159, l. 17: ἐξηγησάμενον ἡμῖν). In these two passages, scholars have generally taken Leontius to be claiming to have received an oral account. Once again, it is not clear from the terms used whether this supposed narration is in oral or written form. Ὑφηγέομαι is elsewhere unattested, and ἐξηγέομαι, while often referring to oral communication, can also be used to describe a written interpretation.[21] (Think of "exegesis.") It may well be the case that scholars have been mistaken, and Leontius never intended to pass off John's testimony as something he received orally.

The Nature of a Possible Written Source

The question then arises concerning the status of Leontius's claim to a written eyewitness source, a concern which I believe has been correctly met with skepticism. Leontius is clearly adhering to hagiographical convention in claiming a good source. But did Leontius have a written source which was not an eyewitness account?

Mango has argued that Leontius indeed had a written source for the episodic material in the second half of the *Life*, positing that this source

18. Festugière, *Vie de Syméon le Fou*, p. 14; so also Mango, "A Byzantine Hagiographer," p. 29.

19. Cf. διήγημα, p. 129 l. 8; LSJ and Lampe, s.v. I thank Alexander Kazhdan for his assistance on this reading.

20. Festugière, *Vie de Syméon le Fou*, p. 14.

21. Lampe, s.v.

was not a previous *vita*, but rather a "paterikon," which he defines as "a collection of disconnected anecdotes."[22] This document, claims Mango, originated in Emesa and was compiled in the 560s. It is this text which Leontius attempts to pass off as the eyewitness account of John the deacon. This allows Mango to account for the great shift in literary style between the first half of the life, which he disparages as "pure verbiage" and ascribes entirely to Leontius, and the second half, which he believes Leontius has taken over from a previous document and only slightly altered. Mango further claims that this paterikon was known to Evagrius—an unlikely proposition, since Evagrius tells us that he knows of no such document.[23] Furthermore, the literary relationship between Evagrius's account of Symeon and Leontius's *Life*, which we will consider below, is sufficiently loose that if they were working from the same source we would have to conclude that either one or both of them reworked the material substantially. While such a conclusion is not impossible, it does not best explain the relationship between the two texts.

Dating the Material in the Second Half of the *Life*

Mango's further arguments for the provenance and date of this posited "paterikon" source need to be examined carefully. He believes that the story in which Symeon invites ten members of the circus faction to a banquet while they are washing their clothes outside the city (pp. 163–64) reflects the actual situation of Emesa, which was two miles from the

22. Mango, "A Byzantine Hagiographer," p. 30. In support of his paterikon argument, Mango cites what he believes to be a parallel example, namely the stories about Daniel of Skete, and claims that John Moschus's *Spiritual Meadow* "presupposes the existence of such collections relating to individual saints" (p. 30 n. 19). But the stories "about" Daniel of Skete are, in fact, a collection of stories about other people whom Daniel of Skete is supposed to have encountered. Each of the accounts is three or four times the length of the average episode in the *Life of Symeon*, and the individual accounts have no relation to each other. The *Life of Daniel of Skete* finds closer generic parallels in such texts as Palladius's *Lausiac History*, the numerous narrative collections of the *Apophthegmata Patrum*, and in John of Ephesus's *Lives of the Eastern Saints*. In each of these texts a number of figures are described in a succession of brief vignettes, a form quite different from a possible "Paterikon of Symeon," presumably a lengthy document entirely devoted to one saint. It is also far from clear that the "sources" for John Moschus were of the sort Mango suggests. In fact, the collection of seemingly disjointed anecdotes about a single saint such as we find in the *Life of Symeon* finds its closest parallels in other full-length *vitae* of the period, such as George of Sykeon's *Life of Theodore of Sykeon*, the various lives of the stylite saints, and Leontius's own *Life of John the Almsgiver*. Leontius uses the word πατερικά (*Life of John* 40) to refer to "Lives of the Fathers" generally.
23. Evagrius, *HE* 4.34.

Orontes. The episode seems contrived. Why would it be necessary for the men of the city to go so far out to do washing when the women could wash in the city? Far from drawing on accurate information about Emesa, this episode is designed to echo the call of the disciples, the parable of the banquet (Mt 22:1–10), and the parable of the wise and foolish virgins (Mt 25:1–13). It is followed by a miraculous feeding. In all likelihood, the episode owes its situation outside the city to a verse from the Book of Revelation in which John of Patmos writes, "Blessed are those who wash their robes, that they may have the right to the tree of life and that they may enter the city by the gates" (Rv 22:14); here the robe washers are placed outside the city. Little else in the text might allow us to argue that Leontius had access to specific knowledge about the topography of Emesa.

Mango's argument for the date of his posited source is based on two factors. First, in one extended episode two monks approach John the hermit (not the deacon) and later Symeon seeking a resolution to their (the monks') debate over the reason for Origen's fall into error (pp. 152–53). Mango argues that this episode makes more sense in the reign of Justinian than one hundred years later in Leontius's time.[24] (Origen was condemned in 553 at the Sixth Ecumenical Council.) This observation, it should be noted, does not argue for fixing the date of the supposed source to the 560s, but actually attempts to date the activities of a historical Symeon to *circa* 550. The *Life of Symeon* is coy concerning Origen, neither criticizing him nor explicitly supporting him, and to my mind does not reflect composition in the period immediately after the Sixth Council. While Justinian was alive, it would have been difficult to discuss Origen without an unambiguous condemnation. The status of Origen's teaching remained an issue in the Church well after Justinian's condemnation, partly for the reasons which the fathers in the *Life of Symeon* outline (p. 152), namely the value of his text-critical and exegetical works. In the mid-seventh century Leontius's contemporary, Maximus the Confessor, was accused of Origenism and defended himself against the charge,[25] and the ongoing popularity of Origen in Syria in this period is well attested.[26] If the issue was no longer relevant in the mid-seventh century (or by the

24. Mango, "A Byzantine Hagiographer," p. 31. Thus also José Grosdidier de Matons, "Les Thèmes d'édification dans la Vie d'André Salos," *Travaux et mémoires* 4 (1970): 290.
25. Maximus, *Relatio motionis* 5, PG 90.120B. Maximus's refutation of Origen can be found in *Ambigua* 7 and 15, PG 91.1068–101, 1216–21. On Maximus's sources for Origenism see Polycarp Sherwood, *The Earlier Ambigua of Saint Maximus the Confessor and His Refutation of Origenism* (Rome: Pontifical Institute, 1955), pp. 72–92. I thank Eric Perl for the reference.
26. On this point see Antoine Guillaumont, Les "Képhalaia Gnostica" d'Évagre le Pontique et l'histoire de l'origénisme chez les grecs et les syriens (Paris: du Seuil, 1962), esp. pp. 173–99.

same token too sensitive), Leontius could have removed it from his text, skipping over it if he had, in fact, found it in a source. The Origen episode in the *Life of Symeon* may thus be taken as evidence not for a sixth-century source, but rather for the continuing relevance of the Origenist controversy in the seventh century.

Indeed, much in the *Life of Symeon* points to a seventh-century date. Other theological concerns expressed in the text can be situated comfortably within the context of seventh-century Cyprus. Leontius's concern with the conversion of Jews (Symeon converts two) reflects imperial policy in the period. Deeply concerned with the loyalty of religious minorities to Byzantine rule after the Persian invasion and conquest of Syria and Egypt (610–29), during which, as we have seen, Jews in Cyprus and Syria sided with the Sassanians, Heraclius issued an edict in 634 demanding the baptism of all Jews.[27] I have already mentioned the account of the Jew who sought baptism on Cyprus during the Arab invasion in the collection attributed to Anastasius the Sinaite. If the treatise entitled *Against the Jews*, surviving sections of which discuss the validity of icons, is correctly attributed to Leontius, it attests to his concern with the presence of Jews and Judaism. If the attribution is false, that text nevertheless reflects mid-seventh-century concerns. In the *Spiritual Meadow*, for instance, John Moschus describes a certain Alexandrian Christian named Cosmas who owned a substantial private library and occupied himself with composing anti-Jewish literature. Cosmas encourages Moschus to engage Jews in discussion in order to convert them.[28] The text known as the *Doctrina Jacobi nuper baptizati*, written in Alexandria around 634 by a Jewish convert to Christianity, provides another example of anti-Jewish propaganda in the period, while at the same time providing further evidence of Jewish conversion.[29]

Another religious group prevalent in the seventh century was the Acephalic Severans, represented in the *Life of Symeon* by the phouska-seller and his wife whom Symeon cajoles into attending the Chalcedonian liturgy. The Acephalic Severans were precisely the group of Monophysites who were the target of Heraclius's experiment with the doctrine of

27. Michael the Syrian, *Chronique* 9.4; cf. F. Dölger, *Regesten der Kaiserurkunden des oströmischen Reiches von 565–1453* (Munich: Oldenbourg, 1924), p. 206.

28. John Moschus, *Spiritual Meadow* 172. Karl Krumbacher suggested (without proof) that this Cosmas encouraged Leontius to write the anti-Jewish tract attributed to him (*Geschichte der Byzantinischen Literatur von Justinian bis zum Ende des oströmischen Reiches (527–1453)* [Munich: Beck, 1897], p. 191).

29. *Doctrina Jacobi nuper baptizati,* ed. F. Nau, *PO* 8 (1912): 745–80. See now the edition of Gilbert Dagron and Vincent Déroche, in "Juifs et Chrétiens dans l'Orient du viie siècle," *Travaux et mémoires* 11 (1991): 70–219.

Monotheletism on Cyprus *circa* 625/6. Paul "the One-eyed," the outspoken leader of this Monophysite communion, was active in Cyprus in the 620s and later was an adversary of Arcadius, archbishop of Constantia.[30] In including Jews and Severans in his narrative, Leontius portrays the world of the mid-seventh century, the anxieties of the fragmented empire, and the local problems of his native Cyprus.

Natural disasters are not precise markers. Mango's second argument for dating the posited paterikon source to the 560s is that the plague of which Symeon has foreknowledge (p. 151) should be identified with the great plague of 542, or perhaps with that of 555. Again, this is ultimately an argument for historical immediacy to the supposed time of Symeon. Plagues, however, returned throughout the rest of the sixth century, during the seventh century, and into the early eighth century.[31] Leontius himself relates a plague in Alexandria during the patriarchate of John the Almsgiver (c. 610–17),[32] and a Syrian chronicle records a devastating plague in the eighteenth Arab year (639) in Palestine[33] in the period immediately preceding the composition of the *Life of Symeon*. Plague was a real concern for Leontius and his audience in the seventh century, and its appearance in his writings should neither be taken as an antiquarian detail nor as a means of dating the subject of his writings. The same applies to earthquakes; it should be remembered that although the earthquake in Evagrius's description of Symeon has been dated by some scholars to the reign of Justinian, Leontius explicitly dates the earthquake in the *Life of Symeon* to the reign of Maurice (582–602; p. 150), a generation after the supposed date of the paterikon which Mango believes he uses as his source.

The three instances of so-called carelessness which Mango identifies at the end of the text[34] do not provide sufficient reason to argue that Leontius was relying heavily on a written source and that he misappropriated it. Mango's first concern, that Symeon visits his "brother" John just before he dies even though it is a long distance from Emesa to the Dead Sea (p. 167), can either be resolved, as Mango himself suggests, by assuming that Symeon traveled to John in spirit rather than in body, or by accepting that Leontius is not particularly troubled by geographical details. Mango's

---

30. On Monophysites in Cyprus in this period see Jan Louis van Dieten, *Geschichte der Patriarchen von Sergios I. bis Johannes VI. (610–715)* (Amsterdam: Hakkert, 1972), pp. 28–30.

31. On the subject of plague in this period see Pauline Allen, "The 'Justinianic' Plague," *Byzantion* 49 (1979): 5–20, esp. pp. 13–14; cf. Evelyne Patlagean, *Pauvreté économique et pauvreté sociale à Byzance 4e–7e siècles* (Paris: Mouton, 1977), pp. 87–91.

32. Leontius, *Life of John* 24.

33. *Chronicon anonymum ad annum domini 819 pertinens*, trans. J.-B. Chabot (Louvain: Durbecq, 1937), p. 200.

34. Mango, "A Byzantine Hagiographer," pp. 31–32.

second problem is that it is unclear which of the two Jews mentioned in the text, the glassblower whose glasses Symeon breaks (p. 163) or the artisan who sees Symeon conversing with angels at the public baths (p. 154), buries Symeon's body (p. 168). The confusion is best explained by suggesting that Leontius never reworked the version we now have to polish it and resolve all inconsistencies.

This solution may also account for Mango's third problem, the fact that although John the deacon is told to look for Symeon's body after three days (p. 167), he does not go to Symeon's hut and only seeks out Symeon's body once it has been buried, discovering an empty grave. Surely biblical typology rather than miscopying accounts for this. The circumstances of Symeon's burial are modeled on the burial of Jesus and the discovery of his empty tomb. Whichever Jew Leontius intends to have buried Symeon is a type for Joseph of Arimathea (Mk 15:43 and parallels), and the Deacon John stands in relation to Peter in the Johannine account of the scene at the tomb (Jn 20:6–7), arriving only in time to find his master's empty garments. We shall return to Leontius's use of the Gospels in the construction of his narrative in chapter 7. Therefore, the so-called confusion in the last chapters of the *Life of Symeon* is inadequately explained by assuming that Leontius is making poor use of a written source. The internal evidence of the *Life of Symeon* does not support Mango's claim that Leontius relied on a source of Emesan provenance datable to the 560s.

Leontius's Versions and the Structure of the *Life*

Having rejected Mango's arguments for Leontius's use of a source close in time to the supposed events of Symeon's life, we are left with the initial concern that the two halves of the life seem to adhere to two very different genres, the feature of the work which suggested multiplicity of authorship to Mango in the first place. Such sharp divisions between the Life and the Miracles were common in early Byzantine hagiography, observes Evelyne Patlagean, citing the *Life of Symeon the Fool* as evidence. She generalizes,

> The division into two of the Lives of saints has not been sufficiently taken into account: first, the acquisition and the inaugural demonstration of miraculous powers, then the exercise of this power in human society, without it ever being endangered or weakened.[35]

35. Patlagean, "Ancient Byzantine Hagiography and Social History," in *Saints and Their Cults: Studies in Religious Sociology, Folklore, and History*, ed. S. Wilson (Cambridge: Cambridge University Press, 1983), p. 107; for the *Life of Symeon* in this pattern, see pp. 116–17 n. 37.

While there is good reason to regard the two halves of the *Life of Symeon* in this way, I believe Leontius's own remarks shed light on the resolution of this problem.

Toward the end of the text, Leontius informs us that the version of the *Life* which we are reading is his second effort at relating the life of Symeon.

> I was eager to commit [Symeon's] miracles and his praiseworthy victory-prize to writing, as far as it is possible for me in my worthlessness, even though I had already done another shorter one [διὰ συντομίας][36] in addition to this, because detailed knowledge of this marvelous story had not yet come to me. (p. 169)

Despite the plain meaning of this passage, Lennart Rydén took Leontius to be referring to the account of Vitalius embedded in Leontius's *Life of John the Almsgiver*.[37] Vitalius was a monk who visited prostitutes in their rooms, appearing to observers to be engaging their services, although he was actually praying for their souls. Presumably on the basis of parallel material in the *Life of Symeon* (pp. 155–56),[38] Rydén argued that in the passage quoted above, Leontius was not conveying that he had written an earlier (now lost) account of Symeon, but rather, that he had written previously on the theme of holy folly.[39] The story of Vitalius, however, is not a tale of holy folly, although it does fall into the broader category of tales of concealed sanctity. Despite the parallel between the two texts, the two accounts are not sufficiently related to convince us that Leontius is referring to the account of Vitalius when he mentions the συντομία. The passage in question must be construed to refer to an earlier life of Symeon.[40] What then can we say about Leontius's earlier version of the text?

Festugière proposed the following solution to the problem of Leontius's two versions. He argued that Leontius wrote a first version that resembled the first part of the extant life.[41] Later he received new material in oral form, presumably a series of anecdotes, which prompted him to write

36. For διὰ συντομίας with the sense of "a shorter version" rather than "earlier" or "in a short while" (as at p. 139 l. 13), cf. Rydén, *Das Leben des heiligen Narren Symeon*, p. 202; see also *idem, Bemerkungen*, p. 141.

37. Leontius, *Life of John* 38. Dawes and Baynes do not translate this chapter in their version (in *Three Byzantine Saints: Contemporary Biographies translated from the Greek*, trans. Elizabeth Dawes and Norman H. Baynes [Crestwood, N.Y.: St. Vladimir's Seminary, 1977], pp. 199–262).

38. I shall discuss these parallels below.

39. Rydén, *Bemerkungen*, pp. 143–44.

40. Thus also Mango, "A Byzantine Hagiographer," p. 29, and Festugière, *Vie de Syméon le Fou*, p. 13.

41. Festugière, *Vie de Syméon le Fou*, pp. 13–15.

a second, fuller version of the life. The assumption here is that Leontius received "reliable" information about Symeon which he could not leave out. (Festugière rejects the possibility that this information was available to Leontius in written form.) But this solution is unlikely. Anecdotal material about Symeon forms the whole of Evagrius's account; Evagrius has no information about Symeon's time before his arrival in Emesa. A narrative about Symeon which said nothing of his folly is inconceivable.

Leontius is unlikely to have written a *Life of Symeon* based on an account without miracles. It is not reasonable to believe that Leontius composed a life of Symeon knowing only of traditions now incorporated in the first part of the *Life;* without anecdotes like those found in Evagrius and in the second half of the *Life of Symeon,* Symeon would not be a subject sufficiently interesting for a saint's life. As I mentioned above, Mango believes that the anecdotal second half was extant first, and that Leontius composed the first half of the *Life* to precede it. In other words, the *Life* was written as an extended introduction to the miracles. With this in mind, I suggest that the reverse of Festugière's argument is more likely, namely that some time after Leontius had written the anecdotal material now in the second half of the *Life,* he invented the rhetorical material in the first half to serve as a frame.

This extended introduction served apologetic purposes. Leontius added the first half of the *Life* as an introduction to the second half in order to show that Symeon had not made a random decision to behave as he did in Emesa. In the episodes related in the second half of the *Life,* Symeon behaves in a manner threatening to the social order. As we shall see in the course of this study, Leontius himself understands some of the material in the second half of the *Life* to be potentially scandalous, and he often attempts to preempt a negative reaction on the part of his audience. Consequently, to discourage others from following Symeon's example, Leontius felt that Symeon should be shown to have gone through elaborate preparations: pilgrimage to Jerusalem, monastic vows, and twenty-nine years living as a grazer (βοσκός) in the desert, conquering his bodily needs.

In the absence of an earlier version of the text, we cannot be sure, but the evidence suggests that Leontius did write two versions, and that the first version consisted largely of the anecdotes in the second half of the *Life.* Later, in response to the reaction of some of his audience, Leontius reworked the *Life,* adding much of the first half of the *Life* as we now know it, and perhaps adding some of the apologetic passages now found in the second half of the *Life.* Here, as before, I believe Leontius's claim to have received reliable information which prompted him to rework the *Life* must be seen as part of the hagiographical topos of the informed witness.

A Possible Written Source

It remains to be determined whether at any stage in his composition of the *Life of Symeon* Leontius relied on a written source. We can know little about oral traditions which may have been available to him, just as we can know little about written sources which have disappeared. Nevertheless, there is one possible written source worthy of our attention, the only other text relating to Symeon extant from Late Antiquity: the passage in the fourth book of Evagrius Scholasticus's *Ecclesiastical History* composed in Antioch during the last decade of the sixth century.[42]

Evagrius's discussion of Symeon is found in a digression from his presentation of events during the reign of Justinian. After a discussion of the Nikē riots in Constantinople in 532, Evagrius shifts his focus to holy men. He writes, "There lived at that season men divinely inspired and workers of distinguished miracles in various parts of the world, but whose glory has shone forth everywhere."[43] Under this heading Evagrius presents short notices of Barsanuphius of Gaza, Symeon of Emesa, and Thomas, who was active in Coele-Syria. Only the account of Symeon concerns us here. Evagrius tells that this certain Symeon appeared insane to those who did not know him, that he lived in solitude, and that no one knew when he fasted and when he ate. Frequently while in the market place he seemed "deprived of his self-possession [ἐκτετράφθαι τοῦ καθεστῶτος]" and often helped himself to food in the local tavern. As the account states,

> But if any one saluted him with an inclination of the head, he would leave the place angrily and hastily, through reluctance that his peculiar virtues should be detected by many persons. Such was the conduct of Symeon in public [κατὰ τὴν ἀγοράν]. But there were some of his acquaintances, with whom he associated without any assumed appearances.[44]

These remarks serve as an introduction to three brief episodes. It is worth noting that all the elements in this introduction are also found scattered about Leontius's *Life of Symeon*. Symeon lives alone in a spare hut (p. 166); his eating habits are a mystery to the residents of Emesa, who see him gorging himself on Holy Thursday (pp. 156–57); he behaves in public in a manner interpreted as insane; he helps himself to food (p. 146); whenever he might be recognized as a holy person, he does something to put others off (p. 147). Finally, Symeon's true identity is known to John, the deacon of

42. Evagrius, *HE* 4.34.
43. Evagrius, *HE* 4.32; trans. p. 415.
44. Evagrius, *HE* 4.34; trans. p. 415.

the church in Emesa, with whom he associates without his manic guise (pp. 160, 166). (The figure of John and his function as "informant" are unknown to Evagrius.)

These are the three episodes which Evagrius relates concerning Symeon: (1) A pregnant girl accused Symeon of being the father of her child. Symeon did not deny this, and pretended to be ashamed. However, when the girl went into a particularly painful labor, Symeon would not allow the baby to be born until she named the real father.[45] (2) Symeon visited a prostitute and remained with her for some time before leaving secretly. To onlookers it appeared that Symeon had engaged her services, although in reality, he had merely brought her food because she was starving. (3) Symeon predicted an earthquake by whipping columns in the agora while raving, "Stand still, if there should be an occasion to dance." When the earthquake did come, only the columns which Symeon whipped remained standing.

The first and third of these episodes have parallels in the *Life of Symeon*. A slave-girl who is pregnant by one of the members of a circus faction accuses Symeon of having raped her (p. 151). As in the version in Evagrius's *History*, the girl can only give birth after she has revealed the true father of the child. Leontius's version is fuller in detail and has the significant difference that instead of pretending to be ashamed, and hiding, Symeon regularly visits the girl during her pregnancy, bringing her bread, meat, and pickled fish. This last element, however, resembles a detail found in Evagrius's second episode, where Symeon feeds the prostitute, and may reflect a conflation of the two stories. On the other hand, Symeon associates with prostitutes elsewhere in the *Life*, although not in episodes which parallel Evagrius (cf. pp. 155–56).[46]

In another episode in the *Life*, Symeon predicts which pillars will stand during an earthquake (which Leontius says occurred during the reign of Maurice) by whipping them and saying, "Your master says, 'Remain standing.' " The narrative continues, "[H]e also went up to one pillar and said to it, 'You neither fall nor stand!' And it was split from top to bottom and bent over a bit and stayed that way" (p. 150). This episode is a version of the earthquake episode related by Evagrius, although there are

---

45. A similar story is told of Macarius in Anan-Isho, *The Paradise of the Fathers* 2.35; ed. with partial Syriac text and a complete English translation: Lady Meux Manuscript No. 6, *Book of Paradise, being the histories and sayings of the monks and ascetics of the Egyptian desert by Palladius, Hieronymous and others. The Syriac texts, according to the recension of Anân Ishô of Bêth Abhê . . .*, ed. and trans. E. A. Wallis Budge, vol. 2 (London: Drugulin, 1904), pp. 417–19. A revised translation appeared in 1934 separating the stories and the sayings under the titles *Stories of the Holy Fathers* and *The Wit and Wisdom of the Christian Fathers of Egypt*.

46. The prostitute episode in Evagrius also parallels the story of Vitalius which Leontius tells in the *Life of John* 38.

no verbal echoes to suggest that Leontius is quoting Evagrius; not even
the precise words of the saint, which one might expect to be preserved,
are the same. Nevertheless the correspondence between these passages,
and particularly between Evagrius's introductory remarks about Symeon
and the various elements of the *Life of Symeon* outlined above, prompts us
to consider a literary relationship between Evagrius's *Ecclesiastical History*
and Leontius's *Life of Symeon the Fool*.

Thus Leontius had Evagrius's account of Symeon available to him as
a source for the *Life of Symeon the Fool*. The fact that all the elements of Evagrius's introductory remarks appear incorporated into Leontius's work
and that two of the three episodes which he relates are found in the *Life of
Symeon* (although in altered form) suggests one of the following possi-
bilities. First, that Leontius and Evagrius drew on the same oral material—something we can never rule out entirely. Second, that Leontius and
Evagrius drew on the same written document. But Evagrius's own observation that the narration of the other deeds which Symeon accomplished
would "require a separate treatise" suggests that he knew of no such written document concerning Symeon of Emesa. Third, that Leontius was familiar with Evagrius's *History* and used it as a bare-bones framework out
of which he constructed his own *Life of Symeon*. This suggestion is further
supported by the fact that in the first half of the *Life*, Leontius presents
Symeon and his friend John as living as grazers (βοσκοί) in the Syrian
desert. An account of such grazers, unrelated to the account of Symeon of
Emesa, can be found in the first book of Evagrius's *History*.[47] As Rydén
has observed, Leontius seems to combine Evagrius's account of the *boskoi*
with the account of Symeon of Emesa when he composes his full-length
vita.[48] Leontius uses the time Symeon "spent" as a *boskos* to account for
how he achieved the state of *apatheia*, so important to Leontius's understanding—indeed his construction—of Symeon.

The fourth possibility for explaining the apparent literary relationship
between Evagrius's *History* and the *Life of Symeon the Fool* is to posit an in-
termediary source which expanded on Evagrius and later found its way
to Leontius's desk. This possibility also can never be completely ruled out,
but it does posit sources which are no longer extant and unnecessarily
complicates a chain of transmission between two authors who wrote
within fifty years of each other. The speculation required for such a model
argues for the likelihood of my third proposition, namely, that Evagrius's

47. Evagrius, *HE* 1.21. Reports of this phenomenon are also found in Sozomen, *Historia
ecclesiastica* (hereafter Sozomen, *HE*) 6.33; and John Moschus, *Spiritual Meadow* 21. Cf. Anan-
Isho, *The Paradise of the Fathers* 2.16a (p. 360) and 2.16d (p. 369).

48. Rydén, "The Holy Fool," in *The Byzantine Saint*, ed. Sergei Hackel (San Bernardino,
Calif.: Borgo, 1983), pp. 108–9.

Ecclesiastical History was Leontius's source for the *Life of Symeon*. That said, I believe it is unnecessary to posit other written sources for the *Life of Symeon*, although there certainly were other influences on Leontius in his composition of the *Life*, as we shall see in the remainder of this study.

The Armenian Synaxary and the *Life of Symeon*

Before we close the discussion of Leontius and his possible sources, the entry for Saint Symeon's day in the Synaxary of the Armenian Church warrants a brief discussion.[49] This lectionary for the liturgical year, based on an eleventh-century collection, was edited by Ter Israel in the thirteenth century. The order and content of the anecdotes related in the reading for St. Symeon's day in this collection are quite similar to those in Leontius, a fact which prompted Festugière to conclude that both Leontius and the citation in the Armenian Synaxary were drawn from the same source.[50] However, the Armenian version includes material found in both the first and second halves of Leontius's *Life of Symeon*. If I am right that Leontius is entirely responsible for both halves, written in somewhat different styles, then it would follow that the Armenian is based solely on Leontius's text. This argument is strengthened by the fact that all the material in the Armenian précis corresponds to passages in Leontius, and the order of events follows that of the *Life of Symeon*, with one exception, a change we can reasonably attribute to the Armenian translator.[51]

Thus the *Life of Symeon the Fool* is the product of the skill and imagination of a mid-seventh-century Cypriot author, Leontius of Neapolis, who, far from slavishly copying sources, composed his work with originality and, as we shall see, a moral purpose. Nevertheless, Leontius did not write without a literary context, and it is to this context that we next turn, for in composing the *Life of Symeon* Leontius was working within an established genre of Late Ancient hagiography, and he drew heavily upon the conventions of that tradition.

49. 15 Hrotits (=21 July), *Le Synaxaire arménien de Ter Israel (XII. mois de Hrotits)*, ed. and trans. G. Bayan, *PO* 21 (1930): 751–60.

50. Festugière, *Vie de Syméon le Fou*, p. 43; Festugière writes, "Ce strict parallélisme dans l'ordre des faits, la ressemblance, ou plutôt l'identité même (*verbatim*), de certaines paroles de Syméon ne permettent pas de douter que et Léontios et le traducteur arménien *n'aient eu entre les mains le même document*" (emphasis in original).

51. Other minor changes (cf. Rydén, *Bemerkungen*, p. 44) should also be attributed to the translator.

· THREE ·

SYMEON AND LATE
ANTIQUE HAGIOGRAPHY

Late Antique hagiography often uses narrative to teach moral lessons. The hagiographer communicates his message to an audience by relating the activities of a holy person. Generally the life narrated is an exemplary life: the saint described serves as a model for others to follow.[1] Athanasius, for instance, presents the *Life of Antony* as an "ideal pattern of the ascetical life."[2] The call to imitate the saint is not, however, universal. In his account of the deeds of Syrian ascetics, including Symeon the Stylite, who spent most of his adulthood atop successively taller pillars in the Syrian desert, Theodoret of Cyrrhus deliberately presents the behavior of some of his heroes as inimitable. He carefully avoids presenting extreme challenges to the body as patterns to be copied. Yet Theodoret takes it for granted that such behavior is glorious and exemplary of Christian virtues.

The case for Symeon the Fool, on the other hand, is far from clear. To be sure, Late Antique saints are reported to have done many strange things: standing on pillars, cross-dressing, donning chains and other iron devices. Nevertheless, it is difficult to see how the *Life of Symeon* might fit established patterns for the representation of holiness or how its hero could be called saintly. After all, Symeon does such things as defecate in

1. On this subject see Peter Brown, "The Saint as Exemplar in Late Antiquity," *Representations* 1.2 (1983): 1–25.
2. Athanasius, *Life of Antony* prologue. Trans. Robert T. Meyer, *The Life of Saint Antony* (New York: Newman, 1978), p. 17.

public, associate freely with prostitutes, and eat gluttonously, especially on fast days. Even when we acknowledge that all saintly behavior deviates from society's norms, Symeon's unsaintly qualities make him stand out among holy men. This chapter explores how Symeon's apparently unsaintly behavior is central to Leontius's construction of the character of Symeon and a key to understanding what Leontius intends when he refers to Symeon as a "Fool for Christ's sake." Closer examination will reveal that much of the *Life* adheres to the patterns which governed the composition of lives of holy people in early Byzantine culture, while other elements of the *Life* are specifically designed to play off such expectations. Our task will then be to recover the resonance and moral value which Symeon's shamelessness had for its Late Antique audience in order to situate the *Life of Symeon* and the peculiar behavior described in it within the traditions of Late Antique Christian hagiography.

Common Hagiographical Patterns in the *Life of Symeon*

By understanding how the *Life of Symeon* conforms to Late Antique canons for sanctity we will be better able to understand the significance of its deviations. Although behavior quite like Symeon's is previously unattested, many aspects of the *Life of Symeon* adhere to conventions known from hagiographical literature.

In its broadest outlines, the *Life of Symeon* is typical of many saints' lives which survive from Late Antiquity.[3] Symeon's relatively high social origins, his "break with the past"[4] and withdrawal from society, his symbolic death in the desert through ascetic practice, his miracles, and his physical death are stock elements of the hagiographical genre.[5] Each of

---

3. On the generic elements of hagiography in Late Antiquity see Alison Goddard Elliot, *Roads to Paradise: Reading the Lives of the Early Saints* (Hanover, N.H.: University Press of New England, 1987), pp. 77–130. Bernard Flusin (*Vie et miracle dans l'oeuvre de Cyrille de Scythopolis* [Paris: Études Augustiniennes, 1983], pp. 87–137) has identified similar motives in the works of the hagiographer Cyril of Scythopolis where he has seen Cyril conforming to models for relating the ascetic life found in Athanasius's *Life of Antony*. See also Giulio Guidorizzi, "Motivi fabieschi nell'agiografia bizantina," in *Studi bizantini e neogreci: Atti del IV congresso nazionale di studi bizantini,* ed. Pietro Luigi Leone (Galatina: Congedo, 1983), pp. 457–67.

4. Elliot, *Roads to Paradise,* p. 81.

5. Robert Browning ("The 'Low Level' Saint's Life in the Early Byzantine World," in *The Byzantine Saint,* ed. Sergei Hackel [San Bernardino, Calif.: Borgo, 1983], pp. 117–27) has observed the following typology to which I am heavily indebted: The holy man withdraws from society; "does not share the needs of ordinary people" for sexual relations and for food; is able to "pass long periods without sleep, in prayer or psalmody"; has no need of shelter;

these conventions is already found in Athanasius's *Life of Antony*, composed in 357, which was one of the earliest, most widely disseminated, and arguably the most influential Late Antique saint's life. Within the next generation these narrative building blocks had become what one might call a hagiographical *koinē*. The conformity of the *Life of Symeon* to patterns established in classic hagiographical texts is striking, particularly in the first half of the *Life*, in which Symeon makes his preparations for his eventual folly. In the second half of the *Life*, Leontius also speaks this hagiographical language even as he inflects it.

Separation from the world is a dominant theme in Late Antique hagiography. In the *Life of Symeon*, Symeon and John withdraw from society in two stages, first by joining the monastery of Abba Gerasimos and later by abandoning the monastery to live as hermits in the desert. Athanasius's Antony makes his withdrawal from the company of others in stages, fleeing first across the Nile to a deserted fortress and later to the more remote "inner mountain" of the desert. This theme of physical withdrawal figures prominently in other popular writings such as the anonymous *History of the Monks of Egypt* (composed c. 395) and various collections of sayings attributed to Egyptian monks known as the *Apophthegmata Patrum*. This trope posits what one scholar has recently called "a dichotomy that separates the complexities of city life from the simplicity of the pastoral setting" and is dependent on the assumption that urban society is generally evil.[6] By fleeing the city, the saint, no longer encumbered by societal obligations, is free to pursue a life of virtue in relative solitude.

Quite often this separation from society demands a severing of family ties. Antony's parents had died shortly before he began to pursue the ascetic life, and he committed his sister to a nunnery before leaving town.[7] In a mid-fifth-century Syriac text, the anonymous "Man of God" escapes his family and his bride, leaving Rome on his wedding day to live as a

---

has no need of clothing; "does not require the support of the family." Browning bases his observations on a sample of full-length Byzantine lives ranging in date from the fifth to the eleventh century. Since the *Life of Symeon* is not included in Browning's sample, its adherence to the model outlined is particularly significant. The article is on the whole excellent. However, Browning's classification of the lives he examines as "low level" is confused. He wishes to use the phrase both to describe the saints' origins as lower class, a characterization which does not hold for all of his examples, and to describe the audience intended for these texts, that is a "popular" audience, presumably in contrast to a highly literate or aristocratic audience. The audiences for Byzantine hagiography are insufficiently understood and require further study. They must be determined on a case-by-case basis before we can generalize. Neither the origins of the saint nor the level of language employed by the author appears to provide faultless criteria for determining a text's audience.

6. James Goehring, "The Encroaching Desert: Literary Production and Ascetic Space in Early Christian Egypt," *JECS* 1 (1993): 282.

7. Athanasius, *Life of Antony* 2–3.

beggar in Edessa.[8] Yet another Symeon, the Syrian Symeon the Younger Stylite, when baptized at the age of two, began repeating, "I have a father and I have not a father; I have a mother and I have not a mother."[9] The early-seventh-century *Life of Theodore of Sykeon* relates that at a young age, following Jesus' command, the saint "fled from his parents and ran to God."[10] Theodore's mother continued to bring him food, but he threw it to the birds and beasts as soon as his mother had gone away. Symeon the Fool's separation from his aged mother is a somewhat more difficult task which causes him much grief. Leontius narrates Symeon's attempts to come to terms with this separation at great length (pp. 130–31, 136–42). Only after God had taken his mother from him was Symeon able to arrive at his "high level [μέτρα μεγάλα]" of virtue (p. 142).

Cultivating this "high level" of virtue involved controlling the body. As part of his strict ascetic regimen, Symeon fasted, abstained from meat and wine, and abstained from sex. Athanasius's Antony fasted continuously and "never bathed his body in water to remove filth."[11] In reward for their endurance and faithfulness, some ascetics of the *History of the Monks of Egypt* are fed heavenly food by the angels.[12] Many ascetics are reported to have cultivated small gardens and eaten only raw vegetables. In a variation on this concept, while in the desert, and before his life of folly, Symeon and John live by "grazing" (p. 133).

Later, in the second half of the *Life,* Leontius deliberately plays with this convention to show how Symeon adheres to it, despite the Emesans' suspicions. Although to the residents of Emesa Symeon appears to have sexual desires (e.g., p. 148) and his appetite appears voracious, even carnivorous (pp. 148, 153), Symeon is "above the burning which is from the Devil," that is, sexual urges (p. 148, cf. p. 155), and secretly keeps a strict ascetic regimen. He eats nothing from the beginning of Lent until Holy Thursday (pp. 156–57). Symeon's diet impresses John the deacon who "felt pity and amazement" at its "indescribable austerity" (p. 148).

Like earlier ascetic types, Symeon has little need for shelter or cloth-

8. *La légende syriaque de saint Alexis, l'homme de Dieu,* ed. and trans. Arthur Amiaud (Paris: Vieweg, 1889). For a discussion of this text see chapter 4.

9. *Life of Symeon the Younger* 5; *La vie ancienne de S. Syméon Stylite le jeune (521–592),* 2 vols., ed. P. van den Ven (Brussels: Société des Bollandistes, 1962–70). Trans. Browning, "'Low-Level' Saint's Life," p. 120. Daniel the Stylite's parents dedicate him to a monastery where he receives a new name (*Life of Daniel* 3).

10. George of Sykeon, *Life of Theodore of Sykeon* 12, cf. 15. Text: *Vie de Théodore de Sykéon,* 2 vols., ed. Festugière (Brussels: Société des Bollandistes, 1970). Translation: in *Three Byzantine Saints,* trans. Elizabeth Dawes and Norman H. Baynes (Crestwood, N.Y.: St. Vladimir's Seminary, 1977), p. 95. Cf. Mt 10:37, 19:29; Lk 14:26.

11. Athanasius, *Life of Antony* 47; trans. Meyer, p. 60.

12. *Historia monachorum in Aegypto* (hereafter *HME*) 2.9 (Abba Or), 8.6 (Abba Apollo), 11.5 (Abba Sourous).

ing. Leontius does not specify what sort of dwelling Symeon and John inhabit in the desert (p. 137), although they spend much of their time praying out of doors. They practice their asceticism "in cold and in heat" (p. 142), a feat of endurance which recalls the harsh austerities of the Syrian ascetics portrayed by Theodoret, many of whom spend their life out of doors. Consider this description of Eusebius of Teleda: "during frost he sits in the shade, in flaming heat he takes the sun and welcomes its flames as if it were a westerly breeze."[13] In Emesa, Symeon lives in a hut (καλύβιον) which contains only a bundle of twigs (p. 166) and wears only an old cloak (παλλίον, cf. Latin *pallium*; p. 147) and a tunic (p. 156). (On the other hand, Symeon's decision to walk naked on the way to the baths [pp. 148–49] and his dancing naked in the streets with prostitutes [p. 156] should probably not be taken to signal the saint's lack of need for clothing.) Symeon can endure the elements; he suffers neither from cold, hunger, nor heat, in Leontius's words, "nearly exceed[ing] the limit of human nature" (p. 142). He is even able to hold live coals in his hands (p. 146).

The discipline of the body allows the ascetic to engage in what may have been his primary activity, the life of prayer. In the desert, Symeon and John pray "unceasingly" (p. 139). While in Emesa he "often passed the night without sleeping, praying until morning, drenching the ground with his tears" (p. 166). Similarly Antony prays constantly in silence, following the teachings of the New Testament (1 Thes 5:17, Mt 6:6, Lk 18:1).[14] Constant prayer figures prominently throughout the lives of hermits and especially in the lives of stylites. The anonymous "Man of God" prays through the night on the steps of the church.[15]

These markers of the holy life find their origin and justification in the biographies and in the teachings of Jesus. Jesus resisted temptation in the desert. Similarly, Jesus commanded a life separated from one's earthly family and taught his followers to pray. I take up the question of the fashioning of the *Life of Symeon* on the life of Jesus in chapter 7, but it is worth noting here the degree to which the lives of the saints are imitations of the lives of the Christ. This is nowhere more evident than in the sort of miracles performed in Late Antique saints' lives.

13. Theodoret, *Historia religiosa* (hereafter Thdt., *HR*) 4.12; trans. R. M. Price, *A History of the Monks of Syria* (Kalamazoo: Cistercian, 1985), p. 55. Cf. 1.2, 16.1, 18.1, 21, 23. This is, of course, the case for the stylites Symeon (Thdt., *HR* 26; cf. Jacob of Serug, *Homily on Symeon the Stylite*, trans. Harvey, in *Ascetic Behavior in Greco-Roman Antiquity: A Sourcebook*, ed. Vincent Winbush [Minneapolis: Fortress, 1990], pp. 19–20) and Daniel (*Life of Daniel the Stylite*, in *Les saints stylites*, ed. Delehaye [Brussels: Société des Bollandistes, 1923], pp. 1–94; Eng. trans. in Dawes and Baynes, *Three Byzantine Saints*, pp. 1–71).

14. Athanasius, *Life of Antony* 3.

15. I take up this topic again in the next chapter. For the centrality of prayer in Syrian Christianity, see Harvey, *Asceticism and Society in Crisis: John of Ephesus and* The Lives of the Eastern Saints (Berkeley: University of California Press, 1990), pp. 8–9.

The extraordinary powers of typical early Byzantine holy men are divine gifts, signs of individual sanctity which mediate God's grace to others.[16] The *Life of Symeon* makes use of motifs and miracle types commonplace in Late Antique literature.[17] After a few years of strenuous ascetic practice in the desert, Leontius relates that Symeon and John "were judged worthy of divine visions, and God's assurances, and miracles" (p. 139). Like so many of the desert ascetics described in the *History of the Monks of Egypt,* and in Theodoret's *Religious History,* Symeon has the gifts of prophecy and clairvoyance.[18] While working as a water carrier in a tavern in Emesa, Symeon is able to discern which wine jar has been poisoned by the Devil (p. 147). He predicts an earthquake (p. 150) and knows in advance which children will die of the plague (p. 151). He knows by clairvoyance whether his friends, the reforming prostitutes, have fornicated while absent from him (p. 156).

More complicated is the question of Symeon's ability to heal, since Symeon seems to afflict people with physical problems as often as he cures them. Miraculous healings, of course, are ubiquitous in hagiography and are perhaps the most important point of contact between holy people and the laity. In addition to the narratives of desert ascetics, miracle stories fill the pages of longer *vitae.* With a repertoire of magical phrases, holy oil, and the sign of the cross, Theodore of Sykeon heals the mute, the lame, the paralyzed, the feverish, and those with dislocated limbs and issues of blood.[19] The sixth-century *Life of Nicholas of Sion* relates how, among other things, the saint cured blindness and constipation.[20] Most of these miracles have antecedents in the gospels. As for Symeon the Fool, after causing a group of girls who make fun of him to become cross-eyed, he heals some of them, but leaves the others cross-eyed, thus preventing the permanently cross-eyed ones from "exceed[ing] all the women of Syria in debauchery" (p. 158), a cure of sorts. In the process of curing a

16. Cf. Harvey, *Asceticism and Society,* p. 14.

17. Among the extraordinary powers of Early Byzantine saints, Browning ("'Low Level' Saint's Life," pp. 121–23) identifies endurance, prophecy and clairvoyance, the power to heal, the ability to overcome demons, control over the forces of nature, visions, ability to provide food miraculously, ability to punish those who question his powers, and longevity. Not all of Browning's saints display all these features, but as he says, "all show some of them, and many show all of them" (p. 126). Again I acknowledge my debt to Browning's typology.

18. *HME* 1.1–3, 10–11, 28; 6.1; 8.48; 10.12; 11.4; 12.11; 22.6–8; Thdt., *HR* 1.3; 2.14; 13.17; 15.4; 21.17; 24.19; cf. George of Sykeon, *Life of Theodore of Sykeon* 54, 119.

19. George of Sykeon, *Life of Theodore of Sykeon* 65, 67, 68, 69, 81, 85, 96. Cf. Athanasius, *Life of Antony* 56–64; *HME* 1.12, 16; 6.1; 7.2; 10.1; 13.9; 21.17; 22.3–4; 26; Thdt., *HR* 2.19, 20; 9.5, 7; 13.9, 13; 14.3; 16.2; 26.16; *Life of Daniel the Stylite* 74.

20. *Life of Nicholas of Sion* 33, 34. Text and translation: *The Life of Saint Nicholas of Sion,* ed. and trans. Ihor Ševčenko and Nancy Patterson Ševčenko (Brookline, Mass.: Hellenic College, 1984).

man with leucoma, Symeon nearly burns the man's eyes in his first attempt, but he does eventually cure him (p. 161). Leontius's narration of Symeon's miracles depends on a reader's expectation of how saints are supposed to perform miracles. Symeon's miracles function not only to show that Symeon is holy, but also to challenge more conventional notions of sanctity. Symeon's deviations and his destructive power are part of Leontius's commentary on the ambiguity of holiness itself.

Closely related to the miracles of healing are tales of exorcism. Much of Athanasius's *Life of Antony* describes his battles with demons; a quarter of this text is devoted to a discourse on the work of the Devil which Antony delivers to his disciples. Casting out demons by methods culled from the gospels or by making the sign of the cross plays a major role in lives of holy men living near small towns, such as Nicholas of Sion and Theodore of Sykeon.[21] Perhaps because of the close association between madness and demon possession, Symeon battles the demonic particularly deftly. Symeon and John overcome demons in the desert (p. 138), "enduring many and unutterable temptations from the Devil and conquering them" (p. 142). And Symeon does battle with demons while in Emesa: he casts out the demon possessing an adulterous youth (pp. 149–50); he chases an unclean spirit (in the form of an Ethiopian) from the phouska-seller's shop (pp. 153–54); and he prevents a demon from attacking townspeople in the agora (p. 157). Symeon is said to have "extraordinary compassion for those possessed by demons" (p. 162).

Another Christ-like miracle of Late Antique saints is the ability to feed the multitudes. Miraculous feedings figure in the descriptions of a number of Egyptian monks, such as Abba Apollo, whose prayers result in lavish Easter banquets of exotic foods and who also multiplies loaves during a famine.[22] Gregory of Nyssa tells of his sister Macrina's "farming miracle" in which "the grain was distributed according to need and showed no sign of diminishing."[23] Symeon the Fool provides banquets miraculously on two occasions (pp. 159, 164). He also gives food away free in the marketplace (p. 146) to feed the poor and hungry.

Miracles can exact justice. Occasionally holy men use their powers to punish wrongdoers and nonbelievers. When a group of pagan girls stares shamelessly at Theodoret's James of Nisibis, he changes their hair to gray. When villagers concoct a ruse that one of them is dead and request that

---

21. *Life of Nicholas of Sion* 26, 61, 63, 65, 66, 73, 74. George of Sykeon, *Life of Theodore of Sykeon* 71, 84, 86, 87, 123. Cf. *HME* 2.6; 10.1; 15.1; 24.10; Thdt., *HR* 3.9, 22; 9.4, 9–10; 13.10; 16.2.

22. *HME* 8. For further discussion of miraculous feeding, see chapter 7.

23. Gregory of Nyssa, *Life of Saint Macrina*, trans. Kevin Corrigan (Toronto: Peregrina, 1987), p. 61.

James resurrect him, the saint says a prayer for the man, during which he actually dies. Later James resurrects the dead man. Julian Saba causes the death of a heretic.[24] Symeon prolongs the labor of a pregnant slave-girl who has accused the fool falsely of paternity (pp. 151–52).[25] Symeon strikes mute the Jewish artisan, who "blasphemed Christ all the time," after the Jew sees Symeon conversing with two angels at the baths (p. 154). Symeon also silences a local village headman who understands that Symeon is holy (p. 156). These ostensibly punitive actions underscore Symeon's hidden sanctity, silencing those who understand his powers and might reveal them.

As this survey makes clear, to a great extent Leontius portrays Symeon within the model of a holy man. The first half of the *Life of Symeon* establishes Symeon's freedom from ordinary needs in a fairly conventional manner. Symeon conforms to the ascetic profile of withdrawal from society in order to focus on a refashioning of the body. The second half of the *Life* portrays Symeon manifesting the power of a more "ordinary" holy man, performing the sorts of deeds found attributed to saints in other texts. Leontius does not challenge the conventional model of the holy man in narrating the *Life of Symeon*; rather he adheres to this model and is able to convey Symeon's holiness to his audience by narrating episodes which his audience understands as signs of Symeon's holiness. So much conforms to established patterns for narrating the life of a holy man that Symeon's seemingly unsaintly behavior appears all the more anomalous. While the next chapter will show that there are precedents for some aspects of Symeon's deviance, we must first consider what Leontius's audience would have made of just that which most deviates from the holy man model, namely, Symeon's shamelessness.

Symeon's Behavior and Ascetic Practice

Symeon's behavior confounds the residents of Emesa. To some, his actions appear as the deeds of a madman. The children who see him dragging a dead dog behind him call out, "Hey, a crazy abba" (p. 145). The residents of Emesa "believed that [Symeon] was just like the many who babbled and prophesied because of demons" (p. 156). When there was a new moon, "he looked at the sky and fell down and thrashed about" (p. 155), a literal lunatic.

Symeon's relation to the Emesans is nothing less than adversarial.

24. Thdt., *HR* 1.4–6, 8–13 (James); 2.21–22 (Julian); cf. 8.9; 9.12; 14.4; 15.3; 26.18.
25. On this common trope, see the discussion in chapter 4.

They respond to Symeon's apparent madness with harsh blows. When he throws nuts at the women in church and overturns the tables of the pastry chefs on his way out, he is nearly beaten to death (p. 146). When the phouska-seller and his wife discover Symeon's empty cash box, showing that Symeon has given their merchandise away for free, they beat him and pull his beard (p. 146). When Symeon breaks a jar of wine which he knows has been poisoned by a snake, the tavern keeper strikes him with a piece of wood (p. 147). When he enters the women's bath, the women beat him and throw him out (p. 149). For some, Symeon's folly is a source of amusement: The townsfolk go to the tavern where Symeon is employed as a water carrier as a diversion, presumably to be entertained by him (p. 147). In short, the residents of Emesa are unaware of Symeon's sanctity and treat him as a madman, which to all appearances he is. The beatings and derision he receives, however, are never unprovoked. The behavior of the other characters in the narrative is always in reaction to some outlandish and often destructive thing which Symeon has done.[26]

The inhabitants of Emesa react to Symeon with righteous indignation. Sometimes people who see him are simply described as "shocked" or "scandalized" (σκανδαλίζω). A monk from a nearby monastery is "scandalized" to see Symeon gorging himself on beans (p. 153); the headman of a nearby village is "scandalized" when he sees Symeon being carried by one prostitute while being whipped by another (p. 156); passersby are "scandalized" to see Symeon gorging himself in a cake shop on the morning of Holy Thursday, when he should be fasting (p. 156); the Deacon John, who knows of Symeon's true nature, claims not to be "scandalized" to see Symeon eating raw meat (p. 158). In each case the shock is in response to Symeon's violation of the norms of Christian ascetic practice and common decency.

The regulation of desires for sex and for food was a proverbial component of the lives of those regarded as holy. In the past decade, the work of Michel Foucault, Aline Rousselle, and Peter Brown has clarified the nature of the ascetic discipline which Late Antique people considered necessary to achieving control over their bodies. Ascetic concerns focused particularly on sexual desire and the consumption of food, concepts which were integrally related, since proper dietary regimen was believed to lead directly to the diminishing of sexual impulses.[27] As Rousselle observes,

26. On the treatment of the insane in Byzantine society see Michael Dols, "Insanity in Byzantine and Islamic Medicine," *DOP* 38 (1984): 135–48.

27. Foucault, *The Care of the Self*, vol. 3 of *The History of Sexuality*, trans. Robert Hurley (New York: Vintage, 1986), esp. pp. 99–144; Aline Rousselle, *Porneia: On Desire and the Body in Antiquity*, trans. Felicia Pheasant (Oxford: Blackwell, 1988), pp. 160–78; Peter Brown, *The*

[F]rom the beginning of the fourth century, the Christian texts are full of
. . . notions of physiology linked with dietetics. They appealed to the
whole Graeco-Roman world. Control of sexuality through a lifestyle
based on physiology and a carefully chosen diet was an everyday concern.[28]

This was all the more true of Christian religious. In fact, achieving control
over their bodies made men and women holy in the eyes of others.

The first half of the *Life of Symeon* presents the saint as the model
desert ascetic. Leontius's language exalts monasticism in conventional
ways: The monks of the monastery of Abba Gerasimos are "angels of
God" (p. 124), the road to the monastery is "the road which leads to life"
(p. 125), and the life pursued there is referred to as "the virtuous life"
(p. 127). When Symeon and John retire to the remote desert to live as hermits, their battles with the temptations of the Devil and devotion to unceasing prayer (p. 139) recall the accounts of the eremitic life in the *Apophthegmata Patrum.*

Particularly important in this model for achieving sanctity is the contrast between desert and city.[29] Leontius articulates this well. Before
Symeon leaves the desert for the city, a journey which he undertakes both
to save souls and to "mock the world [ἐμπαίζω τῷ κόσμῳ]" (p. 142), John
warns him of the dangers of leaving the life of the desert.

> Beware, be on your guard, brother Symeon, unless as the desert gathered
> together, the world disperses; and as silence helped, commotion hinders;
> and as much as keeping watch [through the night] brought, you lose
> through sleep. Be on your guard, brother, lest the delusion of worldly
> things corrupts the prudence of the monastic life. Beware, lest the fruit
> from the privation of women, from whom God has saved you until to-
> day, be destroyed by spending time with them. Beware, lest the love of
> possessions carry off poverty, lest foods fatten the body, which fasting
> has melted away. Beware, brother, lest you lose your compunction
> through laughter and your prayer through your carelessness. Beware,
> please, lest when your face laughs, your mind be dissolved, lest when
> your hands fondle, your soul fondles as well, lest when your mouth eats,
> your heart eats as well, lest when your feet walk, your inner silence
> dances along recklessly, and to speak concisely, lest as much as the body
> does outwardly, the soul does inwardly. (p. 143)

Body and Society: Men, Women, and Sexual Renunciation in Early Christianity (New York: Co-
lumbia University Press, 1988), esp. pp. 213–40, 323–38. Note also Arthur Vööbus, *History of
Asceticism in the Syrian Orient: A Contribution to the History of Culture in the Near East*, vol. 3
(Louvain: Peeters, 1988), and Harvey, *Asceticism and Society*, pp. 43–56.

28. Rousselle, *Porneia*, pp. 177–78.

29. See Goehring, "Encroaching Desert," pp. 281–96.

In addition to listing the components of ascetic practice and its goals (all of which Symeon has achieved), John's speech portrays the city as a place where the practice of asceticism is difficult. While in Emesa, Symeon will necessarily come into contact with food, sexual temptations, and levity, since these are basic elements of lay urban life. By appearances, Symeon's activity in Emesa is the complete antithesis of asceticism, since he appears to engage in sexual activity and to eat large quantities, including proscribed foods.

In many episodes, Symeon appears to the residents of Emesa to have strong sexual desires. He appears to attempt to rape the tavern keeper's wife (p. 148); Symeon plays along with a female slave's claim that he raped and impregnated her (p. 151). Some examples of Symeon's scandalousness are less obvious to the modern reader. When Symeon predicts which schoolboys will die of plague, he kisses each of them saying, "Farewell, my dear [καλέ μου]" (p. 151). If left alone, these farewell kisses would be innocent. But Leontius prefaces the story with the remark that Symeon lived in a manner which appeared "irredeemable [ἀσωτεύεσθαι]" (pp. 150–51), thereby sexually charging the episode. John the deacon invites Symeon to come with him to the baths. Symeon receives this invitation enthusiastically, whereupon he strips off his clothing and wraps it around his head like a turban (p. 148). Thus, with his genitals exposed and his sexuality starkly apparent, he walks past the men's bath and "rushes willingly" into the women's. Symeon skips through the street with "dancing-girls" and "disreputable women" (θυμεκιλή and ἄσεμνα γύναια, pp. 154–55) and is seen regularly with prostitutes (ἑταίρες, p. 155) to whom Leontius refers as Symeon's girlfriends (φίλη, pp. 155–56). He counts among his girlfriends an amulet maker (p. 162). Young girls whom he has caused to be cross-eyed run after Symeon in the streets demanding to be kissed (p. 158).

Similarly, in public, Symeon's eating habits are flagrant violations of ascetic and common social norms. He eats a whole pot of lupines while working in a food stall in the market (p. 146). Later, in a tavern, a monk is scandalized by Symeon's gluttony when he sees Symeon "eating beans like a bear" (p. 153). The tavern keeper exclaims that Symeon "eats meat as if he's godless," for as Leontius explains, "without tasting bread all week, the righteous one often ate meat" (p. 148). Symeon is seen devouring pastries in a cake shop on Holy Thursday (pp. 156–57). On Sundays, when he can be seen eating a string of sausages with mustard, his bingeing lasts from morning on (pp. 160–61). Raw meat is also standard fare (p. 158). Moreover, the consequences of such consumption are equally public. Symeon defecates unabashedly in the marketplace, graphic proof that he has not been fasting.[30]

Given Symeon's tendency to transgress against the conventions established for the behavior of monks and, in many cases, for the laity, it is not difficult to see why Leontius portrays the population of Emesa reacting with horror to Symeon's antics. In his introduction to the *Life*, Leontius writes: "[T]o those more impassioned and more fleshly he seemed to be a defilement, a sort of poison, and an impediment to the virtuous life on account of [his] appearance" (p. 122). Leontius himself understands Symeon's public behavior to be potentially transgressive and incapable of being reconciled with traditional conceptions of sanctity. If it were not for the rigorous ascetic practices which Symeon conducts in private, he would be the crazy man he appears to be. How then does Leontius justify Symeon's behavior?

Symeon's Shamelessness and Leontius's Apologetics

Leontius devotes a good deal of the *Life of Symeon* to Symeon's defense. He offers apologetic statements throughout the introduction (pp. 121–23) and scatters explanatory asides between the anecdotes which make up the second half of the *Life*. Throughout the narration of these transgressions, of course, Leontius's audience is in on the "joke"; they know that the offended residents of Emesa are mistaken and do not perceive that Symeon is, in fact, not disgusting but holy. Most readers must have enjoyed *Life of Symeon* for its slapstick humor.[31] Nevertheless, the work's apologetic tone suggests that Leontius believed some members of his audience would

30. Consider the three epigrams of Agathias (late sixth century) which are said to have been written in a toilet in Smyrna, each of which relates painful defecation to excessive gluttony (*Anthologia Palatina* [hereafter *Anth. Pal.*] 9.642–44). See also Brown, "The Problem of Miraculous Feeding in the Graeco-Roman World," *Center for Hermeneutical Studies: Colloquy* 42 (Berkeley: Graduate Theological Union, 1982), pp. 16–24, esp. p. 17. Artemidorus, author of a second-century book on the interpretation of dreams, believed that dreaming of defecation in public was particularly inauspicious, since it meant that the dreamer would become the object of hatred (Artemidorus, *Oneirocritica* 2.26).

31. Mary Douglas has distinguished between jokes and obscenity. As she says, "The first amuses, the second shocks" ("Jokes," *Implicit Meanings: Essays in Anthropology* [London: Routledge and Kegan Paul, 1975], p. 106). Similarly she distinguishes "the taboo breaker whose polluting act is a real offence to society" and the "joker," a person who is able to say certain things with immunity. In narrating the obscene, the joker transforms the obscene into a joke. This difference between doing the obscene and telling about it separates Symeon from Leontius. Nevertheless, Leontius appears compelled to explain to his audience that they should not be offended by the story he narrates.

indeed have found Symeon's behavior offensive. Leontius's apologetic statements are intended to preempt negative reactions to the episodes which he relates and may even respond to criticisms of his first version of the text. These statements reveal the sorts of criticisms which Leontius anticipated not merely from the fictionalized residents of his narrative's Emesa, but, given the placement and frequency of these statements, from his audience as well. They also provide a clearer sense of the portrayal of Symeon which Leontius wished to impart.[32]

Leontius contrasts the opinion of the residents of Emesa with his own understanding of Symeon. In his introduction Leontius explains that Symeon "rose to the most pure and impassible height" (p. 122) despite appearing to be a defilement. Symeon remains unpolluted by his behavior, like a "pearl which has traveled through slime unsullied" (p. 122). The slime, of course, is the city with all its trappings (cf. p. 143, quoted above). (At the end of the text Leontius compares Symeon in Emesa to Lot in Sodom [p. 169].) Symeon,

> through spending time in the city, hanging around with women, and the rest of the deception of his life . . . truly sought to show a weakness in the virtuous life to the slothful and pretentious and the power granted by God to those who truly serve against the spirits of evil with all their souls. (p. 122)

Through sharing his narration with them, Leontius fashions his audience to be like "those who truly serve against the spirits of evil" and unlike the slothful and pretentious, for they are able to see in Symeon the "power granted by God." Leontius requests that his audience "regard [his] writings with fear of the Lord" and with Christian faith, since he knows that "to the most senseless and disdainful [he seems] to be relating something incredible and worthy of laughter" (p. 122).

Symeon's behavior and especially his deception of the residents of Emesa is justified by the fact that he was able to perform the deeds of a holy man while under cover. "There was this for the glorification and admiration of God: the gestures which caused some to believe that Symeon led an irredeemable life were often those through which he displayed his miracles" (pp. 150–51). By pretending to be crazy, Symeon converts heretics, Jews, fornicators, prostitutes, and other sinners; and by

---

32. If the first half of the *Life of Symeon* is the product of a second stage of composition, as I suggested in chapter 2, the defensive passages there may well reflect actual audience reaction to the earlier parts of the text. The possibility remains that the asides which fall (occasionally awkwardly) between anecdotes in the second half of the text are also part of a second stage of composition.

this method he is also able to keep his holiness concealed. After the incident in which Symeon enters the women's bath, Leontius remarks, "Some of his deeds the righteous one did out of compassion for the salvation of humans, and others he did to hide his way of life" (p. 149). Symeon wishes to hide his ascetic practice and the level of impassivity which he has achieved through this practice.

With this in mind we can understand Leontius's apologetics for Symeon's apparent sexual and gastronomic indulgence. In an episode alluded to earlier, John the deacon invites Symeon to join him in a refreshing bath. On the way to the bathhouse, Symeon strips naked and places his garment on his head like a turban. He passes the entrance to the men's bath and proceeds toward the women's. In response to John's protests, Symeon replies, "Leave me alone, you idiot, there's hot and cold water here, and there's hot and cold water there, and it doesn't matter at all whether [I use] this one or that" (p. 149). Despite the segregation which is determined by convention, for Symeon there is no inherent difference between the men's and women's baths. Later, Symeon, no longer feigning madness, explains to John about the event, "I felt neither that I had a body nor that I had entered among bodies, but the whole of my mind was on God's work, and I did not part from him" (p. 149). In short, Symeon was no longer affected by sexual desire. Elsewhere in the *Life*, Leontius writes,

> The blessed one advanced to such a level of purity and impassivity [ἀπάθεια] that he often skipped and danced, holding hands with one dancing-girl on this side and another on that, and he associated with them and played with them in the middle of the whole circus, so that the disreputable women threw their hands into his lap, fondled him, poked him, and pinched him. But the monk, like pure gold, was not defiled by them at all. (pp. 154–55)

Leontius further relates that Symeon had had a vision in the desert in which the Abba Nikon appeared to him and sprinkled Symeon's genitals with holy water while making the sign of the cross, thus purifying Symeon and making him free from the nuisance of erections and all sexual desire (p. 155). Perhaps Leontius alludes to this event in his introduction when he writes that Symeon "quenched the burning of the flesh with the dew of the Holy Spirit" (p. 123). Leontius's defense of Symeon highlights his concealed sanctity.

As for the matter of Symeon's public gluttony, although he eats meat in public, he abstains completely from bread (p. 148). While in Emesa, he maintained a regimen of "indescribable austerity" and "possessed the gift of abstinence [ἐγκράτεια] in a way not many of the saints do" (p. 156). He does not eat through the entirety of Lent (pp. 148, 156–57). Similarly, when the monks discover Symeon gorging himself on lupines in the tavern, Symeon remarks that they had been soaked for forty days (p. 153) during which, presumably, he had eaten nothing.

Symeon's shamelessness is predicated on his blessedness. Immediately before the bathhouse episode, in connection with Symeon's defecation in public, Leontius relates that Symeon was "entirely as if he had no body [ὥσπερ ἀσώματος]" (p. 148), an assertion which parallels his earlier statement that Symeon "perceived himself fearing neither suffering, nor cold, nor hunger, nor burning heat, but rather nearly [σχεδόν] exceeded the limit of human nature" (p. 142). Leontius does not claim that Symeon had achieved a state of bodilessness, merely that he *approached* that state.

These claims, of course, are concerned not so much with social convention as with theological self-understanding. Christian theological anthropology understood the spiritual freedom which came through strict *askēsis*. For many Late Ancient Christians, Leontius included, the term "bodiless" (ἀσώματος) described the angels.[33] Ascetics, in their practice, regularly aspired to approach the state of the angels, a state which was, among other things, sexless.[34] One finds parallels for Leontius's claims about Symeon in a wide range of Late Antique sources, including the writings of Evagrius Ponticus. Evagrius argued,

> To separate the body from the soul is the privilege only of the One who has joined them together. But to separate the soul from the body lies as well in the power of the man who pursues virtue. For our Fathers gave to the meditation of death and to the flight from the body a special name: *anachoresis*.[35]

Symeon had practiced this "flight from the body" for twenty-nine years in the Judean desert and had been so successful that he was granted the ability to appear shameless while maintaining his spiritual perfection.

33. *Life of Symeon*, pp. 135.5, 168.23, 170.7; cf. Lampe, s.v.
34. On the angelic state in Late Antiquity see Brown, *Body and Society*, pp. 325–32.
35. Evagrius Ponticus, *Praktikos* 52; trans. John Eudes Bamberger, *The Praktikos and Chapters on Prayer* (Spencer, Mass.: Cistercian, 1970), p. 30. On the goals of asceticism in the writings of Evagrius see Elizabeth A. Clark, "New Perspectives on the Origenist Controversy: Human Embodiment and Ascetic Strategies," *Church History* 59 (1990): 145–62, and Michael Wallace O'Laughlin, "Origenism in the Desert: Anthropology and Integration in Evagrius Ponticus" (Th.D. diss., Harvard University, 1987). The popularity of Evagrius, especially in Syriac-speaking circles, beyond 553 is well attested. Many of Evagrius's teachings were condemned at the Fifth Ecumenical Council in 553 for their association with the teachings of Origen. (Cf. Antoine Guillaumont, *Les "Képhalaia Gnostica" d'Évagre le Pontique et l'histoire de l'origénisme chez les grecs et chez les syriens* [Paris: du Seuil, 1962].) Leontius's treatment of Origen and the Origenist controversy fall far short of condemnation and might lead one to speculate that the character of Symeon the Fool is drawn with an Origenist model in mind.

It is also tempting to associate the behavior of Symeon the Fool with the conception of human perfection found in the anonymous collection of late-fourth- or early-fifth-century Syriac sermons known as the *Liber Graduum* or *Book of Degrees* (*Ktava demasqatha*), often regarded as heterodox.[36] According to the author of these sermons, ascetics could achieve a state of perfection, at which point they acquired tremendous license to behave as they might. Peter Brown has written, "For them there were no boundaries, no social statuses, no objects of avoidance. For them no thing was unclean. . . . Filled with the Spirit, they felt as little shame at the robust profanity of urban life as a child wandering through a brothel."[37] Such a theological stance might explain how a "historical" Symeon's behavior would have appeared to an onlooker. But in his literary efforts Leontius does not go so far; he makes it plain that Symeon never rejected his extreme ascetic practice in private and that it would have been undesirable for him to do so. Furthermore, Symeon's apparent license is never presented as a model either for Leontius's lay audience or for other ascetics.

Leontius's language is better understood within the common vocabulary of ascetic practice described by writers generally regarded as orthodox by the Chalcedonian hierarchy of the period. One of the Pseudo-Macarian sermons describes successful ascetics thus: "At . . . times they are like incorporeal angels [ὥσπερ ἄγγελοι ἀσώματοι], they are so light and transcendent, even in the body."[38] We find similar statements in the writings of Basil of Caesarea, John Chrysostom, Isidore of Pelusium, and Theodoret of Cyrrhus.[39]

Concerning the mix of public indulgence and private austerity in the *Life of Symeon* Patlagean has suggested, "[T]he whole story is constructed on an ascetic reversal of the values of ascesis."[40] Ironically, to the extent

36. Brown, *Body and Society*, pp. 334–36; text: *Liber Graduum*, ed. Michael Kmosko (Paris: Firmin-Didot, 1926). Kmosko has associated the *Liber Graduum* with Messalianism. But Robert Ratcliff has argued convincingly against identifying the *Liber Graduum* with the Messalian movement; see Ratcliff, "Steps along the Way to Perfection: The *Liber Graduum* and Early Syrian Monasticism" (Ph.D. diss., Emory University, 1988), pp. 33–93; cf. Arthur Vööbus, *History of Asceticism in the Syrian Orient*, p. 2. On the conception of human perfection in the *Liber Graduum*, see now Aleksander Kowalski, *Perfezione e guistizia di Adamo nel Liber Graduum* (Rome: Pontificum Institutum Orientale, 1989), pp. 35–115.

37. Brown, *Body and Society*, p. 335; with reference to *Liber Graduum* 7.15, 22.3, and 15.4.

38. Pseudo-Macarius, *Spiritual Homilies* 18.7; trans. George A. Maloney, *Intoxicated with God: Fifty Spiritual Homilies of Macarius* (Denville, N.J.: Dimension, 1978), p. 126.

39. Basil *Sermo asceticus* 1.2 (PG 31.873b); John Chrysostom, *Homilia in Matt* 70.5 (PG 58.660); Isidore of Pelusium, *Epistulae* 1.477 (PG 78.444a); Thdt., *HE* 3.24.1 (PG 82.1117).

40. Evelyne Patlagean, "Ancient Byzantine Hagiography and Social History," in *Saints and Their Cults: Studies in Religious Sociology, Folklore, and History*, ed. S. Wilson (Cambridge: Cambridge University Press, 1983), p. 110.

that his odd behavior prevents Symeon from indulging in the acclaim of others, it *is* an ascetic discipline. But Leontius does not present Symeon's apparently antiascetic behavior as an acceptable substitute for more conventional ascetic practice; for while Symeon's actions are based on the reversal of practices associated with achieving the status of holiness in Late Antiquity, Leontius presents Symeon's public behavior in Emesa as abominable. In presenting Symeon as profane in public, yet ultimately holy in his private practices, Leontius affirms the conventional asceticism of Late Antique Christianity, an asceticism which, as we have seen, Symeon follows diligently in the desert and does not reject when he goes to the city.

Symeon goes to Emesa in order to save souls. He asks John, "What more benefit do we derive, brother, from passing time in this desert? But if you hear me, get up, let us depart; let us save others. For as we are, we do not benefit anyone except ourselves, and we have not brought anyone else to salvation" (p. 142). Far from rejecting ascetic conventions or criticizing monasticism, Symeon's remarks underscore the importance of proper ascetic comportment. The success of Symeon's ascetic practice is firmly attested and is a precondition for his ability to assist others in their salvation, a point to which we shall return.

Leontius's defense of Symeon, of course, is not limited to his explicit apologies for Symeon's behavior. In addition to his antiascetic behavior, Symeon engages in activities which were conventional for Late Antique holy men. Through the miracles he performs and the conversions he effects, Symeon's status as holy is guaranteed. For Leontius, the difference between Symeon's profane appearance and the reality of his sanctity provide an occasion to conclude his narrative with a moral lesson. "Truly no one knows a person's deeds without knowing the person's spirit. Truly we must not judge someone before the time, O friends of Christ, before the Lord comes and illuminates everything" (p. 169). To understand that Symeon was holy is to be party to a revealed truth hidden from the ordinary Christian. Symeon's deception becomes another manifestation of his sacred power. Although Symeon deviates from the conventional patterns of the holy man, Leontius conveys to his audience that Symeon is a holy man nonetheless.

Symeon's Shamelessness in Byzantine Tradition

The ways in which Leontius intended his readers to interpret Symeon's behavior and the way in which actual readers did interpret it may have diverged. Evidence suggests that some found it too racy. A more complete picture develops when examining how later Byzantine readers treated Symeon the Fool, in particular paraphrasers ($\mu\epsilon\tau\alpha\phi\rho\alpha\sigma\tau\acute{\epsilon}s$), liturgists, and hagiographers.

A paraphrase of the *Life of Symeon* is included in an anonymous collection of lives, or menologium, compiled late in the tenth century for use in churches.[41] The paraphraser provides shortened versions of most of the episodes in Leontius's *Life of Symeon*, reducing the length of the entire account to about one-sixth of Leontius's *Life*. The paraphraser updates Leontius's vocabulary, particularly words with colloquial usage or obscure meaning.[42] Most of the menologium text is devoted to a précis of the second half of the *Life of Symeon*, and the text leaves the impression of being a listing of Symeon's miracles.[43]

The omissions are instructive. The paraphraser reduces Symeon's activity to his miracles, excising all explanations of Symeon's behavior. The condensed version leaves out Symeon's defecation in public (p. 148), the episode where Symeon attends the theater and throws stones at the juggler (p. 150), and condenses a series of episodes dealing with Symeon's lack of sexual desire and his encounter with prostitutes (pp. 154.28–156.22) into a short notice explaining that Symeon reformed prostitutes. An even briefer Armenian epitome of the *Life of Symeon* includes an account of Symeon's gorging himself on Holy Thursday and his visit to the baths naked, but omits stories about prostitutes or defecating in public.[44]

To the paraphrasers, it seems, attempts to theologize and thereby defend Symeon's shamelessness only aggravated the anomaly of Symeon's behavior. In abandoning explanations, these new versions avoided calling special attention to the potentially troubling implications of Symeon's actions. The metaphrastic project of the tenth century was, above all, con-

41. *Menologii anonymi byzantini saeculi X*, ed. Basilius Latyšev (St. Petersburg, 1912), pp. 194–202. Shortened versions of saints' lives were compiled from the middle of the tenth century in collections generally called menologia. These texts, often heavily edited, could be used as sermons on each particular saint's day, and in their compilation reflect the tastes and concerns of Church leaders. Leontius's *Life of Symeon the Fool* does not appear in the earliest of these collections, that compiled by Symeon Metaphrastes (who died c. 1000).

42. A similar process is also reflected in the manuscript tradition for the *Life of Symeon*. Cf. Rydén, *Das Leben des heiligen Narren Symeon*, esp. p. 116.

43. The menologium text follows Leontius's order, with some noticeable gaps. The paraphraser leaves out two large blocks of material corresponding to pp. 157.11–159.15 and pp. 163.16–166.4 in Rydén's edition. Although it is possible that pages were missing from the paraphraser's copy, it is unlikely that page divisions corresponded neatly to divisions between episodes, and there is no evidence that any episodes were available to him only in fragmentary form. I suggest that the episodes left out were deemed superfluous given the volume of miracles already to be included in the epitome.

44. Found in the Armenian Synaxarium (properly a menologium) discussed in chapter 2. *Le Synaxaire arménien de Ter Israel*, pp. 751–58.

cerned to provide the Church with versions of the lives of the saints acceptable for use during worship services. In order to achieve this goal, the metaphrasts sought to bring the accounts of the saints into conformity with each other. It is precisely what was distinctive about the *Life of Symeon* which would have to be toned down or excised in order to present a Symeon worthy of inclusion in a calendar of saints. It is no surprise, therefore, that Symeon's behavior, an apparent rejection of asceticism, was toned down, ignored, or, when presented, dealt with as if it were not problematic.

Another tenth-century liturgical text passed by Symeon's outrageousness in silence. The *Synaxarium of Constantinople* summarizes Symeon's public activity as follows:[45]

> He went to the city of Emesa. He played the part of madness and performed many miracles under this pretense, which not even the most clever people recognized at first, but which they discerned after his death. And when others narrated these things, everyone believed. And everything was set forth toward a common benefit and teaching.[46]

The blandness of this précis's treatment of Symeon's activity in Emesa is underwhelming. The liturgist has chosen not to relate any anecdotes about Symeon's antic behavior but, ironically, has retained the apologetic tone of Leontius's account, preempting any possible criticism of Symeon's activities by asserting his worthy goals.[47]

It is difficult to say with confidence whether the liturgists of the middle Byzantine period made a concerted effort to excise Symeon's

---

45. The *Synaxarium of Constantinople* probably dates from the tenth century. This collection contains briefer readings about the saints. The place of these readings within the liturgy of the period in which they were compiled remains uncertain. From the middle of the thirteenth century the Orthodox Church read these passages during the canon of matins (*orthros*) between the sixth and seventh odes, or occasionally after third ode, a practice which continues to this day. The *Synaxarium*'s second notice for July 21 gives an account of the lives of Saints Symeon "τοῦ διὰ Χριστὸν σαλοῦ" and John. Comprising forty-seven lines in the modern edition, the text gives a condensed version of the first half of Leontius's *Life of Symeon* (23 lines). On the dates of various Byzantine synaxaria and menologia, see Delehaye, *Synaxaires byzantins, ménologes, typica* (London: Variorum, 1977).

46. *Synaxarium ecclesiae Constantinopolitanae*, ed. Delehaye (Brussels: Société des Bollandistes, 1902), cols. 833–34. The next nineteen lines are devoted to relating the miraculous circumstances of Symeon's death, including some material not found in Leontius. It is common for the notices in the *Synaxarium of Constantinople* to concentrate on the circumstances of a saint's death, particularly in the case of martyrs.

47. A briefer text which probably derives from the no longer extant second half of the *Menologium of Basil II* (which is properly a synaxarium), and therefore is perhaps datable to the turn of the eleventh century, truncates the text of the *Synaxarium of Constantinople* concerning Symeon. Of Symeon's strange behavior, this text relates only: "He returned to the city. And he played the part of madness, performing many miracles under this pretense." *Menologium of Basil II*, PG 117.552.

shamelessness from liturgical celebrations, or whether Symeon's story suffered through the same process of truncation which all the saints' lives experienced in the preparation of these liturgical books. In any case, the Symeon of the liturgy seems to have lost his shamelessness and his ability to shock.

Another strategy for reinterpreting Symeon's behavior is found in the *Life of Andrew the Fool* written in the middle of the tenth century.[48] The author of the *Life of Andrew* was familiar with the *Life of Symeon*. He makes reference to Symeon, echoes Leontius's language, and borrows episodes from the *Life of Symeon* in the construction of his own narrative.[49] Like Symeon, Andrew defecates in public,[50] he gorges himself in the market,[51] and associates freely with women.[52] For the author of the *Life of Andrew* such accounts have become the elements of narrating the life of a holy fool. What is of greatest interest for our purposes is that this author does not avoid such material, as did the liturgists, but rather is willing to borrow these themes from Leontius. We must conclude that the author of the *Life of Andrew* did not consider this material to be too shocking to relate to his audience. On the other hand, although the behavior itself did not seem to bother Andrew's hagiographer, the status of the perpetrator did. The author of the *Life of Andrew* changed a significant element of the fool's tale: Andrew is not a monk. Unlike Symeon, Andrew has not made vows which would raise an audience's expectations about his commitment to avoid the pleasures of the body, both sexual and dietary.[53]

The legacy of Symeon in the middle Byzantine period confirms some of Leontius's own intuitions about his narrative. Later liturgists' whitewashing of Symeon's shamelessness might lead us to conclude that middle Byzantines were significantly more prudish than early Byzantines. Yet we cannot escape the fact that Leontius himself felt compelled to defend Symeon's behavior in order to mollify an audience's reaction to his off-color tale. We must conclude that without some theological

48. Rydén, "The Date of the *Life of Andreas Salos*," *DOP* 32 (1978): 129–55. For debate on the date of this text see chapter 1, n. 5.

49. See S. Murray, *A Study of the Life of Andreas* (Borna-Leipzig: Noske, 1910), pp. 54–63, and Rydén, "Style and Historical Fiction in the Life of St. Andreas Salos," *JÖB* 32 (1982): 175–83. On the *Life of Andrew* generally, see also John Wortley, "The *Vita Sancti Andreae Sali* as a Source of Byzantine Social History," *Societas* 4 (1974): 1–20.

50. *Life of Andrew the Fool*, PG 111.708.

51. PG 111.713.

52. Cf. PG 111.653 and 652.

53. Furthermore, there is no evidence that the author intended this text to be used in a liturgical context, and it seems more likely that the *Life of Andrew* is a literary novel intended for a lay audience outside of a religious setting.

justification for Symeon's antics, Leontius's seventh-century Cypriot parishioners would have been shocked. Thus Symeon's lengthy preparations in the desert, the claim that he had nearly achieved the angelic state of bodilessness, and the assertion, constant throughout the text, that his shamelessness was a ruse all contribute to the construction of "holy folly" by undergirding his holiness. Leontius guarantees his audience that, for the most part, Symeon was like any other holy man—especially in private. Symeon is a saint, then, not because of his shamelessness, but rather in spite of it. Ironically, rather than challenging a Late Antique definition of holiness, Leontius affirms it, and then uses it as a precondition for his fool's salvific agenda as well as his own. How are we to understand the place of Symeon's folly in this agenda? What system of values was the bishop of Neapolis trying to communicate by combining traditional markers of sanctity with such acts of transgression in a single tale? Why is Symeon's holiness veiled behind his folly? In pursuit of these questions we turn next to the theme of concealed sanctity in Late Ancient Christian literature.

· FOUR ·

HOLY FOOLS AND
SECRET SAINTS

Holy folly and the more general concept of concealed sanctity advance a search for a literary and religious context for Leontius's tale of a holy man's public deviance. Our concern here is not to construct a history of folly-oriented praxis, but rather to consider the history of the composition of stories of folly and concealed sanctity in Late Antique and Early Byzantine culture. Long before Leontius of Neapolis composed the *Life of Symeon the Fool*, tales of Christian holy men and women who pretended to be crazy were common.[1] Much briefer than the *Life of Symeon*, each of these accounts is no more than a cursory attempt to explain the unusual behavior described. Nevertheless these stories share a number of themes with the *Life of Symeon*.

The oldest surviving Christian account of a holy person who feigns madness is found in the thirty-fourth chapter of Palladius's anthology of desert ascetics' lives, the *Lausiac History*, written around 420.[2] Here Palla-

---

1. These tales have been discussed most thoroughly by José Grosdidier de Matons, "Les Thèmes d'édification dans la Vie d'André Salos," *Travaux et mémoires* 4 (1970): 277–329. See also S. Murray, *A Study of the Life of Andreas* (Borna-Leipzig: Noske, 1910), pp. 11–16; Festugière, *Vie de Syméon le Fou*, pp. 15–27; Irina Goraïnoff, *Les Fols en Christ dans la tradition Orthodoxe* ([Paris]: Desclée de Brouwer, 1983), pp. 29–42; John Saward, *Perfect Fools: Folly for Christ's Sake in Catholic and Orthodox Spirituality* (Oxford: Oxford University Press, 1980), pp. 12–19; and Michel de Certeau, *La Fable mystique: XVIᵉ–XVIIᵉ siècle* (Paris: Gallimard, 1982), pp. 48–70.

2. On the passage in Palladius about the nun who feigned madness, see the enlightening discussion by Kari Vogt, "La Moniale folle du monastère des Tabbenésiotes: Une inter-

dius relates how the monk Piteroum once visited a nunnery at Tabennisi where he encountered a nun who feigned madness and demonic possession. None of the sisters ever saw her eat, and she was never angry, although she was often abused. Instructed in a vision to seek her out, Piteroum asked the sisters about her and was told that she was σαλή, "mad."[3] The monk then revealed the woman's true nature, after which she disappeared, "unable to bear the praise and honor of her sisters." Despite Palladius's initial statement that she feigned madness, there is little to suggest that she was not, in fact, mad. Like Symeon, the nun shuns recognition, yet in important ways, she differs from Symeon, whose disguise is elaborately calculated and who actively and aggressively confronts others under the guise.

As an appendix to his edition of the Syriac version of John Rufus's *Plerophoriae*, F. Nau published a rare fragment of the original Greek text, which was composed in the second decade of the sixth century. In one episode, Rufus tells how in Silvanus's monastery near Eleutheropolis (lower Egypt) there was a monk who pretended to be mad (προσποιούμενος μωρίαν).[4] He laughed when others came near him. When three visitors came to the monastery and asked to see all the monks, Silvanus told them not to try to see the σαλός, the "crazy one," because he would scandalize them (σκανδαλίζω). They demanded to see him, and found him in his cell where he was putting pebbles in two baskets. He answered their questions by laughing at them. Later he explained to Silvanus that he picked up each pebble and placed it in the basket on the right or the one on the left depending on whether it prompted him to think a good thought or a bad one. At the end of the day, if there were more pebbles in the good basket than in the bad, he would eat; otherwise, he would not. Silvanus alone perceives the monk's virtue. In the *Life of Symeon*, Symeon also makes fun of those who try to talk with him. And like those who see this monk, Symeon scandalizes those who watch him. Nevertheless, Rufus's monk seems gentle rather than raucous, and as in Palladius's narrative, Rufus appears more than anything else to be constructing an apology for the sorts of peculiar figures engaging in cenobitic life in Late Antiquity.

In contrast to these rural tales of holy folly, late-sixth-century tales of people who feigned madness are decidedly urban. The first is Evagrius's

---

prétation du chapitre 34 de l'Historia Lausiaca de Pallade," *Symbolae Osloenses* 62 (1987): 95–108.

3. On other possible meanings of this term, see below.

4. John Rufus, *Plerophoriae*, ed. F. Nau, *PO* 8 (1912): 178–79 . This passage is rarely included in discussions of holy folly in Late Antiquity and merits further study. The passage is discussed briefly by Grosdidier de Matons in "Les Thèmes d'édification," pp. 285–86. A similar story is included in Anan-Isho, *The Paradise of the Fathers* 2.22 (pp. 388–90).

account of Symeon of Emesa, discussed in the second chapter, and which I have argued served, in some loose fashion, as Leontius's source for the *Life of Symeon*. In considering this tale, we should regard Evagrius's Symeon as a separate character from Leontius's. Evagrius introduces his narration, "There lived also at Emesa Symeon, a man who had so un-clothed himself of vainglory as to appear insane [παράφορος] to those who did not know him, although filled with all wisdom and divine grace."[5] Here, as in Leontius's *Life of Symeon*, the point of the story is Symeon's humility. He has chosen to humble himself in order to *appear* other than he is. In secret, Evagrius's Symeon is a good monk, maintaining the demands of the ascetic life. In public (literally "in the agora," i.e., the marketplace) Symeon shuns recognition. Evagrius then narrates the three episodes discussed above. After this story, Evagrius notes that there was another man like Symeon named Thomas, but he offers no details, creating the impression that monks who behaved oddly were not uncommon in late-sixth-century cities.

In a similar vein, the so-called *Life of Daniel of Skete* relates the story of Mark the Fool. When Daniel and one of his disciples went to Alexandria to celebrate Easter, they encountered a monk who pretended to be a fool and who was known throughout the city. He walked around the agora naked except for a loincloth. And when Daniel and his disciple saw him,

> The brother [Daniel] said that he was pretending that he was a fool, and there were other fools also with him. And the brother who was [pretending to be] a fool [ὡς σαλός] and acting crazy turned around, and seized things in the market and handed [them] out to the other fools.[6]

Eventually, Mark admits that after having spent fifteen years as a monk in the desert, enslaved to the demon of lust, he decided to go to Alexandria and spend eight years being a fool. The eight years are now over, and Mark dies the night after his confession. Unlike Palladius's and John Rufus's fools, both Symeon and Mark operate in an urban environment, where they are notorious among the inhabitants. Like Mark, Leontius's Symeon distributes food in the marketplace (p. 146), an act disruptive of commercial activity designed to provide for those whom society shuns. Mark feeds the *truly* insane "street people" of Alexandria with whom he associates.

Despite the similar location of the activities of the fools in Daniel of Skete's account of Mark and Leontius's *Life of Symeon*, the authors' attitudes toward the urban environment is quite different. Mark is unable to

---

5. Evagrius, *HE* 4.34; trans. p. 415, slightly modified.
6. Daniel of Skete, *Vie (et récits) de l'Abbé Daniel le Scétiote*, ed. Léon Clugnet (Paris: Picard et Fils, 1901), p. 12.

conquer his desires in the desert, and thus he comes to the city as an elaborate penance. Mark is then able to achieve holiness in the city. In contrast, Symeon does not go to the city until he has conquered lust and reached a state of *apatheia*. For Leontius the city is to be feared because it is likely to aggravate lust, a point which Symeon's fellow hermit John makes at some length (p. 143). While Mark is primarily concerned with his own salvation, Symeon is devoted to the salvation of others.

Another common feature in all but one of these stories is that the fool's true identity is known only to authority figures in the Church; everyone else is duped. There is not a direct parallel in Evagrius's account of Symeon although he is known to some for what he is. Leontius's character John the deacon also perceives the truth of Symeon's nature:

> For concerning this Deacon John, when the two found themselves alone together, the old man [Symeon] did not act like a fool at all, but he conversed with him so gracefully and with such compunction, that often perfume came from his mouth, as this Deacon John maintained, "such that I almost doubted that he had been a fool [σαλός] only moments before." (p. 160)

Some characters in the *Life of Symeon* have a suspicion about Symeon's true identity, but their inklings are quickly confounded because Symeon immediately does something shameful before them, as before the tavern keeper (p. 148) and the owner of the pregnant slave-girl (p. 152). Others Symeon miraculously prevents from being able to reveal him, such as the Jew whom Symeon strikes mute (p. 154), the boy whom he frees from the demon adultery (p. 150), the juggler whom Symeon forces to abandon his profession (p. 150), and the headman of a nearby village whose tongue Symeon binds (p. 156). The perception of sainthood is privileged and usually available only to persons of relative virtue and, not accidentally, ecclesiastical position; this knowledge is power.

The denouement of each of these stories is the revelation of the saint's holiness, although the function of the pretended folly differs significantly. In the case of Palladius and the *Life of Daniel,* the revelation of the fool's true identity is followed by the fool's disappearance or death. What is revealed in each case is that the pretending fool is in fact holier than the others around him or her, especially the more ordinary religious. However, it is not always clear whether the fool is made holier because of his or her behavior, or whether he or she feigns holiness in order to conceal a particularly close relationship with God. In the case of Mark the Fool, feigned folly seems to be a particular sort of asceticism which helps him conquer the demon lust. This contrasts with the *Life of Symeon,* where Symeon's outward behavior is portrayed not as a form of asceticism but as the antithesis of ascetic practice. Nevertheless, we can generalize that the pretense of folly is justified because it allows the monastics in these stories to achieve and maintain a state of humility.

Although these stories may have a basis in history, it is worthwhile examining them first and foremost as literary works, rather than as actual records.[7] These accounts should be taken as evidence that stories of this sort circulated widely in Late Antiquity and that authors considered them sufficiently entertaining and instructive to share them with their respective audiences. The fact that three of these stories of feigned madness are set in Egypt might lead one to suspect, as has been commonly assumed, that stories of this type were primarily of Egyptian provenance. Those intent on discovering "real people" behind these tales have argued that "holy folly" as a religious practice started in Egypt, whence it traveled to Syria.[8] We must not lose sight, however, of the literary nature of these works, or of their international dissemination. Palladius's *Lausiac History* presents itself as a memoir of a journey which the author took during the 390s and of the stories he heard while traveling; it was written a generation later (c. 420) for the court of Theodosius II in Constantinople, a collection of wondrous exotica for aristocrats that was intended to entertain as well as exhort. Disseminated from the capital, this text appears to have circulated widely throughout the empire. That Palladius's *Lausiac History* circulated in Syria is shown by the fact that the work was translated into Syriac twice in the course of the seventh century.[9] In the late sixth century, stories concerning feigned madness were composed in Syria and Egypt. Evagrius, writing in Antioch, of course, relates the earliest version of the story of Symeon of Emesa. The *Life of Daniel of Skete*, composed in Egypt, was also translated into Syriac; however, the dates of the various translations of this work have yet to be determined.[10] Thus, the fluidity of the

7. While some might be tempted to construct a brief history of the phenomenon of "holy folly" from these accounts, I am particularly skeptical about the possibility of reconstructing a history for a type of actual ascetic practice engaged in by "real," historical persons. In their own ways, each of these sources presents serious problems for those who would wish to extract "historicity" from them.

8. Thus Grosdidier de Matons, "Les Thèmes d'édification," p. 279. Cf. Saward, *Perfect Fools*, pp. 14–19.

9. See the introduction to Palladius's *Lausiac History*, trans. Robert T. Meyer (New York: Newman, 1964), pp. 9–10. The only version of Anan-Isho's translation yet edited does not contain the story of the nun who feigned madness. It does, however, contain similar stories which are not found in the Greek versions of Palladius. Wallis Budge's edition of Anan-Isho, *The Paradise of the Fathers* (Lady Meux Manuscript No. 6, *Book of Paradise*) is based only on a single manuscript.

10. The earliest manuscript dates from the tenth century. Selected passages of the Syriac manuscripts which F. Nau edited can be found in Clugnet, *Vie (et récits) de l'Abbé Daniel le Scétiote*, pp. 68–82. Clugnet and Nau include a list of Syriac manuscripts on p. xxxi.

texts in their many translations make it difficult to establish a "provenance" for stories of holy folly. Moreover, since such stories were known in Constantinople, Egypt, and Syria prior to Leontius's composition of the *Life of Symeon*, and since all these places had regular contact with Cyprus, it is impossible to trace Leontius's acquaintance with the phenomenon of stories of feigned madness to a particular place. Tales of this type were known throughout the Early Byzantine empire.[11]

These tales are part of a continuum of strange behavior described in Late Ancient hagiography, and they share a strong affinity with tales associated with modes of ascetic piety generally associated with Syria in which holy men and women go to great extremes either in the pursuit of *apatheia* or in its demonstration. One thinks again of the peculiar feats of the monks described in Theodoret's *Religious History*, of the stylites, and of various figures who debased themselves publicly in pursuit of holiness. Many of these forms of piety originated in Syria, but it is important to remember that by Leontius's time, stories of these figures were widely disseminated throughout the Eastern Mediterranean, both through the circulation of texts and through the degree to which certain practices were taken up in disparate parts of the empire. In the course of the second half of the fifth century, stylitism, for instance, had traveled from Syria, where it originated with Symeon the Elder, to Constantinople where Daniel the Stylite's pillar overlooked the Bosphorus. By the seventh century, the practice had been taken up in Egypt, Cyprus, and southern Gaul.[12] Thus we cannot discount the successful promulgation of Syrian literature and models of asceticism in the centuries before the Arab conquest. Leontius drew on these elements because they constituted an international hagiographical vocabulary.

The Word *Salos* and Holy Folly

The evidence just presented suggests that a tradition of tales of folly existed as an identifiable genre by Leontius's time. Nevertheless, the themes

---

11. Although a discussion of a motif of holy folly is inconclusive, and while the small size of the sample makes generalization difficult, one significant observation does seem justified: There does appear to be a shift in the location of these stories over time, such that the fifth- and early-sixth-century examples take place in rural monasteries, while the late-sixth- and seventh-century examples take place in urban environments.

12. Egypt: P.Turner 54 (late sixth century) and John of Nikiu, *Chronicle* (cf. Hippolyte Delehaye, *Les saints stylites* [Brussels: Société des Bollandistes, 1923], p. cxxiv); Cyprus: *The Vision of Kaioumos* 3, ed. F. Halkin, "La vision de Kaioumos et le sort éternal de Philentolos Olympiou," *AB* (1945): 63; Gaul: J. Nasrallah, "Survie de Saint Siméon Stylite l'alépin dans les gaules," *Syria* 51 (1974): 171–97.

expressed in these tales were not fixed, nor was the vocabulary used to describe the principal characters. For example, the Greek version of the *Life of Daniel* contains a story of a nun who feigned drunkenness (μεθύ-στρια); in the Syriac version, however, the word is translated as "madness" (*shanitha*).[13] Thus, the concept of pretended madness as such was quite fluid.

Extreme caution is also warranted with regard to the term *salos* (σαλός), usually used to describe holy folly in both the modern scholarly literature and the Orthodox churches. The word *salos,* translated usually as "fool," is of uncertain origin. It is not to be confused with the Greek word σάλος, "tossed" or "agitated."[14] As Grosdidier de Matons has observed, *salos* appears to have had a principally colloquial usage at first.[15] It first appears in written sources in the early fifth century CE in Palladius's *Lausiac History* 34, the well-known story of the nun in a monastery in Tabennisi who feigned madness (μωρία) and demonic possession. The nuns in the monastery tell the narrator that the woman is σαλή, a term which Palladius glosses after its first usage, presumably because the word was unfamiliar to his audience, explaining that this is the word they use "to describe those women who are afflicted." Although we do find the theme of sanctity concealed by madness in this story, nothing suggests that the term *salos* has been connected with her practice as a technical term.

In four anecdotes in the alphabetical collection of the *Apophthegmata Patrum,* redacted in the sixth century, the word is either used sincerely to

13. Greek text, Clugnet, *Vie (et récits) de Daniel,* pp. 22–27; Syriac text, pp. 68–72. English translation of the Syriac: Sebastian Brock and Susan Ashbrook Harvey, *Holy Women of the Syrian Orient* (Berkeley: University of California Press, 1987), pp. 143–45.

14. Attempts to show a Syriac derivation for the word have proven inconclusive. It was once believed that the word was derived from the Syriac *sakla,* used to translate the Greek μῶρος in the Peshitta version at 1 Cor 3:18 ("Let him become a fool that he may become wise"). The Peshitta uses *shatayya* at 1 Cor 4:10 ("We are fools for Christ's sake"), although the version used by Ishodad of Merv in his ninth-century commentary on 1 Cor used *sakla* here. (See Ishodad of Merv, *The Commentaries,* ed. Margaret Dunlop Gibson, vol. 5, pt. 1 [Cambridge: Cambridge University Press, 1916], p. 42 l. 15.) An argument for this Syriac derivation, presumably following Rosweyde, is alluded to by Peter Hauptmann in "Die 'Narren um Christi Willen' in der Ostkirche," *Kirche im Osten* 2 (1959): 34 n. 40, and is assumed by Thomas Spidlík, "Fous pour le Christ en Orient," *DS* 5 (1964): col. 753. Such a derivation is to be rejected, as is clear from M. A. Guillaumont's observations quoted by Grosdidier de Matons, "Les Thèmes d'édification," p. 279 n. 7. So also Rydén has written, "[T]he similarity between *salos* and *sakla* is not very striking, and there does not seem to be any other convincing Syriac etymology" (Rydén, "The Holy Fool," in *The Byzantine Saint,* ed. Sergei Hackel [San Bernardino, Calif.: Borgo, 1983], p. 107).

15. On the history of the use of the word, see Grosdidier de Matons, "Les Thèmes d'édification," pp. 279–92. His discussion reviews all the citations listed in H. Estienne, *Thesaurus Linguae Grecae,* vol. 7 (1572; ed. A. Firmin-Didot [Paris: F. Didot frères, 1865]), s.v., as well as others.

describe someone who appears crazy (and may well be) or as an insult. The term has a slang quality to it, and a recent English translator of the *Apophthegmata* has rendered it variously "mad," "distraught," "silly," and "fool."[16] Here too the word clearly has no technical meaning suggesting the pretense of insanity as a form of ascetic practice. The word occurs with a notably abusive sense in a recently published letter from Oxyrhynchus dated to the late fifth century. While discussing business matters connected with a mill at Orthoniu the author of the letter refers to a third party as "that imbecile [σαλός] Horus."[17]

In John Moschus's *Spiritual Meadow,* which dates from the early seventh century, the word *salos* is used to describe a mendicant whom John says he and his companion Sophronius encountered on the steps of the Church of Theodosius in Alexandria. The beggar "appears as if he is crazy [ὡς σαλός]"; however, nothing in the anecdote suggests that the man is a holy man or that he is merely pretending to be crazy.[18]

It is puzzling that Evagrius Scholasticus, at the end of the sixth century, never uses the term *salos* in his description of Symeon. Grosdidier de Matons, who interprets this omission to indicate the word's status as a colloquialism, argues that Evagrius avoided the word since it was inappropriate to his "bon style."[19] However, we cannot rule out the possibility that Evagrius was unfamiliar with the word. Further confusion is introduced by the tale of Mark the Fool, one of the stories included in the *Life of Daniel of Skete*, a text roughly contemporary with Evagrius Scholasticus's *Ecclesiastical History.* Here the author describes Mark as a *salos*; however, he also uses the term to describe the truly insane people with whom Mark associates.[20]

As we have seen, stories of feigned madness were widespread in the

16. *Apophthegmata Patrum,* alphabetic series (PG 65), Ammonas 9; Eulogius the Priest 1; John, Disciple of Abba Paul 1; Moses 8. English translation by Benedicta Ward, *The Sayings of the Desert Fathers* (Kalamazoo: Cistercian, 1975), pp. 27, 61, 109, 140.

17. *P.Oxy.* LVI 3865.57. To my knowledge this is the only occurrence in papyri published to date. I thank Leslie MacCoull for calling this document to my attention.

18. John Moschus, *Spiritual Meadow* 111, PG 87/3.2976. The passage is of interest to the study of Leontius's works since in his prologue to the *Life of John the Almsgiver,* Leontius relates that he has written in order to supplement the previously extant biography of the Patriarch which was written by John Moschus and Sophronius (Leontius, *Life of John the Almsgiver,* prologue, ll. 30ff.). An epitome of this earlier biography has survived, and as Cyril Mango has concluded, we can be reasonably sure that Leontius had indeed read this work ("A Byzantine Hagiographer at Work: Leontios of Neapolis," in *Byzanz und der Westen: Studien zur Kunst des europäischen Mittelalters,* ed. Imgard Hutter [Vienna: Österreichischen Akademie der Wissenschaften, 1984], pp. 33–35). It remains for later scholars to discover whether Leontius knew of other works by Moschus, including the *Spiritual Meadow.*

19. Grosdidier de Matons, "Les Thèmes d'édification," pp. 279–80.

20. *Vie (et récits) de Daniel,* pp. 12–15. See especially p. 12 ll. 10–11.

period from the early fifth through mid-seventh century; however, the term σαλός was not always used in these stories. Moreover, none of these stories demonstrates a developed sense of the *salos* as a technical category, nor for that matter of feigned madness as a well-defined form of spiritual expression. The term *salos*, therefore, should not be understood as the equivalent of "holy fool" in Late Antiquity.

In the *Life of Symeon the Fool*, we find a more extensive treatment of this term. Leontius works out for the first time a definition of holy folly through his attempt to establish a theological justification as well as a cultural precedent for holy folly. Leontius uses the term σαλός often. He writes that Symeon "played all sorts of roles foolish and indecent [σαλῶν καὶ ἀσχήμων]" (p. 155). *Salos* is used as an epithet: "Go away, Fool!" (p. 166); the girls of Emesa use the word in the vocative Σαλέ, calling him "Fool" as if it were his name. And Symeon is not the only one to be called a *salos*; Symeon refers to his friend the monk John with this term (p. 153).[21] Leontius also twice uses the verb σαλίζω, previously unattested, apparently to mean "playing the fool."[22] But while Leontius makes frequent use of the word *salos*, it does not, in itself, have a technical sense. What is crucial for Leontius is the fact that Symeon is a σαλός διὰ Χριστὸν, "a Fool for Christ's sake." The first time he is seen by the residents of Emesa, school children run after him and call him not a *salos*, but a *mōros* (μωρός) (p. 145). Later Leontius describes Symeon as one who "simulates μωρία for Christ's sake" (pp. 155–56), recalling Paul's wording in 1 Corinthians 4:10. For Leontius *salos* and *mōros* are largely interchangeable. His innovation is not to give *salos* a technical usage, but to define his folly as διὰ Χριστὸν, "for Christ's sake."

Despite the Pauline overtones, Leontius's conception of the Fool for Christ's Sake is not particularly Pauline.[23] In Palladius's remarks introducing the story of the nun who feigned madness, Palladius claims that in behaving as she does the nun was fulfilling the passage from 1 Corinthians (3:18): "If anyone among you thinks that he is wise in this age, let him become a fool that he may become wise." Rydén has seen that Palladius willfully misinterprets this passage from Paul.[24] Paul contrasts the term with wisdom in a significantly different context. Paul was surely not advocating a pretense to insanity, and there is no indication that Palladius's

21. Cf. Festugière, *Vie de Syméon le Fou*, p. 201; Rydén, *Das Leben des heiligen Narren Symeon*, p. 200, s.v.
22. Leontius, *Life of Symeon*, p. 154 l. 19; p. 157 l. 15. Cf. Rydén, *Das Leben des heiligen Narren Symeon*, pp. 78–79.
23. A discussion of Paul's use of the phrase can be found in Saward's *Perfect Fools*, pp. 2–7.
24. See Rydén, "The Holy Fool," p. 106–7.

nun achieved wisdom. The same prooftext is also used by Leontius in his introduction to the *Life of Symeon* (p. 122) where it similarly stands in an awkward relationship with the story about to be narrated. Perhaps more significant for Leontius is a second passage from 1 Corinthians, "We are fools [μωροί] for Christ's sake, but you are wise in Christ" (1 Cor 4:10), where Paul seems to concede that his first-century Christian communities are breaking social conventions. Leontius uses 1 Corinthians 4:10 as a prooftext as well (p. 122), and he modifies the phrase in his title for the work, "The Life and Conduct of Abba Symeon Called the Fool [σαλός] for the Sake of Christ."[25] Here he replaces *mōros* with *salos*. While Leontius does not attempt to recover Paul's sense of the phrase, he does use Paul's language to establish biblical authority for Symeon's extraordinary behavior.

The Theme of Concealed Sanctity

Related to the theme of madness in the *Life of Symeon the Fool* is the fact that Symeon's true nature is concealed; that he is a holy man is known only to a few residents of Emesa. The Syrian homilist Isaac of Nineveh, writing a generation or two after Leontius, grouped those who pretended to be fools with other types of ascetics who humbled themselves by acquiring a mistaken reputation for depravity.

> A man who is truly humble is not troubled when he is wronged and he says nothing to justify himself against the injustice, but he accepts slander as truth; he does not attempt to persuade men that he is calumniated, but he begs forgiveness. Some have voluntarily drawn upon themselves the repute of being licentious, while they are not such; others have endured the charge of adultery, being far from it, and proclaimed by their tears that they bear the fruit of the sin they had not committed, and have wept, asking their offenders' forgiveness for the iniquity they had not done, their souls all the while being crowned with all purity and chastity; others, lest they be glorified because of the virtuous state which they have hidden within them, have pretended to be lunatics, while in truth they were permeated with divine salt and securely fixed in serenity, so that, because of their uttermost perfection, they had holy angels as heralds of their deeds of valour.[26]

25. For the titles of the work in the various manuscripts see Rydén, *Das Leben des heiligen Narren Symeon*, pp. 31–42. The phrase τοῦ διὰ Χριστὸν . . . σαλοῦ occurs in all of them.

26. Isaac the Syrian, *The Ascetical Homilies* 6, trans. the Holy Transfiguration Monastery [D. Miller] (Boston: Holy Transfiguration Monastery, 1984), p. 55. I thank Susan Harvey for bringing this marvelous passage to my attention. It is quite possible that Isaac was familiar with Leontius's *Life of Symeon*.

The theme of concealed sanctity was widespread in Late Ancient hagiography and provides a broader context for understanding Leontius's objectives in composing the *Life of Symeon*.

The *Life of John the Almsgiver* reveals Leontius's ongoing interest in the broader theme of concealed sanctity, stories in which a holy person pretends to be something he or she is not. In an extensive digression in the *Life of John*, Leontius relates the story of the monk Vitalius who came to Alexandria and solicited prostitutes. In each case, after paying the woman for her time, he spent the night in a corner of her room, praying for her soul. Vitalius forbade the women to tell what had actually transpired during the night, and the townspeople were scandalized by what the monk appeared to be doing. Many of the prostitutes became nuns, others married and raised families. The saint's pretense here is an instrument for the salvation of others.

The story of a monk who converts prostitutes or other disreputable men and women such as actors and actresses has numerous analogues. Anan-Isho's Syriac version of the *Lausiac History* contains an account of how Sarapion converted an unnamed prostitute as well as a similar story about a subdeacon.[27] There are also numerous versions of the story of how Sarapion converted the actress and courtesan Thaïs.[28] The story of Vitalius has a parallel in the *Life of Symeon the Fool*. Symeon gives courtesans gold (which God has provided him for this purpose) and extracts promises from these women not to be unfaithful to him, thus reforming many of them (pp. 155–56).

Leontius himself shows considerable interest in traditions about the monk Sarapion. He writes in the *Life of John* that the patriarch enjoyed reading the life of Sarapion and in his admiration summoned his officials in order to read them passages from the life. Leontius specifically mentions the story in which "a widow woman asked the holy Sarapion for alms because her children were hungry, and as he had nothing whatever to give her, he obliged her to sell him to some pagan actors, and these he converted to Christianity in a few days."[29] An earlier version of this story appears in Palladius's *Lausiac History*. In that version, Sarapion sells himself to a family of pagan actors and keeps the money on his own person since he has no master to reimburse.[30] After Sarapion converts them, the actors still cannot recognize that he is in fact a holy monk, even when he

27. Anan-Isho, *The Paradise of the Fathers*, pp. 413–15.

28. See F. Nau, "Histoire de Thaïs," *Annales du Musée Guimet* 30 (1903): 51–114.

29. Leontius, *Life of John* 22. Trans. Dawes and Baynes in *Three Byzantine Saints*, p. 232, slightly modified.

30. Palladius, *Lausiac History* (hereafter *LH*) 37. On Sarapion see Richard Reitzenstein, *Hellenistische Wundererzählungen* (Leipzig: Teubner, 1906), pp. 64–80.

washes their feet. Once baptized and having given up the stage, the actors, out of compassion, wish to set Sarapion free "since" as they say, "you freed us from our shameful slavery." Sarapion then·reveals that he is in
· fact a free man and an ascetic. He explains, "I sold myself for the sake of your salvation. Now since God did this through my humiliation, I rejoice. Take your money that I may go and help others." When they cannot persuade him to stay with them as their spiritual leader, the former actors tell Sarapion to give to the poor the money with which they had bought him as a token of their salvation.

This story depends on ironic twists. When Sarapion sells himself, he is not only concealing his sanctity, he is engaging in playacting. He is pretending to be a slave, but in fact it is the family of actors who are slaves, since they are slaves to sin, both because they are pagans and because they are involved in the theater. The early-sixth-century metrical homilies of Jacob of Serug (modern Suruç, southwest of Urfa), composed in Syriac, reveal a Christian leader's reasons for condemning the theatrical spectacles of the time. The plays depict pagan myths, especially the immoral exploits of the Greek gods. Moreover, in these plays men play the parts of women and behave in a shameless manner. The theater thus disseminates lies and encourages immorality.[31] No wonder that in Palladius's tale of Sarapion, the saint endeavors to convert actors away from paganism and from the stage. Nevertheless, Sarapion's own playacting is not problematic, since his "humiliation" is the work of God. In playing the part of a slave, Sarapion emulates Christ who, as in the hymn quoted by Paul in the epistle to the Philippians, "emptied himself, taking the form of a slave" (Phil 2:7) in order to effect the salvation of others. Finally, in the Sarapion vignette almsgiving is presented as the appropriate response of those who have received salvation.

Often tales of the conversion of actresses or prostitutes focus attention on the women themselves. The widely circulated *Life of Pelagia the Harlot* tells of how a famous celebrity confessed her sins to Nonnus, the bishop of Antioch. While making penance in preparation for baptism, she gave up all her wealth and freed her slaves. One week after her baptism Pelagia left the nunnery where she had been staying, and wearing the bishop's hair shirt and mantle, she left Antioch in a new sort of costume, dressed as a man. She arrived in Jerusalem and entombed herself in a cell on the Mount of Olives, where she became known as the monk Pelagius, a eunuch. Only years later when they sought to anoint her body for burial after her death did the clergy and monks of Jerusalem discover that the

---

31. Texts and translations appear in C. Moss, "Jacob of Serugh's Homilies on the Spectacles of the Theatre," *Muséon* 48 (1935): 87–112.

famous hermit was, in fact, a woman.[32] In addition to themes of playacting and transvestism, this tale, like those of other fallen women, including Thaïs, Mary of Egypt, and Mary the Niece of Abraham of Qidun, stresses that repentance can transform even the most depraved sinner.[33]

Another story of concealed sanctity involving actors appears in John of Ephesus's Syriac *Lives of the Eastern Saints*, composed *circa* 560. John narrates the story of two well-born Antiochenes, Theophilus and Maria, who dress as a mime-actor (*mimos*) and a prostitute (*pornē*) and perform as clowns in the courtyard of the church in Amida (modern Diyarbakir, on the Tigris, northwest of Urfa), "jesting at the clergymen and everyone, and being boxed on their heads by everyone as mime-actors." The men of Amida are filled with lust for Maria and search for her throughout the night, desiring to have sex with her. They search, however, in vain, since Theophilus and Maria spend the night perched on the city wall praying with their arms outstretched.[34]

The theme of concealed sanctity finds its most intriguing form in the anonymous legend of the "Man of God of Edessa," later known as Alexis, written either in the late fifth or early sixth century.[35] The anonymous author, setting his story during Rabbula's tenure as bishop of Edessa (411–35), writes of a wealthy Roman who leaves his own wedding and

32. Text: *Pélagie la Pénitente: Metamorphoses d'une légende*, vol. 1, *Les textes et leur histoire* (Paris: Études Augustiniennes, 1981). Translation from Syriac: Brock and Harvey, *Holy Women of the Syrian Orient*, pp. 40–62. For a study of this and related texts, see Benedicta Ward, *Harlots of the Desert: A Study of Repentance in Early Monastic Sources* (Kalamazoo: Cistercian, 1987).

33. For these texts, see Ward, *Harlots of the Desert*.

34. John of Ephesus, *Lives of the Eastern Saints* (hereafter *Lives*) 52, ed. and trans. E. W. Brooks, PO 19 (1925): 164–79. Elsewhere in the *Lives*, John writes of Kashish, the bishop of the island of Chios who had lived for thirteen years as a wanderer, traveling to Egypt, Greece, and Rome, having "changed the monastic habit for lay attire, in order that he might not on account of the habit be venerated or honoured by any man, but as an ordinary poor man he went about everywhere among poor ordinary needy men; and consequently he suffered blows and distresses in a laborious, distressing, severe, and hard life of peregrination" (John of Ephesus, *Lives* 51, trans. Brooks, p. 160). Concealed sanctity also plays a part in the story of Mary and Euphemia (John of Ephesus, *Lives* 12; cf. Brock and Harvey, *Holy Women of the Syrian Orient*, pp. 122–33).

35. *La légende syriaque de saint Alexis, l'homme de Dieu*, ed. and trans. Arthur Amiaud (Paris: Vieweg, 1889). This edition contains the Syriac text and a French translation. "Story of the Man of God" survives in Syriac in a number of manuscripts, three of which Amiaud dated to the first half of the sixth century. For a discussion of the text, see Harvey, *Asceticism and Society in Crisis: John of Ephesus and* The Lives of the Eastern Saints (Berkeley: University of California Press, 1990), pp. 18–21; Han J. W. Drijvers, "Hellenistic and Oriental Origins," in *The Byzantine Saint*, ed. Sergei Hackel (San Bernardino, Calif.: Borgo, 1983), pp. 26–28; and *idem*, "Die Legende des heiligen Alexius und der Typus des Gottesmannes in syrischen Christentum," in *Typus, Symbol, Allegorie bei den östlichen Vätern und ihren Parallelen im Mittelalter*, ed. Margot Schmidt and Carl Friedrich Geyer (Regensburg: Pustet, 1982), pp. 187–217.

sails to Edessa (modern Urfa, in Turkish Mesopotamia) where he lives as
a beggar on the steps of the church. He reveals his true identity only to
one doorkeeper, who observes the man praying at night with his arms
outstretched. Only after his death is the man's identity and his status as
holy revealed to the rest of the inhabitants of the city, including Bishop
Rabbula. When the man's tomb is opened, only the rags that served as his
clothes can be found.

The tales of concealed sanctity discussed here share a number of features.
While some of the tales do not have all of the following elements, they are
found repeatedly, allowing us to describe a generic literary type.

1. The holiness of the saint is usually "witnessed" by an informant
   who then "tells" the story to the narrator. Tales of concealed sanctity depend on someone knowing the true story, so that this story
   can be "revealed." In Leontius's *Life of Symeon*, Symeon's identity
   is known only to John the deacon, who eventually "narrates" the
   story. In many ways, these stories recall Jesus' own futile attempts
   to conceal his identity and his powers throughout the Gospel
   of Mark.

2. These stories nearly always involve not only the concealing of
   sanctity, but also the concealing of high social status in the garb of
   low social status. The highborn become beggars, monks become
   slaves, virgins become prostitutes, and holy men become johns.
   This intentional humbling reenacts an aspect of the incarnation of
   the Christ as presented in the hymn in Philippians 2, a text which
   Leontius quotes in his introduction to the *Life of Symeon* (p. 123).
   This suggests that economic humiliation is a key component of
   sainthood. Both Symeon the Fool and his companion John the
   hermit are from wealthy Syrian families. When Symeon goes to
   Emesa under the guise of a madman he humbles himself not
   merely through a shift in economic status, but especially because
   in behaving shamelessly he places himself decisively among the
   outcasts.

3. In some cases these texts are quite explicitly about role playing, as
   in the case of Palladius's account of Sarapion Sidonites, the monk
   who sells himself into slavery to an acting troop, and in John of
   Ephesus's *Lives of the Eastern Saints*, where Maria is an actress who
   pretends to be a prostitute but is really a holy woman. Symeon of
   Emesa pretends to be a fool. The fact that in each case the holy one
   engages in deception does not seem to present moral problems

for the various authors, nor does it appear to have implications for the authors' Christology, although one might infer (heretically) that Christ also was only playacting in taking the form of a human. Symeon himself engages in a form of street theater.

4. A recurrent theme in these stories is the saints' praying through the night. This feature is found in the *Life of Symeon the Fool,* each of the stories about the conversion of prostitutes, the story of Theophilus and Maria, and the story of the Man of God. Under cover of darkness, their sanctity is visible.

5. Central to each story is the problem of identifying the holy. Holy men and women appear in profane roles: as insane, as fornicators, as actors, and as poor beggars. And yet, the narrators insist these people are not as they appear; they are, in fact, holy.

6. Since in each of the stories, holiness appears where it is least expected, these stories teach compassion for those on the margins of society—particularly the poor. These stories of concealed sanctity are not only entertaining but edifying. Within these stories, characters are converted to a better way of life. The narration of these stories is intended to effect similar conversions in the audience.

7. In each of the stories irony plays a large role, both for the characters within the narrative, separating those who do not know the holy person's identity from those who do, and for the audience, which can take delight in the themes of disguise and revelation. Such irony binds the author to the audience in a common, although ostensibly esoteric, understanding of the nature of sanctity.

It is important to remember that Symeon the Fool is not a fool at all. Rather, he is a holy man who plays the fool. His outrageous behavior is an elaborate disguise. In this way, the *Life of Symeon the Fool* shares traits with a number of Late Antique Christian works which edify through narrating the exploits of one who is secretly holy. These works provide a context for understanding Symeon's *pretense* of folly as a literary device which can be exploited to encourage an audience to reflect on a range of religious and ethical matters. Nevertheless, this context cannot fully account for the nature of the folly which Symeon pretends. While Symeon's folly does conform to the pattern of humiliation which elevates, the specific meaning of Symeon's shamelessness remains enigmatic. How did Leontius expect Symeon's behavior to be instructive? To address this aspect of the *Life of Symeon,* we must look beyond the explicitly Christian context to the legacy of Greco-Roman Cynicism. Therefore, it is to the context provided by Diogenes of Sinope that we turn next.

FIVE

DIOGENES IN LATE ANTIQUITY

In many ways, the *Life of Symeon the Fool* conforms to patterns for narrating the lives of holy men in Late Antiquity. The broad outlines of the text share much with more widely studied Late Antique saints' lives, such as Athanasius's *Life of Antony,* Theodoret's portrait of Symeon the Stylite, or the *Life of Theodore of Sykeon.* Even Symeon's antics can be understood both as a reversal of ascetic practice and as thematically related to stories of secret sanctity found in a number of earlier Christian texts. The magnitude of Symeon's shameless behavior, however, is distinctive, and precedents for the playful, even burlesque elements in the text warrant further exploration. If the canons of Christian hagiography do not fully provide a context for understanding Symeon's shamelessness, what elements of Late Ancient culture do? The Greco-Roman Cynic tradition provides part of the answer.

Diogenes of Sinope lived in Athens during the fourth century BCE. According to the account given by Diogenes Laertius in his *Lives of the Philosophers,* the Cynic tradition started with Antisthenes, a student of Socrates. The movement gained notoriety with Antisthenes' disciple, Diogenes, an exile from Sinope, a city on the Black Sea coast of Asia Minor. Although the colorful anecdotes reported about Diogenes in the *Lives of the Philosophers* and other ancient writings are of little value for reconstructing the life of the historical Diogenes of Sinope,[1] the tradition tended to portray him walking the streets, dressed in a philosopher's robe, carry-

---

1. Donald R. Dudley (*A History of Cynicism from Diogenes to the Sixth Century A.D.* [London: Methuen, 1937], p. 20) still found it possible to discuss Diogenes as a historical figure whose actions had specific content, although he realized that anecdotes and teachings attrib-

ing a wallet and a staff. He upbraided passersby for their hypocrisy, and from time to time he performed deeds considered shocking: eating in the market or at public lectures, farting loudly in crowded places, urinating, masturbating, and even defecating wherever he chose.[2]

The parallels between Symeon and Diogenes are striking. As we shall see in the next chapter, Leontius carefully models Symeon's behavior on that attributed to this Cynic philosopher in both pagan and Christian lore. In order to understand the significance of the connection between Symeon the Fool and Diogenes the Cynic, however, we must leave Symeon aside for the moment and consider the place of Diogenes in Christian intellectual history.[3] Therefore, this chapter considers the atti-

---

uted to Diogenes by Epictetus, Dio Chrysostom, and Julian were of little value in the attempt to reconstruct the origins of Cynicism.

2. Eating in public: Diogenes Laertius, *Lives of the Philosophers* (hereafter D. L.) 6.57, 58, 61. Farting: D. L. 6.48; cf. D. L. 6.94; Julian, *Or.* 6.202b; cf. Epictetus, *Disc.* 3.22.80. Urinating: D. L. 6.46. Masturbating: D. L. 6.46, 69; *Epp. Diog.* 35, 42, 44; Dio Chrys., *Disc.* 6.16–20; Athenaeus, *Deip.* 4.145ff. Defecating: Dio Chrys., *Disc.* 8.36; Julian, *Or.* 6.202b, c.

3. On the history of Cynicism in general see Dudley, *History of Cynicism.* Léonce Paquet, *Les Cyniques grecs* (Ottawa: Éditions de l'Université d'Ottawa, 1975) collects anecdotes relating to each major Cynic. An overview of Cynic thought and ways of life can be found in Ferrand Sayre, *Greek Cynicism and Sources of Cynicism* (Baltimore: Furst, 1948); and Heinrich Niehues-Pröbsting, *Der Kynismus des Diogenes und der Begriff des Zynismus* (Munich: Funk, 1979). Studies of individual topics include Ragnar Höïstad, *Cynic Hero and Cynic King* (Uppsala: Gleerup, 1948); Harold W. Attridge, *First Century Cynicism in the Epistles of Heraclitus* (Missoula, Mont.: Scholars, 1976); I. Nachov, "Der Mensch in der Philosophie der Kyniker," in *Der Mensch als Mass der Dinge,* ed. R. Müller (Berlin: Akademie-Verlag, 1976), pp. 361–98; Abraham J. Malherbe, "Self-Definition among Epicureans and Cynics," in *Jewish and Christian Self-Definition in the Greco-Roman World,* vol. 3, ed. B. F. Meyer and E. P. Sanders (Philadelphia: Fortress, 1983), pp. 46–59; Jean-Marie Meillard, "L'Anti-intellectuelisme de Diogène le Cynique," *RevThPh* 115 (1983): 233–46; Marie-Odile Goulet-Cazé, *L'Ascèse cynique: Un commentaire de Diogène Laërce VI:70–71* (Paris: Vrin, 1986); Margarethe Billerbeck, *Epiktet, Vom Kynismus: Herausgegeben und Übersetzung mit einem Kommentar* (Leiden: Brill, 1978); and Rudolf Asmus, "Der Kyniker Sallustius bei Damascius," *Neue Jarbücher für das klassisch altertum Geschichte und deutsche Literatur* 25 (1910): 504–22. For students of the history of Christianity, the study of Cynicism has contributed to an understanding of the reception of pagan literary genres such as the diatribe and the *chreia* by the authors of various writings in the New Testament. The classic study is Rudolf Bultmann, *Der Stil der paulinischen Predigt und die kynisch-stoische Diatribe* (Göttingen: Vanderhoeck und Ruprecht, 1910). Abraham Malherbe's writings on Paul and the Cynics are now collected in *Paul and the Thessalonians* (Philadelphia: Fortress, 1987), and in *Paul and the Popular Philosophers* (Minneapolis: Fortress, 1989). F. Gerald Downing, *Cynics and Christian Origins* (Edinburgh: T. & T. Clark, 1992), collects many of his earlier articles. See also J. S. Kloppenborg, *The Formation of Q* (Philadelphia: Fortress, 1987), pp. 306–25, and Burton Mack, *The Myth of Innocence* (Philadelphia: Fortress, 1988), pp. 67–69. For a consideration of post–New Testament Christian attitudes toward Cynicism, see my "Diogenes the Cynic among the Fourth-Century Fathers," *VC* 47 (1993): 29–49; and my "The Bawdy and Society: The Shamelessness of Diogenes in Roman Imperial Culture," in *The Cynics: The Movement in Antiquity and Its Legacy for Europe,* ed. R. Bracht Branham and Marie-Odile Goulet-Cazé, forthcoming.

tudes of Christian writers from the second half of the fourth century to the
early seventh century toward traditions about Diogenes of Sinope, the
Cynic philosopher.

The Survival of Diogenes Traditions in Late Antiquity

The preservation of traditions about Diogenes in the school curriculum in
Late Antiquity provides a suitable starting point for surveying comments
about Diogenes and Cynicism in the writings of fourth-century Christians. Only then can we begin to understand what the figure of Diogenes
meant to the architects of an emerging Christian intellectual culture. By
the time of the early empire, Diogenes had become a cultural type, a
πρόσωπον, a recognizable stock character. As such, he appears in works
by a number of authors from the first and second centuries, including Dio
Chrysostom, Epictetus, Plutarch, as well as in a collection of pseudepi-
graphical letters.[4] Each of these writers had access to a loosely organized
body of traditions about Diogenes which circulated both in oral and in
written forms.[5]

Familiarity with the figure of Diogenes did not fade away with the
coming of Christianity. Sayings attributed to Diogenes and anecdotes
about him were preserved (and even generated), particularly in the
schools of grammar and rhetoric located in cities throughout the Mediterranean world.[6] Diogenes, as a cultural type, became an element in Christian culture, an example from the past to be referred to in discussion of a
range of topics, a bit of cultural property whose meaning and significance
were widely debated. Christians' exploitation of Diogenes' meaning was
part of their synthesis of the cultural legacy of the pagan past.

Traditions about Diogenes were preserved in the rhetorical exercises,
particular in *chreia* (χρεία), the sayings and anecdotes which formed the
building blocks of rhetorical education and hence had direct bearing on

4. We also find him earlier in the writings of Cicero and elsewhere. Dio Chrysostom,
Epictetus, Plutarch, and Cicero are available in the Loeb Classical Library. The corpus of
pseudepigraphic letters is available with translation in Abraham J. Malherbe, *The Cynic
Epistles: A Study Edition* (Missoula, Mont.: Scholars, 1977).

5. Gunnar Rudberg, "Zur Diogenes Tradition" and "Zum Diogenes Typus," *Symbolae
Osloenses* 14 (1935): 22–43; 15 (1936): 1–18. Using methods parallel to those developed by
Rudolf Bultmann, Rudberg tried to describe the development of the Cynic tradition through
the history of these formal units. For a more specialized discussion of gnomic anthologies
which include Diogenes traditions, see J. Barns, "A New Gnomologium," *Classical Quarterly,*
44 (1950): 127–37; 45 (1951): 1–19.

6. M. Luz, "A Description of the Greek Cynic in the Jerusalem Talmud," *JSJ* 20 (1989):
49–60, has recently shown that the rabbis were familiar with traditions about the Cynics.

the very art of speech making.[7] Drawing on literally thousands of sayings and anecdotes attributed or attributable to various ancient personages, teachers developed their students' oratorical skills. Many *chreiai* were attributed to Socrates, Isocrates, and Menander. Perhaps the greatest number were attributed to Diogenes. One scholar estimated that, in all their variations and permutations, the *chreiai* attributed to Diogenes number more than a thousand.[8]

Chreiai attributed to Diogenes also appeared in other literary contexts. In the *Lives of the Philosophers,* Diogenes Laertius gathers a number of earlier collections of *chreiai* specifically concerned with Diogenes of Sinope in compiling his anecdotal "life" of the Cynic.[9] In this and other collections, there was little concern that the attributions should be accurate, only that they should be apt.[10] The requirement of apt attribution presupposes that the conception of a given character ($\pi\rho\acute{o}\sigma\omega\pi\text{ov}$) was well developed and well understood. In order to attribute a saying to Diogenes, for instance, one first had to consider whether it was appropriate to his character. This character was based in large part on what had been attributed to Diogenes in other *chreiai,* the materials which formed a Diogenes tradition. *Chreiai* attributed to Diogenes shared a "family resemblance," in that they portrayed Diogenes as a certain sort of character determined by a set of

7. Ronald F. Hock and Edward N. O'Neil, *The Chreia in Ancient Rhetoric,* vol. 1, *The Pro-gymnasmata* (Atlanta: Scholars, 1986), contains all the chapters on the *chreia* found in ancient textbooks, with English translations. According to a textbook on rhetoric written by Theon of Alexandria in the second half of the first century, the *chreia* is "a concise statement or action which is attributed with aptness [$\varepsilon\dot{v}\sigma\tauo\chi\acute{\iota}\alpha$] to some specified character [$\pi\rho\acute{o}\sigma\omega\pi\text{ov}$] or to something analogous to a character" (Hock and O'Neil, *The Chreia,* pp. 82–83, text and translation). See also Krueger, "Diogenes the Cynic," pp. 31–32.

8. Henry A. Fischel, "Studies in Cynicism and the Ancient Near East: The Transformation of a *Chria*" [*sic*], in *Religions in Antiquity: Essays in Memory of Erwin Ramsdell Goodenough,* ed. J. Neusner (Leiden: Brill, 1968), p. 374. In Theon's discussion of the *chreia,* seven of the twenty-nine *chreiai* which he uses as examples are attributed to Diogenes. Diogenes is also well represented in later textbooks. Hermogenes, writing in the second century, has one *chreia* attributed to Diogenes out of three examples; Aphthonius of Antioch (late fourth, early fifth century), who appears to be dependent on Hermogenes for his selection, has one Diogenes *chreia* of four; Nicholas of Myra, writing in the sixth century, uses one of eight. Although Aphthonius became the standard rhetorical textbook sometime after the first half of the sixth century, Theon continued to be read (cf. Hock and O'Neil, *The Chreia,* p. 212).

9. Diogenes Laertius cites a certain "Sale of Diogenes" by Menippus (6.29) and a book of the same title by Eubulus (6.31), as well as books of *chreiai* by Hecato (6.32) and Metrocles (6.33) as his sources. On Diogenes Laertius's sources for Diogenes of Sinope see K. von Fritz, *Quellenuntersuchung zu Leben und Philosophie des Diogenes von Sinope* (Leipzig: Dietrich, 1926); Hoïstad, *Cynic Hero,* p. 116; Richard Hope, *The Book of Diogenes Laertius* (New York: Columbia University Press, 1930). See also Rudberg, "Zum Diogenes Tradition" and "Zum Diogenes Typus."

10. Studies attempting to assess the authenticity of these and other sayings and deeds attributed to Diogenes are ultimately futile, since the whole point of the school exercises was to manipulate these statements and thus change them.

loosely related "biographical" details which were commonly "known" to have happened in Diogenes' life, such as his exile from Sinope, his arrival in Athens, the fact that he carried a wallet and a staff and wore a white robe. Chief among the details were witty sayings, an ascetic way of life, and shameless acts.[11]

The wide dissemination of Diogenes traditions is exemplified in the work of the fifth-century pagan author John of Stobi, who compiled an anthology of poetry and prose from over 450 Greek authors.[12] As Photius relates, John presented "opinions, sayings, and maxims" as "precepts to discipline and improve his son."[13] John's anthology was copied frequently in the Byzantine world and has long served scholars because it preserves fragments of many texts now lost. Diogenes figures prominently in this collection; there are over sixty of his sayings, making him one of the most cited sources in the anthology.[14] Reading through the Diogenes *chreiai* in the anthology can give us a sense of what constituted the character of Diogenes in the fifth century. Here are some typical examples:

> When someone asked how can one become master of himself, Diogenes said, "When those things which he reproves in others he reproves even more in himself." (3.1.55)

> Diogenes mocked those who lock up their storehouses with bolts, keys, and seals, but who open up all the doors and windows of their bodies, through their mouth, their genitals, their ears, and their eyes. (3.6.17.)

> Diogenes said that virtue can reside neither in a wealthy city nor a wealthy house. (4.31c.88)

As in Diogenes *chreiai* elsewhere, John of Stobi's Diogenes challenges hypocrisy and praises the virtue of poverty. He embodies the problem of living a moral life for the urban elite.

Throughout the Byzantine era, Diogenes remained an important figure in rhetorical handbooks. Twelve Diogenes *chreiai* appear in John of Damascus's anthology known as the *Sacra Parallela*, consisting mostly of sayings attributed to Christian authors compiled early in the eighth cen-

11. The full range of such details can be found in Diogenes Laertius's life of Diogenes, *Lives of the Philosophers* 6.20–81.

12. The edition cited here is John of Stobi, *Anthologium*, 5 vols., 2nd. ed., ed. C. Wachsmuth and O. Hense (Berlin: Weidmann, 1958). Of continuing usefulness is John of Stobi, *Florilegium*, 4 vols., ed. Augustus Meineke (Leipzig: Taubner, 1855–57); this edition uses a different numbering system from Wachsmuth and Hense.

13. Photius, *Bibl.* cod. 167.

14. For an index of these citations, see Wachsmuth and Hense. Most of the Diogenes material has been translated into French by Léonce Paquet and appears interspersed throughout his own Diogenes anthology in *Les Cyniques grecs*, pp. 59–108.

tury.[15] Rhetors continued to employ the *chreiai* in their speeches, and their audiences continued to be familiar with Diogenes and the meaning that his character came to embody.[16]

School exercises, of course, were not the only factor in the preservation of traditions about Diogenes in Late Antiquity. The writings of the church fathers, as well as the Emperor Julian and the Neoplatonist philosopher Damascius, give evidence for the existence of practicing Cynics in Late Antiquity.[17] Some of the Cynics are known to us by name. Julian attacked a Cynic named Heraclius for misrepresenting the gods.[18] Patriarch Gregory of Nazianzus preached in praise of Maximus, a Christian priest from Alexandria who *also* identified himself as a Cynic and who arrived in Constantinople in 380.[19] Damascius's *Life of Isidorus* gives a spare account of a Cynic and Neoplatonic philosopher named Sallustius who was born around 430 and seems to have survived into the early decades of the sixth century.[20] Moreover, sources from the period either address or

15. During the eighth century John of Damascus, often regarded as the last writer of the Patristic period, compiled an anthology in much the same style as John of Stobi's anthology, grouping quotations under various headings. John of Damascus, however, drew his material primarily from Christian authors, mostly theologians. Materials from "profane" and non-Christian sources make up a small part of the *Sacred Parallels,* but among these pieces of the pagan world are twelve sayings attributed to Diogenes. Selections from the "profane" authors are included in the fourth volume of Meineke's edition of John of Stobi. See John of Damascus, *Sacra Parallela,* PG 95–96. Karl Holl ("Die *Sacra Parallela* des Johannes Damascenus," *Texte und Untersuchungen* 16 [1897]: 1–392) argued convincingly for the authenticity of the work. Also worthy of mention are the few sayings of Diogenes in the so-called *Florilegium Monacense* once attributed to a seventh-century writer named Maximus—most likely not Maximus the Confessor—for which a date as late as the late ninth through early eleventh century has also been suggested. The text is included in Meineke's edition of John of Stobi's *Anthology,* 4:267–90. On the date see A. Ehrhard, "Zu den 'Sacra Parallela' des Johannes Damascenus und dem Florilegium des 'Maximus,'" *BZ* 10 (1901): 394–415. On further discussion of this question and on Patristic florilegia in general see Marcel Richard, "Florilèges spirituels grecs," *DS.*

16. I do not mean to suggest that the transmission of traditions about Diogenes in Late Antiquity was limited to his survival among educated elites. We must imagine that oral traditions contributed to the preservation and dissemination of anecdotes about Diogenes.

17. Although Dudley's *History of Cynicism* (pp. 202–8) devotes only seven pages to the period from the third to the sixth centuries, the evidence suggests that practicing Cynics continued to be a feature of urban life until the decades immediately preceding the reign of Justinian.

18. Julian, *Or.* 7. For Julian, the speech against Heraclius was an occasion to praise the value of mythology—a mythology which had been rejected by the growing number of Christians around him. Julian advocates a purer Cynicism which could be part of a pagan front against the Christians. Cf. Johannes Geffcken, *The Last Days of Greco-Roman Paganism,* trans. Sabine MacCormack (Amsterdam: North Holland, 1978), p. 151.

19. On Gregory and Maximus, see below.

20. Damascius's *Life of Isidorus* has been reconstructed from fragments appearing in Photius and in the *Suda. Damascii vitae Isidori reliquiae,* ed. Clemens Zintzen (Hildesheim: Olms, 1967).

refer to groups of nameless practitioners of Cynicism. Julian composed a
speech scolding the Cynics of his day for failing to understand Diogenes
and achieve his objectives.[21] Augustine was also aware of the continued
existence of Cynics.[22] The Cynic way of life continued to have a powerful
appeal into the fifth century.

Nevertheless, after the "army of the dog" had ceased to attract recruits, it
was rhetorical education which guaranteed familiarity with Diogenes into
the seventh century and beyond. Leontius, himself, had had such rhetorical training, as is evidenced not only by his allusions to Diogenes in the
Life of Symeon, but also by its lengthy rhetorical introduction. Clearly
Leontius had mastered the tools necessary to make a speech. What sort of
Christian interpretation of Diogenes and Cynicism might he have received with his education? To consider this aspect of Leontius's intellectual heritage, we must turn to the interpretations of Diogenes among
Christians and pagans of the fourth century, since it was the reflections of
such figures as Basil the Great, John Chrysostom, Gregory of Nazianzus,
and even the Emperor Julian which framed the debate over the relevance
of the Hellenistic curriculum for Christians.

Attitudes toward Diogenes

Already in the third century, Origen had cited the Cynics with favor to
justify the Christian practice of preaching in public and the life of voluntary poverty.[23] The fourth century brought changes in the status of Christianity in aristocratic and hence in intellectual circles. As the relationship
between Christianity and traditions of pagan learning was renegotiated,
the figure of Diogenes was revalued. Basil of Caesarea, it seems, was quite
fond of Diogenes the Cynic. In a casual note to a wealthy friend written
around 358, Basil thanks his friend for gifts, joking that his beloved
Poverty has been driven away. He muses that Poverty would object, since
she had decided to live with Basil in the first place because he praised
Zeno and Cleanthes and had donned the philosopher's cloak. "As for Diogenes," protests Poverty,

21. Julian, *Or.* 6.
22. Augustine, *Civ. Dei* 14.20.
23. Origen, *Contra Celsum* 3.50.

[Basil] has never ceased to admire him, who, endeavoring to be satisfied by the things derived from nature alone threw away even his drinking cup, after he learned from a boy how to bend over and drink from the hollow of his hands.[24]

As he appears here, Diogenes might be taken for just one of many elements of the literary culture which Late Roman gentlemen shared and to which they might make witty reference. Basil's commitment to the traditions which transmitted this literary culture, articulated in his *Letter to Young Men on How They Might Benefit from Pagan Literature,* is evidence for a balance struck between Christianity and Greek *paideia* in Christian intellectual circles. Basil's formulation of the balance between Christian values and pagan culture had crucial consequences for the whole of Christian intellectual history in the East. With Basil, Diogenes became firmly rooted in a Christian intellectual tradition. Basil's *Letter to Young Men* had tremendous influence in Late Antiquity and in Byzantine times, shaping a Christian philosophy of education that accommodated prevailing Late Antique pagan curricula.[25]

Basil felt that the example of Diogenes which was presented in the educational curriculum was instructive and worthy of inclusion in the canon of information to be passed on to Christian students. In Basil's letter on pagan literature, among references to Homer and Hesiod, Plato and Plutarch, are passages based on *chreiai* attributed to Diogenes of Sinope. Diogenes exemplified a form of behavior which Basil felt was desirable for Christian youths. Basil writes,

[T]o spend one's time, beyond what is necessary, on the care of the hair or on dress, is, according to the saying of Diogenes, the mark of men who are either unfortunate or doing wrong.[26] Hence, to be a dandy and get the name of being one ought, I maintain, to be considered by persons so inclined just as disgraceful as to keep company with harlots or to seduce other men's wives. For what difference should it make, at least to a man of sense, whether he is clothed in a costly robe or wears a cheap work-

24. Basil, *Ep.* 4. Variants of this *chreia* include Plutarch, *Mor.* 79e; D. L. 6.37; *Ep. Diog.* 6.
25. Cf. H. I. Marrou, *A History of Education in Antiquity,* trans. George Lamb (1956; rpt., Madison: University of Wisconsin Press, 1982), pp. 321–22, 340–42. While Marrou is right to observe that Basil is warning against the dangers inherent in reading pagan literature, he underestimates the degree to which Basil is presenting a defense of the extant canon. The letter was addressed to Basil's nephews, and it is unclear whether Basil intended it for wide circulation. Numerous manuscripts survive from the late ninth century on, by which time it had become widely used as a school text. The existence of Syriac translations of the text, the first from the fifth century and the second from the seventh, suggests that Basil's letter was widely read. On the history of the text and translations, see N. G. Wilson, *Saint Basil on the Value of Greek Literature* (London: Duckworth, 1975), pp. 72–73.
26. Cf. D. L. 6.54 and Stobaeus, 3.6.38.

man's cloak, so long as what he has on gives adequate protection against
the cold of winter and the heat of summer?[27]

And later,

> I admire also the scorn of Diogenes for all human good without excep-
> tion, who declared himself richer than the Great King [Alexander the
> Great] by reason of the fact that he needed less for living than the King.[28]

Thus, Diogenes' simple comportment—rather than his shameless acts—
received Basil's praise.

Not only was Diogenes a moral exemplar, he was also an instrument
of polemic. The pagan tradition, of course, was not static in this era, and
the meaning of the figure of Diogenes was debated by pagans as well as
Christians. There is no better evidence of the pagan concern to revalue
the legacy of the Cynic tradition in this era than the writings of the Emperor Julian. Julian's oration directed against "uneducated Cynics" was
probably composed in Constantinople, late in the spring of 362.[29] In this
speech Julian defended Diogenes from criticisms which had been directed
against him by contemporary Cynics, especially that Diogenes was foolish when he ingested raw octopus. Julian defended this deed, as well as
many of Diogenes' acts of shamelessness, by arguing that Diogenes' intent was to determine which activities humans engaged in on account of
nature, and which they engaged in merely to conform to social convention (δόξα).[30] Julian presents Diogenes as a model against which to judge
contemporary Cynics, and in fact all philosophers. For Julian, Diogenes is
the ideal pagan philosophical type, and Diogenes' shameless acts are an
essential and even laudable aspect of his character. Although Julian states
he is responding to Cynic allegations against Diogenes in this oration,
criticism was also leveled at Diogenes by Christians, and Julian seems to
have taken on the defense of a pagan philosophical type in order to present Diogenes as an alternative to Christian asceticism.

27. Basil, *Leg. lib. gent.* 9.3, 4. Text and English translation, *Letters*, vol. 4, ed. and trans.
Roy J. Deferrari and Martin R. P. McGuire (Cambridge: Harvard University Press, 1962), pp.
415–17.
28. Basil, *Leg. lib. gent.* 9.20; trans. Deferrari and McGuire, pp. 425–27. Dio Chrys. *Or.*
6.6 ff. is an expansion of the *chreia* which stands behind this statement. See also Plutarch,
Mor. 499b and 604c.
29. Julian, *Or.* 6. The date is suggested by Julian's reference to the summer solstice in
the opening of the speech (181a). Cf. G. W. Bowersock, *Julian the Apostate* (Cambridge: Harvard University Press, 1978), p. 71.
30. On the terms δόξα and ἄδοξος in Cynicism see Malherbe, "Ps-Heraclitus, Ep. 4: The
Divinization of the Wise Man," *JAC* 21 (1978): 60.

Shortly after he composed this oration against the "uneducated Cynics," Julian spent time in residence at Antioch. When Julian's remarks about Diogenes are read against the comments of John Chrysostom, a monk and later presbyter at Antioch, we can see that the value of Diogenes as a model for moral behavior was part of the larger debate between pagans and Christians in the second half of the fourth century over which community was the legitimate heir of Greco-Roman educational and philosophical traditions.

Although his writings have led one modern critic to suggest that he "retained little admiration" for the poets and philosophers he had read in the pagan curriculum, Chrysostom had been widely educated in classical authors and would refer to them in his own writings to make a point.[31] Certainly Chrysostom was not indifferent to all aspects of Greek philosophy, for while he was concerned to show that Greek philosophers compared badly with Christian thinkers, he was quick to cite the achievements of individual philosophers who had led lives which, at least in part, could be regarded as exemplary. Diogenes the Cynic received both Chrysostom's criticism and his praise.

In his treatise *Against the Enemies of the Monastic Life*, John Chrysostom praises the ascetic virtues of Diogenes as well as Socrates and Plato. He writes,

> Do you know how much money Alexander [the Great] would have given to Diogenes, if he wanted to accept it? But he did not want it. And Alexander tried hard and did everything so that he might some day come to Diogenes's riches.[32]

He concludes, "That other philosopher, the one from Sinope, was richer by far than these and countless other such kings."[33] Ironically, Chrysostom invokes Diogenes as an exemplar of the ascetic life in his defense of Christian monasticism. Chrysostom assumes that his audience is familiar with the story of Diogenes and Alexander, and that it was already inclined to think well of Diogenes.[34] Chrysostom argues that if Diogenes was respected by educated Christians for his way of life, despite the fact that he

31. P. R. Coleman-Norton, "St. Chrysostom and the Greek Philosophers," *Classical Philology* 25 (1930): 305. On Diogenes and other Cynics, see pp. 307–9.

32. John Chrysostom, *Adversus oppugnatores vitae monasticae* 2.4, PG 47.337.

33. John Chrysostom, *Ad. op. vit. monast.* 2.5, PG 47.339.

34. Furthermore, Chrysostom, ever suspicious of pretension, praised Diogenes and Crates, as well as Socrates, for not having mastered the art of eloquence—an ironic point perhaps in light of Chrysostom's rhetorical skill. John Chrysostom, *Ad. op. vit. monast.* 3.11, PG 47.367. Socrates, of course, was remembered as an opponent of the Sophists.

was a pagan, how much more should the Christian ascetic be worthy of respect.[35]

While Diogenes' legendary impurity and shamelessness seem to have been overlooked by Basil, Chrysostom voiced his disapproval. In his *Discourse on the Blessed Babylas,* composed in Antioch around 378, Chrysostom compares the murdered bishop of Antioch to ancient philosophers. Of course, Babylas is superior to these men. Chrysostom accuses the pagan philosophers of "vain-glory, impudence, and puerility" and praises Babylas because "he did not shut himself up in a large wine cask, nor did he go round the market place clothed in rags." The reference, of course, is to Diogenes.[36] Chrysostom chides Diogenes for his audacity in asking Alexander the Great to step out of his light. When Chrysostom's imaginary interlocutor protests that "'the man from Sinope was also temperate and lived abstinently, even refusing to contract a legitimate marriage,'" Chrysostom responds, "But add how and in what way! You will not add it, but prefer to deprive him of praise for temperance than tell the mode of his temperance, so foul and full of so much shame."[37] The reference here is most likely to stories about Diogenes' tendency to masturbate in public.[38] After condemning the approving attitudes of Aristotle, Chrysippus, Socrates, and Plato toward various sex acts, Chrysostom accuses Diogenes of being indifferent to cannibalism. Chrysostom presents Diogenes as licentious and morally irresponsible, hardly worthy of comparison with a Christian saint. What is most intriguing is that Chrysostom's argument proceeds by countering a position which he assumes to be commonplace: that Diogenes' way of life—his poverty, freedom, and temperance—was laudable.

The speech in praise of the martyr Babylas is directed "against Julian and against the pagans." It is probable that Chrysostom was familiar with Julian's oration against the "uneducated Cynics." Julian argued that Di-

35. Chrysostom's invocation of Diogenes in defense of monasticism needs to be considered in light of the considerable suspicion against asceticism among Christian elites. The decision to adopt the monastic life was seen as a radical break with the privileges and duties of the life of the upper classes throughout the Mediterranean world. Parents in particular resisted their children's impulses to retire from the world. (Cf. the *Life of Melania the Younger* and the remarks of Elizabeth A. Clark in "Ascetic Renunciation and Feminine Advancement: A Paradox of Late Ancient Christianity," *Anglican Theological Review* 63 [1981]: 240–57. The subject of parental resistance to the ascetic life deserves further study.)

36. John Chrysostom, *De sanctum Babyla contra Julianum et contra Gentiles* 8, PG 50.545; English trans. by Margaret A. Shatkin in *Saint John Chrysostom, Apologist* (Washington, D.C.: Catholic University Press, 1985), pp. 100–1. On the date of the text, see Shatkin's introduction, pp. 15–16.

37. John Chrysostom, *De s. Babyla* 9, PG 50.545; trans. Shatkin, pp. 102–3.

38. Cf. D. L. 6.46, 69.

ogenes had rejected common opinion in favor of a life according to the principles of nature, a standard interpretation of Diogenes' behavior found already in the pseudepigraphic epistles.[39] But the Greek word *doxa* (δόξα), which Julian and the epistles use to mean "social convention" or "opinion," also means "glory" or "honor," a concept related to renown or repute.[40] For Chrysostom, glory was for God alone and was to be rejected by the saints. Chrysostom's letter to a young widow argues that a number of ancient philosophers rejected wealth in pursuit of "glory from everyone [τῆς δόξης τῆς παρὰ τῶν πολλῶν]," that is, public recognition or common good opinion. It is precisely this virtue of the rejection of *doxa* which Chrysostom wishes to instill in the widow.[41] In arguing here that Diogenes sought *doxa,* Chrysostom contradicts the commonplace assertion found in Julian that he did not. For Chrysostom, the notion that Diogenes had been motivated by *doxa* was sufficient grounds to condemn him. In a homily on First Corinthians, Chrysostom says that the apostles did not seek glory,

> Not like him of Sinope, who clothed in rags and living in a cask to no good end, astonished many, but profited none: whereas Paul did none of these things; (for neither had he an eye to ostentation;) but was both clothed in ordinary apparel with all decency, and lived in a house continually, and displayed all exactness in the practice of all other virtue; which the Cynic despised, living impurely and publicly disgracing himself, and dragged away by his mad passion for glory [δόξα]. For if any one ask the reason of his living in a cask, he will find no other but vain-glory alone.[42]

Here and elsewhere, when John Chrysostom compared Cynics and Christians, the Cynics were to be faulted for their failure to achieve the virtues of early Christians. Chrysostom is thus refuting a *contemporary* pagan evaluation of Diogenes and the meaning of the Cynic tradition in order to prove the superiority of Christianity. In fact, Chrysostom is specifically interested in discrediting this pagan exemplar who most seems to embody Christian ideals.

John Chrysostom's rejection of Diogenes as unworthy of a Christian's praise stands in great contrast to the opinions of his predecessor as patri-

39. Julian, *Or.* 6.193d, 202c. Cf. *Epp. Diog.* 6, 42.

40. Cf. Lampe, s.v. This meaning can be found in Christian liturgical texts.

41. John Chrysostom, *Ad viduam juniorem* 6, PG 48.607; cf. NPNF (first series) IX, p. 126. On the question of how widespread familiarity with Diogenes was in Late Antiquity, we note that Chrysostom writes to this widow that she did not need to learn who the pagan philosophers he was referring to were from him, since "you know Epaminondas, Socrates, Aristeides, Diogenes, and Crates . . . better than I do."

42. John Chrysostom, *Homiliae in 1 Cor* 35.4, PG 61.302; English trans. NPNF (first series) XII, p. 212.

arch of Constantinople, Gregory of Nazianzus. In a letter composed after he had been removed from the patriarchate and returned to his home town, Gregory addressed the civic administrators of Nazianzus, seeking to obtain a tax exemption for a local priest.

> It seems to me that you would not spare Diogenes of Sinope's wallet, if it were up to you; rather if [only] you could lay your hand on *it* also, and regard his cloak, staff, and his lack of all possessions on account of his philosophy as a profession, his habit of going from door to door, living life however it comes . . . [thus you would also tax this poor priest who serves the community.][43]

Diogenes here, as we have seen elsewhere, is a paradigm for a person living in voluntary poverty for the sake of others. Such a person is worthy of regard by civil officials and therefore by the town in general. Gregory's reference to Diogenes has much in common with that in the personal letter of Basil's quoted above. Diogenes was part of these gentlemen's culture, and Gregory's opinion of Diogenes was not unlike that of his friend and fellow Cappadocian.

This similarity is all the more remarkable given Gregory's previous experiences with a flesh and blood Cynic. In 380 a certain Maximus arrived in Constantinople from Alexandria. Before his conversion to Christianity, Gregory explains, Maximus had practiced Cynicism. When he arrived in Constantinople he still had long hair and carried a staff.[44] It is clear from his garb as well as from Gregory's description that, although Maximus had become a Christian, he remained in some sense a Cynic. The Nicene bishop of Constantinople, soon to be patriarch, Gregory of Nazianzus preached two panegyrics in his honor referring to him as a "philosopher."[45] These two orations in honor of Maximus are, in fact, a defense and praise of philosophy, albeit a conditional one. These neglected speeches are exceptionally good evidence for a late-fourth-century synthesis of pagan learning and Christian culture, a synthesis which the Cappadocians played a leading role in creating. Gregory's treatment of philosophy was far more positive than anything that would be found in John Chrysostom. Gregory refers to philosophers in general as "witnesses

43. Gregory of Nazianzus (hereafter Greg. Naz.), *Ep.* 98; *Briefe,* ed. Paul Gallay (Berlin: Akademie-Verlag, 1969), pp. 80–81.

44. Greg. Naz., *De vita sua,* ed. Christoph Junck (Heidelberg: Winter, 1974), ll. 767–68; English trans. Denis Molaise Meehan, *Three Poems* (Washington, D.C.: Catholic University Press, 1987), p. 99.

45. Greg. Naz., *Orations* 25, 26. The identification of the Maximus of *De vita sua* with the hero of *Orations* 25 and 26 is certain. On the Maximus affair see the excellent discussion by Justin Mossay in his edition, *Discours* (Paris: Cerf, 1978), pp. 120–41.

[μαρτύρες] to the truth."[46] He continues, "Their splendid robes are angelic as is the radiance which they express in outward form in their bodies."[47] The language here recalls that used of Christian monastics (and late Neo-platonist pagan philosophers). This speech was given when, of all philosophical types, a Cynic was on hand. Gregory was not just referring to the martyred Socrates. In Gregory's eyes the aims of Maximus's philosophy and his Christianity were compatible. For Gregory, this Cynic Christian was a "defender of the truth and a champion of the Trinity,"[48] worthy of comparison with the martyrs. Gregory refers to Maximus many times as a "dog," punning on the commonly accepted etymology for the word "Cynic" (κυνικός, which can also mean "doglike"),[49] and says that he is a

> dog [κύων], not by shamelessness, but by courage [παρρησία], nor by gluttony, but by living day by day, nor by barking [ὑλακή], but by guarding [φυλακή] the good and keeping watch over souls, and by wagging your tail at whatever belongs to the family of virtue and barking at whatever does not.[50]

The connection between Cynics and dogs is exploited most fully in praising the philosopher. Even in this high praise, however, we can see another vision of the Cynics, one characterized by accusations of shamelessness and gluttony. Maximus had, Gregory tells us, risen above the peculiar practices of his pagan predecessors—Antisthenes' arrogance, Diogenes' vegetarianism, and Crates' fondness for group marriage—and was quite different from them in his prudence, continence, modesty, affability, sense of community, and love of humanity.[51]

Gregory's affection for Maximus did not last long. A few months after Maximus arrived in Constantinople, he attempted to unseat the bishop and have himself installed in Gregory's place. He bribed a priest who was a member of Gregory's staff to help him and gained the support of a mob of sailors from the Alexandrian fleet, recently moored at Constantinople.

---

46. One thinks, of course, of Socrates. On Christian attitudes toward Socrates, see J. Geffcken, *Sokrates und das alte Christentum* (Heidelberg: C. Winter, 1908).

47. Greg. Naz., *Or.* 25.2, ed. Mossay, p. 158.

48. Greg. Naz., *Or.* 25.3.

49. On Cynics as dogs, see Ferrand Sayre, *Greek Cynicism,* pp. 4–5. Serious doubts concerning the etymology of the term "Cynic" and a discussion of the ancient (non-Christian) interpretations of the title can be found in Heinz Schulz-Falkenthal, "Kyniker—Zur inhaltlichen Deutung des Namens," *Wissenschaftliche Zeitschrift Martin-Luther Universität, Halle-Wittenberg* (Gesellschaftsreihe) 26.2 (1977): 41–49. For dog = Cynic in collections of Cynic *chreiai,* see D. L. 6.33, 40, 61, 77; *Gnomologium Vaticanum* 175, 194; Athenaeus, *Deip.* 5.216b; *Florilegium Monacense* 155 = Meinecke 4:278; Stobaeus, 4.55.11; *Anth. Pal.* 7.63–68.

50. Greg. Naz., *Or.* 25.2, ed. Mossay, pp. 158–60.

51. Greg. Naz., *Or.* 25.7.

His plan failed, thanks to loyal citizens who interrupted Maximus's sham consecration ceremony. Gregory was understandably furious, and not long after, when he had resigned his post and retired to his native Cappadocia, he expressed his wrath in his autobiographical poem *De vita sua*, devoting a quarter of the work to this incident.[52] Explaining his error in praising Maximus earlier, Gregory writes, "It was a great thing for me when a dog trod in my courtyard and worshipped Christ instead of Herakles."[53] But Gregory only condemned the man, not his philosophy. Concluding his narration of this episode he says, "Such is the philosophy of our modern dogs: barking dogs, and dogs in this alone. In what way are they like Diogenes or Antisthenes? What has Crates to do with you?"[54] Gregory echoes Julian in rejecting the Cynics of his own day because they did not live up to the examples of the great Cynics of the past.

In his later years, when he spent much of his time composing poetry, Gregory continued to hold that Christians could learn from virtuous nonbelievers, "like gathering roses from among the thorns."[55] In this way, he continued to make reference to the example of Diogenes.

> Who has not heard of the Sinopean dog? What else needs be said but that he was someone thus, simple and moderate in life, and giving these laws to himself, not observing laws from God, and not on account of any hope, so that he had one possession, his staff, an open-air house in the middle of the town, a round barrel, an escape from the force of the wind, which for him was better than dwellings laden with gold, and food nearby, not prepared with toil.[56]

For the retired patriarch, Diogenes' life remained a romanticized ideal. Despite Gregory's troubles with his Cynic contemporary, Diogenes continued to be proverbial for his virtuous poverty.[57] His obvious shortcoming was that he was not motivated by the love or laws of God.

Ambivalence beyond the Fourth Century

Basil's and Gregory's enthusiasm should not be taken as representative of all educated Christians of the Later Roman Empire. In his monumental

---

52. Greg. Naz., *De vita sua*, ll. 750–1043.

53. Greg. Naz., *De vita sua*, ll. 974–75. Herakles was a hero for the Cynics. See Dio Chrys., *Disc.* 1.59–84; Malherbe, "Ps.-Heraclitus Ep. 4," *passim*.

54. Greg. Naz., *De vita sua*, ll. 1030–33.

55. Greg. Naz., *Poems* 1.2.10, ll. 215–16, PG 37.696.

56. Greg. Naz., *Poems* 1.2.10, ll. 218–27.

57. For a general treatment of Gregory's attitudes toward wealth and poverty, see Bernard Coulie, *Les Richesses dans l'oeuvre de Saint Grégoire de Nazianze* (Louvain: Institut Orientaliste, 1985).

antipagan treatise *The Cure of Pagan Maladies,* Theodoret of Cyrrhus demonstrates his ambivalence toward the Cynic. Subtitled *The Truth of the Gospels Proved from Greek Philosophy,* the work dates from the second quarter of the fifth century.[58] Theodoret refers to Diogenes of Sinope six times in the course of the treatise.[59] His reproaches are numerous: Theodoret regarded Diogenes as "a slave to pleasure." "He mingled with prostitutes in public, and he set a bad example for those who saw him." Diogenes "lived lewdly, without restraint."[60] Unlike the Christian "athletes of virtue,"[61] Diogenes, it seems, missed the mark, and was therefore an inappropriate model for the Christian seeking to live the moral life. Theodoret's protests imply that for many Christians Diogenes remained a model of virtue.[62]

Christians did not share a unified stance toward Diogenes, nor was the position of any particular Christian toward Diogenes entirely consistent. Ultimately Diogenes' shamelessness was the stumbling block for a number of Christian writers. In this regard it is worth citing the opinions of Augustine of Hippo, who argued in *City of God* that Diogenes behaved shamelessly "because he imagined that his school of philosophy would gain more publicity if its indecency were more startlingly impressed on the memory of mankind."[63] Augustine, however, claimed that this practice was not continued when modesty prevailed over the mistaken notion that "men should make it their ambition to resemble dogs." He continues,

> Hence I am inclined to think that even Diogenes himself, and the others about whom this story is told, merely went through the motions of lying together before the eyes of men who had no means of knowing what was really going on under the philosopher's cloak.[64]

58. Thdt., *Graecarum affectionum curatio,* 2 vols., ed. and French trans. Pierre Canivet (Paris: Cerf, 1958). Canivet dates the work from the early 420s; however, this may be too early. Cf. Canivet, *Histoire d'une enterprise apologétique au ve siècle* (Paris: Bloud et Gay, 1957), p. v. Canivet has shown that Theodoret is greatly dependent on Clement of Alexandria's *Stromata* and Eusebius's *Preparatio Evangelica.*

59. Thdt., *Affect.* 1.24, 50; 3.53; 6.20; 12.32, 48–49.

60. Thdt., *Affect.* 12.48. Theodoret (*Affect.* 12.49; cf. Clem., *Strom.* 4.19.121) remembers that Crates had surrendered to passion and "consummated his dog's marriage [κυνογαμία] in public." The Cynics were examples who prove the rule that "the road to virtue is rough, steep, and difficult" (*Affect.* 12.46).

61. Thdt., *Affect.* 12.32.

62. In fact, in his *Discourse on Providence,* written for an Antiochene audience sometime after 435, Theodoret lists Socrates, Diogenes, and Anaxarchus as examples of people who renounced wealth in favor of poverty. Thdt., *Provid.* 6, PG 83.649; French trans. Yvan Azéma, *Discours sur la providence* (Paris: Les Belles Lettres, 1954), p. 207.

63. Augustine, *Cīv. Dei* 14.20; trans. John O'Meara, *City of God* (London: Penguin, 1984), pp. 581–82.

64. Trans. O'Meara, p. 582.

Rather unimaginative indeed is Augustine's remark: "I doubt whether the pleasure of that act could have been successfully achieved with spectators crowding round." In what I believe is an otherwise unattested twist on the ancient *chreiai*, Augustine was willing not only to defend the Cynic's shameless behavior, but to go so far as to deny it by claiming that Diogenes was only pretending to do something unseemly. We can only wonder whether this attempt to vindicate Diogenes was persuasive. For Augustine, the Cynic's achievements were too important to allow them to be discredited by lewd stories.[65]

Interest in Cynicism did not wane in the period between these authors and Leontius. The late fifth and early sixth centuries witnessed a revival of interest in Cynicism among pagan Neoplatonists.[66] In his *Life of Isidorus*, Damascius praises the Neoplatonist and Cynic Sallustius, a native of Emesa (born c. 430), who practiced Cynicism in Alexandria and appears to have survived into the sixth century. Moreover, Simplicius, a student of Damascius, who chose voluntary exile in Persia after Justinian closed the schools in Athens in 529, refers to Diogenes quite favorably in his *Commentary on the Enchiridion of Epictetus*.[67]

In addition, one of the most cultivated authors of the first half of the seventh century was Theophylact Simocatta. Better known for his history of the reign of the Emperor Maurice, he also wrote *Ethical Epistles,* a collection of eighty-five fictitious letters purportedly written by and addressed to a variety of historical and mythical personages.[68] The work probably dates from the first decade of the seventh century. Theophylact attributes four letters in the collection to Diogenes.[69]

Into the seventh century Diogenes remained an element of literary culture,[70] a complex cultural type who stood forever outside the norm,

65. Concerning Cynics in his own time, Augustine writes, "Even now we see that there are still Cynic philosophers about. . . . [N]one of them dares to act like Diogenes. If any of them were to venture to do so they would be overwhelmed, if not with a hail of stones, at any rate with a shower of spittle from the disgusted public." Trans. O'Meara, p. 582.

66. On this question, see Asmus, "Der Kyniker Sallustius." Moreover, earlier Platonists were neither ignorant nor universally condemning of the Cynics. Cf. Eunapius, *Lives of the Sophists,* ed. and trans. W. C. Wright (Cambridge: Harvard University Press, 1952), pp. 346–49.

67. Simplicius, *Commentary on the Enchiridion of Epictetus,* in *Theophrasti Charactares, Marci Antonii Commentarii Epicteti . . . et Enchiridion cum Commentario Simplicii,* ed. F. Dübner (Paris: Firmin-Didot, 1872), pp. 40, 45, 49.

68. Theophylact Simocatta, *Epistulae,* ed. Joseph Zanetto (Leipzig: Teubner, 1985). A very brief description of the work appears in Michael and Mary Whitby, *The History of Theophylact Simocatta* (Oxford: Clarendon, 1986), p. xv.

69. Diogenes "wrote" epp. 19, 43, 46, 76, and is mentioned in ep. 60. He "writes" against wealth and effeminacy.

70. The continued relevance of Diogenes in later Byzantine intellectual culture is attested by Michael Psellus's references to Diogenes in his praise of Symeon Metaphrastes written during the eleventh century. Michael Psellus, "Encomium on Symeon Metaphrastes," *Scripta minora,* vol. 1, ed. Edward Kurtz (Milan: Società editrice "vita e pensiero," 1936), p. 97.

chastising those who held too tenaciously the common values of the educated classes. Gentlemen continued to reflect upon him in the course of
their studies and beyond. Although some Christians rejected him out-
right, others harnessed the power of his critique and incorporated it into
Christian moral exhortation. He was invoked in treatise, homily, and private correspondence. The next chapter considers his invocation in hagiography, in Leontius's *Life of Symeon the Fool.* What attitudes toward Diogenes might Leontius have inherited? The portrait is decidedly mixed. On
the basis of the evidence examined here, we can make the general observation that Late Ancient Christians invoked Diogenes positively to support their arguments in favor of the life of poverty and self-control, and
negatively to argue against surrendering to passion and lust. This Christian lack of consistency with regard to Diogenes should not be surprising.
Christians presented a varied picture of Diogenes because they had received a varied picture. The variety of ways in which Christians employed the *chreiai* attributed to Diogenes reflected the diversity within the
figure of Diogenes which the *chreiai* preserved. The figure of Diogenes
was a blend of asceticism and shamelessness. And it was this composite
which attracted Leontius.

· SIX ·

SYMEON AND THE CYNICS

When Symeon first arrived in Emesa, he discovered a dead dog lying on a dunghill just outside the city. He tied the dog's leg to his belt and then entered the city gate, dragging the dog behind him (p. 145). Symeon's entry into Emesa is his first act as a *salos*, the first time he plays the fool. The placement of this event within the course of the narrative is significant. It sets up all the antics to come. This act is outrageous, a madcap, crazy thing to do. More significantly, the dog, proverbial for its tendency toward indecent activity, becomes a symbol of Symeon's own shamelessness. This event marks the transition in Symeon's life from desert to city, from proper ascetic comportment to antiascetic insanity. As Symeon enters the city gate, he crosses the border beyond civil behavior. Symeon enters where he does not belong. A holy man in the city? Shamelessness in the ascetic life? The dead, rotting, dung-encrusted dog represents the crossing of boundaries—impurity, defilement, matter out of place. The dog is also a pun.

Writing on the eve of the Second World War, Ernst Benz suggested that there was a connection between the Byzantine fools' lives and "the tradition of wandering Cynic preachers." Benz considered it significant that Symeon began his activity in Emesa with a dead dog, a figure for the Cynics.[1] Benz's suggestion has not found favor with more recent scholars and has never been tested either for its validity or considered for its implications. The previous discussion of Diogenes invites us to examine Benz's suggestion anew.

1. Ernst Benz, "Heilige Narrheit," *Kyrios* 3 (1938): 18.

In his introduction to the first modern edition of the *Life of Symeon*, Rydén dismisses any Cynic influence on the *Life*. He writes, "It seems clear that we encounter here an un-Greek ascetic type, who, despite certain external similarities, has nothing to do with the Cynics."[2] In his commentary on the text, Rydén has written that

> the connection between the *Life of Antony* and the lives of philosophers, which [others] have already proven, has, as far as the *Life of Symeon* is concerned, of course, no parallel. I admit that Symeon's seemingly ridiculous appearance in Emesa occasionally recalls the conventional disdain of the Cynics; in fact, however, this might be treated as a parallel phenomenon.[3]

Thus Rydén rules out the possibility of direct influence of Cynic lives on the *Life of Symeon the Fool*.

A cross-cultural approach to the similarities between Symeon and the Cynics might, of course, prove fruitful. Alexander Syrkin, for instance, sought to understand the phenomenon of the "fool for Christ's sake" in the Eastern Orthodox tradition by comparing Symeon with similar figures in later Orthodox as well as Hindu traditions. Syrkin described holy folly as "a peculiar kind of religious practice . . . that is characterized by eccentric acts which violate moral precepts and etiquette and are often accompanied by comic effects."[4] Diogenes of Sinope could no doubt be shown to adhere to the same pattern. But comparing Symeon's behavior to Diogenes' apart from their discrete historical contexts is problematic. Such an approach attempts to consider "historical figures" for which we have little reliable "historical" evidence, or else it treats the evidence we have for these figures as popular folklore, rather than as literary texts.

A brief description of a monk named Symeon who feigned madness, presumably the same as the subject of Leontius's narrative, appears in Evagrius Scholasticus's *Ecclesiastical History*. However, there is nothing in Evagrius's account of Symeon of Emesa which draws parallels between Symeon and the Cynics.[5] Moreover, this chapter does not suggest that the behavior of a sixth-century saint was motivated or influenced by Cynics

2. Rydén, *Das Leben des heiligen Narren Symeon*, pp. 17–18; my translation.

3. Rydén, *Bemerkungen zum Leben des heiligen Narren Symeon von Leontios von Neapolis* (Uppsala: Almquist and Wiksell, 1970), pp. 17–18; my translation. In such a fashion, Richard Reitzenstein (*Hellenistische Wundererzählungen* [Leipzig: Teubner, 1906], pp. 67–72) argued that the stories of Sarapion found in Palladius's *Lausiac History* and in its expanded Syriac version share a similarity of spirit. Sarapion has often been seen by students of holy folly as a precursor to Symeon in the development of the concept of the holy fool in Christianity. Cf. Festugière, *Vie de Syméon le Fou*, p. 16.

4. Alexander Y. Syrkin, "On the Behavior of the 'Fool for Christ's Sake,'" *History of Religions* 22 (1982): 150.

5. Evagrius, *HE* 4.34.

or Cynicism. Instead, it is a comparison of texts, which explores a literary relationship between Leontius of Neapolis's *Life of Symeon the Fool* and literary traditions about Diogenes of Sinope, the Cynic philosopher, a relationship which has serious implications for our understanding of Symeon's behavior—both his shamelessness and his asceticism—as well as Leontius's conception of folly for the sake of Christ.

Symeon and the Cynics

In the last chapter we saw that in Late Antiquity educated Christians were introduced to the figure of Diogenes through their school training, which made extensive use of Diogenes *chreiai* in grammatical and rhetorical exercises, and that Christian writers were particularly interested in Diogenes, especially because he presented a pagan model of the ascetic life. These Christians also tended to be concerned about Diogenes' shamelessness. The evidence which follows confirms that Leontius also was familiar with Diogenes. While it is possible that Leontius's familiarity with the Cynic hero derived solely from the assimilation of Cynic material into Christian popular culture, the specificity of the allusions to Diogenes suggests otherwise. Leontius's knowledge of Cynicism betrays exposure to *chreiai* he would almost certainly have encountered in the course of schooling in the standard Late Antique curriculum. That this Cypriot bishop had had such a formation is evident from his use of a studied rhetorical writing style in the first half of the *Life of Symeon*.

Although Leontius never refers to Diogenes or the Cynics by name, he does allude to Diogenes' characteristic behavior in several places. Of particular relevance are the passages in which Symeon defecates in public, eats lupines, eats raw meat, and arrives in Emesa, dragging a dead dog.

Defecation in Public

Leontius relates that Symeon regularly defecated in public. This activity gives physical (and even graphic) proof that Symeon had not been fasting, that Symeon violated ascetic norms for food consumption.[6] Leontius informs his reader that Symeon defecates in public in an explanatory aside, placed after a raucous anecdote in which Symeon pretends that he will rape the tavern keeper's wife. As such, the aside breaks the general pat-

6. On the model ascetic's desire to avoid being seen defecating, see Thdt., *HR* 21.5.

tern of this portion of the *Life* which flows from episode to episode, each of which narrates a single unseemly occurrence. Presumably the aside is presented as an explanation for the troubling incident which precedes it, intended to allay the audience's fears about Symeon's behavior. Lest Leontius's reader be concerned that Symeon capitulated to carnal desires, he explains that Symeon had none, and furthermore, that Symeon had no regard for social conventions regarding basic bodily functions. Leontius writes:

> It was entirely as if Symeon had no body, and he paid no attention to what might be judged disgraceful conduct either by humans or by nature. Often, indeed, when his belly sought to do its private function, immediately, and without blushing, he squatted [ἐκαθέζετο] in the market place, wherever he found himself, in front of everyone, wishing to persuade [others] by this, that he did this because he had lost his natural [κατὰ φύσιν] sense. (p. 148)

By performing a private deed in public, Symeon challenges the boundary between public and private, perhaps the most prominent division in the Late Antique city. Two features of this passage merit attention here: the act of defecating in public and the assertion that this was done in order to appear as if he had lost his natural sense, literally, "the sense in accord with nature."

Diogenes the Cynic also was said to have defecated in public. In the Eighth Discourse of Dio Chrysostom, a sophistic orator of the late first and early second centuries CE who often composed speeches set in the mouths of figures from the past,[7] Diogenes praises the virtues of Herakles before a crowd. Referring to the labor in which Herakles cleaned away the dung in the Augean stable, an unsavory task which had not been performed for thirty years, Dio's Diogenes claims Herakles did this "because he believed that he should fight hard no less in the battle against common opinion [δόξα] than against wild beasts and the evil deeds of humanity."[8] Diogenes' point was that mucking the stalls was unpleasant only because people held it to be so. The crowd was pleased with Diogenes' oration; whereupon, Dio continues, "thinking of the deeds of Herakles, and having finished his speech, he squatted [καθεζόμενος] on the ground and did something indecent [τί τῶν ἀδόξων]. At this point the crowd scorned him and called him crazy."[9] Dio Chrysostom writes that Diogenes had done "something indecent" (τί τῶν ἀδόξων), literally "something not *doxa*,"

7. On Dio Chrysostom generally, see Christopher P. Jones, *The Roman World of Dio Chrysostom* (Cambridge: Harvard University Press, 1978).
8. Dio Chrys., *Or.* 8.35.
9. Dio Chrys., *Or.* 8.36.

against common opinion.[10] Defecation in itself, of course, is not remarkable; what makes this act indecent is that it is done in public. As in the *Life
of Symeon*, Dio uses the euphemism καθέζω, "to squat." Before Diogenes
performs this deed, the crowd's opinion of him is favorable. His action effects a complete change in the audience. He even is accused of being crazy
(μαίνεσθαι). So also in the passage from the *Life of Symeon*, the assumption is that each time Symeon defecates in public, he changes what people
think of him. He persuades them that he is behaving as if he had lost his
senses (φρενῶν ἐξεστηκώς).

The Emperor Julian's oration "To the Uneducated Cynics" sheds further light on this episode. For Julian, as for Dio, defecation in public was
an activity strongly associated with Diogenes. Writing in 362, Julian argued that the key to understanding Diogenes was his rejection of *nomos*,
probably best translated here as "social convention," and his adherence to
a life in accord with *phusis*, or "nature."[11] Thus Julian sought to explain
some of Diogenes of Sinope's more peculiar behavior. Julian's Diogenes
claimed that the conventions by which the majority led their lives were
foolish, and he felt it was his duty to refute common misconceptions
about the behavior natural to humans.[12] The instruments of this refutation
were the functions natural to the human body itself.

> Let [Diogenes] trample on conceit; let him ridicule [καταπαιζέτω] those
> who although they conceal in darkness the necessary functions of our na-
> ture—I am speaking of the expulsion of excrement—yet in the center of
> the marketplace and of our cities carry out most violent [deeds] which
> are not proper to our nature: robbery of money, false accusations, unjust
> indictments, and the pursuit of other such vulgar business. When Di-
> ogenes farted [ἀπέπαρδεν] or went to the bathroom [ἀπεπάτησεν][13] or
> did other things like this in the marketplace, which they say he did, he
> did these things to trample on the delusion of those men and to teach
> them that they carried out [deeds] far more sordid and dangerous than
> his. For what he did was according to our common nature, while what
> they did was not, so to speak, in accord with everyone's nature [πᾶσι
> κατὰ φύσιν], but were all carried out because of perversion.[14]

10. On δόξα and ἄδοξα in Cynicism, see Abraham J. Malherbe, "Ps.-Heraclitus, Ep. 4:
The Divinization of the Wise Man," *JAC* 21 (1978): 60.

11. Discussions of φύσις, especially as it is distinct from νόμος (convention), were common in Socratic and Sophistic debate. See especially Plato's *Gorgias*. On the history of the
concept in ancient philosophy see F. P. Hargar, *Historisches Wörterbuch der Philosophie* (Basel:
Schwebe, 1971–), s.v. "Natur."

12. Cf. Julian, *Or.* 6.191d.

13. ἀποπατέω, a common euphemism, literally meaning "to go off the path." Its use
here is ironic: Diogenes does not go off, but rather stays in public view. Julian no doubt intends his audience to appreciate the onomatopoeic qualities of the scatological words in this
passage.

14. Julian, *Or.* 6.202b, c.

For Julian (at least for the sake of argument here), public defecation is in accord with nature (*kata phusin*). Leontius *presents* Symeon's defecation as unnatural—behavior which is intended to demonstrate that Symeon has been abandoned by the sense which is in accord with nature. In some ways this treatment is disingenuous—intentionally contradicting popular notions about the Cynics, that is, those who defecate in public. Furthermore, as in the *Life of Symeon,* Diogenes' defecation is presented as habitual.[15] Like Diogenes', Symeon's profaning actions in the marketplace comment on society's hypocrisy, iniquity, and economic injustice.

That Cynicism was "the life in accord with nature" was a commonplace in the ancient sources, as is reflected in texts ranging from the pseudepigraphic Cynic epistles[16] to the writings of the late Neoplatonic philosopher Simplicius in the sixth century. According to one "Diogenes" epistle, "[C]ynicism . . . is an investigation of nature."[17] Furthermore, this investigation was not without its spiritual significance. As another letter explains, "Nature [$\phi\acute{v}\sigma\iota\varsigma$] is mighty and, since it has been banished from life by appearance [$\delta\acute{o}\xi\alpha$], it is what we restore for the salvation of mankind."[18] Simplicius had studied Neoplatonic philosophy in Alexandria and Athens in the years just before 529. In his *Commentary on the Enchiridion of Epictetus,* he regards Herakles, Theseus, Diogenes, and Socrates (all traditional Cynic heroes) as men of virtue who rose above the beasts and human evils by "pushing on toward most simple heights and the life in accord with nature."[19]

When Leontius relates that Symeon defecated in public, although he explains that, in doing so, Symeon wished to persuade people that he was

15. These details, among others, raise questions about Leontius's sources for Diogenes. Leontius was no doubt familiar with Diogenes *chreiai* from his school education, but the parallels between the passage from the *Life of Symeon* quoted above, the passage from Dio Chrysostom, and this passage from Julian are striking. Thus it is possible that Leontius was familiar with the works of Dio and Julian. On the reception of Dio Chrysostom see Aldo Brancacci, *Rhetorike philosophousa: Dione Crisostomo nella cultura antica e bizantina* (Rome: Bibliopolis, 1986). On survival of the works of Julian, see N. G. Wilson, *Scholars of Byzantium* (Baltimore: Johns Hopkins University Press, 1983), pp. 12, 115 (on Photius), 130–32 (on Arethas).

16. On the Diogenes epistles and their probable date, see Malherbe, *The Cynic Epistles: A Study Edition* (Missoula, Mont.: Scholars, 1977), pp. 14–18.

17. *Ep. Diog.* 42.

18. *Ep. Diog.* 6.

19. Simplicius, *Commentary on the Enchiridion of Epictetus,* ed. Dübner, p. 40; cf. pp. 45, 49. Simplicius's praise of Diogenes is particularly enthusiastic (*In Ench.,* pp. 53–54):

"Why," he [i.e., Epictetus] asked, "were Diogenes and Heraclitus despised, [since] they were divine and worthy to be called so?" For they were divine and living according to excellence [$\kappa\alpha\tau\grave{\alpha}$ $\tau\grave{o}$ $\check{\alpha}\kappa\rho\sigma\nu$], and setting free that which was within them. For they were in all ways excellent and divine, for God is more excellent than all things.

behaving as if he had lost his natural (*kata phusin*) sense, Leontius is, in fact, associating Symeon's behavior with the behavior of a Cynic philosopher. In doing so, Leontius calls up a number of themes associated with the figure of Diogenes. Diogenes' public shamelessness was a bit of street theater which expressed a rejection of social conventions. The retelling of these anecdotes functioned as a form of cultural criticism. In fact, tradition held that Diogenes had performed a wide range of shameless deeds in public, including, in addition to defecating, masturbating[20] and urinating.[21] In the same vein, Leontius relates that after performing miracles, it was Symeon's practice to go quickly to another part of town and "do something inappropriate [ἄκαιρον]" (p. 147). The euphemism leaves the reader to imagine the specific deed or deeds Leontius has in mind.

Leontius goes so far as to suggest that Symeon exceeded the Cynics in shamelessness. Symeon "paid no attention to what might be judged disgraceful either by humans or by nature" (p. 148). That is, not only did he violate normal human conventions for decency—in the manner of the Cynics, who rejected human conventions in favor of those determined by nature—he also violated those things held to be indecent by *nature*, by implication, at least, also therefore violating Cynic "standards" of decency. In part, of course, this is because Symeon behaves in accord with a divine convention.

Eating Lupines

On two occasions in the *Life of Symeon*, the saint eats a legume called θέρμια or "lupines."[22] Shortly after arriving in Emesa, Symeon is offered a job by the proprietor of a soup stand in the agora. In addition to this humble fare, the proprietor also sold lupines and boiled lentils.[23]

20. D. L. 6.46, 69; *Epp. Diog.* 35, 42, 44; Dio Chrys., *Or.* 6.16–20; Athenaeus, *Deip.* 4.145 ff.
21. D. L. 6.46.
22. This is a diminutive of θέρμος, also "lupines," to be distinguished from θερμός, the adjective meaning "warm," and its derivatives. Nevertheless, the popular lore about the physical effects of lupines is no doubt enhanced by the fact that their name is a pun for "heating." Heated foods were believed to lead to flatulence as well as to increased sexual desire. Cf. Foucault, *The Care of the Self*, vol. 3 of *The History of Sexuality*, trans. Robert Hurley (New York: Vintage, 1986), p. 132.
23. The φουσκάριος sold a soup called φούσκα, which was made with vinegar. (Cf. Latin *posca*, a mixture of vinegar, hot water, and eggs.) He is not a "wine merchant" as others have conjectured. On this point, see also Rydén, "Style and Historical Fiction in the Life of St. Andreas Salos," *JÖB* 32 (1982): 175–83. An epigram in the *Greek Anthology* includes lupines in the description of a dinner party in which only vegetables are served. The poet deems the selection more fit for sheep than for friends. *Anth. Pal.* 11.413.

According to God's plan, a phouska-seller saw [Symeon not knowing] that he was playing the fool [σαλός]. And he said to him (for it seemed that he was sane), "Would you like, my Lord Abba,[24] instead of wandering about, to be set up to sell lupines [θέρμια]?" And he said, "Yes." (p. 146)

While on the job, Symeon began to give the food away, and he himself began to eat insatiably. The proprietor's wife observed Symeon eating a whole pot full of lupines, causing her to remark, "Where did you find us this abba? If he eats like this, it's no use trying to sell anything!" (p. 146). In a second episode, Symeon is sought out by two monks who are debating the reason for Origen's fall into heresy. They find Symeon in the phouska-seller's shop "eating lupines like a bear" (p. 153).

Symeon's robust appetite is less noteworthy in these stories than are the lupines themselves. The lupine is a legume which was known for its ability to induce flatulence.[25] Ostentatious farting was a trademark of Diogenes. Diogenes Laertius relates stories about both Diogenes and Crates which involve lupines, suggesting that lupines held a special place in Cynic lore. Consider the following anecdote about Diogenes:

> A young man was delivering a set speech, when Diogenes, having filled the front fold of his dress with lupins [sic], began to eat them, standing right opposite to him. Having thus drawn off the attention of the assemblage, he said he was greatly surprised that they should desert the orator to look at himself.[26]

The significance of the ingestion of lupines as a commentary on the content of the speech in this passage is made clear by an anecdote concerning Crates, a follower of Diogenes the Cynic, related in Diogenes Laertius's life of Metrocles.

> While [Metrocles] was practicing a speech, he farted. Out of desperation, he shut himself up in his house and tried to starve himself to death. On learning of this, Crates came to visit him as he had been asked to do. After having purposely eaten lupines, Crates tried to convince Metrocles that he had done nothing wrong, for it would have been a marvel if he had not answered the winds in accord with nature [κατὰ φύσιν]. But at

24. *Mari Abba* is a Greek transliteration of the Syriac "mry ab'," meaning "my Lord Abba."

25. See for example the Hippocratic *Regimen in Acute Diseases (Appendix)* 47: "All pulses produce flatulence. . . . The lupin is the least injurious of the pulses" (*Hippocrates,* trans. Paul Potter, vol. 6 [Cambridge: Harvard University Press, 1988], pp. 308–9). Cf. *Regimen* 2.45 (*Hippocrates* 4:314–17), where lupines are grouped under the heading of κυάμοι, here "legumes" in general, which produce flatulence.

26. D. L. 6.48, trans. R. D. Hicks, *Diogenes Laertius,* vol. 2 (London: Heinemann, 1932), pp. 49–51.

last Crates also farted, thus lifting Metrocles from his depression, consoled by the similarity of the deeds.[27]

From this moment Metrocles became a student of Crates and a Cynic. This
remarkable tale of the conversion of Metrocles makes it clear that lupines
were notorious for causing gas. In order to appreciate these stories fully
we must consider lupines as the rough equivalent of our baked beans. The
anecdote about Diogenes eating lupines at a public lecture depends on the
audience's expectations. In addition to breaking social codes by eating in
a public place,[28] Diogenes distracted the audience because of the specific
food he was eating. No doubt the audience was fixated on Diogenes,
awaiting the result of his ingestion. He therefore provided not only a vi-
sual alternative to the speaker, but, in time, could be expected to provide
an audible alternative as well. Thus, Diogenes is able to use his bodily
functions to comment on the situation at hand. The speech to which Diogenes is listening is nothing more, if you will, than hot air.

Although in these stories about Diogenes and Crates flatulence is intentionally induced, the act of farting is regarded in the passage concerning Crates as completely natural. It is only on account of social convention
that one is embarrassed by such natural acts. Farting in public is one of
the shameless activities associated with Diogenes the Cynic elsewhere. Julian mentions farting along with defecating as activities which Diogenes
performed in the market place.[29] And Diogenes Laertius even attributes to
Diogenes a treatise with the title *Pordalos*, derived from the word πορδή,
"a fart."[30] Epictetus complained that the second-rate Cynics of his day imitated their predecessors in nothing other than producing farts.[31] Thus
when Leontius portrayed Symeon as an avid eater of lupines, he was once
again drawing a connection between Symeon and Diogenes. Eating legumes which cause one to fart, it should be noted, was a particularly un-
philosophical thing to do. Pythagoras is said to have forbidden his followers to eat broad beans (κύαμος), another legume, because they caused
gas and interfered with proper breathing.[32] Thus in eating lupines, Diog-

---

27. D. L. 6.94; my translation.
28. Other examples of Diogenes causing a stir by eating in public include D. L. 6.57
(eating salt fish at a lecture); 6.58, 61 (eating in the market place).
29. Julian, *Or.* 6.202b.
30. D. L. 6.20, 80. Diogenes Laertius seems to have regarded the work as authentic! On
farting in ancient times generally see Ludwig Radermacher, *"Pordē,"* in *RE* 22.235–40; Jef-
fery Henderson, *The Maculate Muse: Obscene Language in Attic Comedy* (New Haven: Yale
University Press, 1975), pp. 195–99; and J. N. Adams, *The Latin Sexual Vocabulary* (Baltimore:
Johns Hopkins University Press, 1982), pp. 249–50.
31. Epictetus, *Disc.* 3.22.80.
32. D. L. 8.24. Cf. Pliny the Elder, *HN* 28.18; Cicero, *Div.* 1.62; Aulus Gellius, *NA* 4.2.3.
Other reasons for the prohibition are given by Porphyry, *Vita Pyth.* 44; Iamblichus, *Vita Pyth.*

enes contradicts the practice of more respectable philosophers,[33] and Symeon contradicts the behavior of a good ascetic in that he gorges himself when he should probably be fasting.[34]

Eating Raw Meat

Another element of Symeon's diet, raw meat, should be counted among Leontius's allusions to Diogenes of Sinope.

> Once [Symeon's] friend, Deacon John, invited him to lunch, and they were hanging salted meats there. So Abba Symeon began to knock down the raw meat and eat it. The all-wise John, not wanting to say anything to him with a loud voice, drew near his ear and said to him, "You really don't scandalize me, [even] if you eat raw camel. Do whatever you'd like with the rest." (p. 158)[35]

Traditions about Diogenes eating raw meat are widely attested.[36] Diogenes Laertius reports that Diogenes "attempted to eat raw meat, but he

---

109. On the Pythagorean avoidance of broad beans, see Mirko D. Grmek, *Diseases of the Ancient Greek World,* trans. Mireille Muellner and Leonard Muellner (Baltimore: Johns Hopkins University Press, 1989), pp. 210–24. Grmek sees the prohibition against eating the beans as only part of an elaborate taboo against the plant, forbidding touching the bean or walking through a field of bean plants. Celsus seems to have understood Pythagorean avoidance of *kuamos* to have been much like Jewish food taboos (Origen, *Contra Cels.* 5.41). I have been unable to find evidence that this concern to avoid foods which cause flatulence was carried into Christian monastic practice in the East. On the contrary, legumes (pulses) constituted a major element of the monastic diet. See Maria Dembińska, "Diet: A Comparison of Food Consumption between Some Eastern and Western Monasteries in the 4th–12th Centuries," *Byzantion* 55 (1985): 431–62, and esp. p. 440.

33. In an epigram attributed to Lucian an unnamed Cynic avoids lupines, although he does eat a sow's womb; *Anth. Pal.* 11.410.

34. The lupines in the Origen episode function as they do in the anecdote about Diogenes, as a commentary on the discussion at hand, dismissing debates concerning Origen's orthodoxy. The question of Leontius's possible sympathy for Origenism, which is beyond the scope of this study, is a subject worthy of further investigation. Despite the condemnation of Origen at the council of Constantinople in 553 at Justinian's behest, debate over the status of Origen was still possible in the mid-seventh century, as witnessed by the trial of Maximus the Confessor. Cf. Sebastian Brock, "An Early Syriac Life of Maximus the Confessor," *AB* 91 (1973): 299–346; and also Antoine Guillaumont, *Les "Képhalaia Gnostica" d'Évagre le Pontique et l'histoire de l'origénisme chez les grecs et chez les syriens* (Paris: du Seuil, 1962).

35. The notion that eating raw camel was particularly disgusting recalls Thdt., *HR* 26 where Symeon the Stylite is credited with influencing the pagan Ishmaelites to such a degree that in assimilating to Greco-Roman culture and converting to Christianity they gave up their ancestral custom of eating "wild asses and camels."

36. Plutarch, *Mor. (Whether Water or Fire Is More Useful)* 956b, and *Mor. (On the Eating of Flesh)* 995d; Lucian, *Vitarum Auctio (Philosophies for Sale)* 10. The *chreia* on which Plutarch is dependent suggests that Diogenes ate raw squid for the salvation of others.

could not digest it."[37] Laertius includes the eating of raw octopus among the several differing accounts of Diogenes' death. "He was seized with colic [or perhaps 'cholera'] after eating an octopus raw and so met his end."[38] Controversy over the merits of such action served as the focal point for Julian's defense of Diogenes, referred to earlier. Julian argues at great length that in eating raw octopus, Diogenes was behaving in accord with nature, following the same pattern assigned to all the other animals.[39] According to Julian, Diogenes had reasoned further that if raw foods alone caused him nausea, it was because he was enslaved to vain opinion (*doxa kenē*) rather than reason (*logos*). This act of eating raw flesh articulates what Julian considered to be the core of Cynic philosophy, namely the life in accord with nature, and Leontius's inclusion of an episode in which Symeon eats raw flesh must allude to Cynicism. Thus Leontius harnesses Diogenes' significance as a critic of social convention.

A Saint and His Dog

All of this brings us to Symeon's dog. Symeon's tying of a dead dog to his belt in order to enter the city is perhaps the most emblematic episode in Symeon's career as a fool. While the anecdote contains elements of the burlesque, it also has deeper meaning. Ewald Kislinger has attempted to explain Symeon's dog as a figure for Cerberus, the watchdog of Hades, or for Charon, who ferried the dead souls to the underworld.[40] Charon, it seems, was originally portrayed as a dog. Kislinger also invokes Anubis, the jackal-headed Egyptian deity with a similar role. Kislinger sees the dog as "a symbol of the passage from this world to the other."[41] The entry into Emesa is, in Kislinger's reading, a parody of the soul's entry into Hades. Instead of the dog conveying the dead soul, here we have the saint conveying the dead dog. Kislinger expresses wonder that the pagan religious symbolism on which his reading depends was accessible in the seventh (or sixth) century, but offers no proof of the relevance of such a myth in the culture of the period. Kislinger's thesis is too far removed from the *Life of Symeon*. Without allusions to pagan myths, Leontius's text does not support such an allegorical reading. For all its failings, the city of Emesa is never portrayed as a city of the dead, or as a cipher for Hades.

---

37. D. L. 6.34.
38. D. L. 6.76. "Colic" is a particularly satisfying translation, since it implies an inability to flatulate.
39. Julian, *Or.* 6.191c et seq.
40. Ewald Kislinger, "Symeon Salos' Hund," *JÖB* 38 (1988): 165–70.
41. Kislinger, "Symeon Salos' Hund," p. 168; my translation.

One need look no farther than the elements of pagan philosophy preserved in the school tradition. In specifying a dog, I suggest, Leontius is
referring to the Cynic tradition. The use of the word *kuōn* (κύων, genitive
κυνός), "dog," to describe a Cynic is a commonplace in writing concerning the Cynics throughout Late Antiquity.[42] The usage depends on a pun
grounded in a popular etymology for the word *kunikos* (κυνικός), "Cynic,"
which claimed that the term was derived from the word *kuōn*. Cynics
were so named because they behaved like dogs.[43] They urinated and defecated, ate, masturbated, and copulated in public. Moreover, the usage of
kuōn to describe Cynics was not exclusively negative, and the two terms
kuōn and *kunikos*, "dog" and "Cynic," were used interchangeably when
referring to Cynics.

The fact that "dog" could mean "Cynic" became a trope in Late Antique discussions of rhetoric, even among Jewish and Christian writers,
and is well attested in grammar books, lexica, and in the writings of the
church fathers. In the treatise *Noah's Work as a Planter*, Philo discusses the
difference between synonymy, where many words refer to the same thing,
and homonymy, where the same word means a variety of things. His first
example of homonymy is the word "dog" (*kuōn*). On land a "dog" is a
barking animal, in the sea it is a monster, and in the heavens it is a star. He
continues, "The name 'dog' . . . moreover [signifies] a philosopher who
proceeds from the Cynic sect, Aristippus, Diogenes, and countless others
who thought it fit to practice these things."[44] In book 8 of the *Stromata*,
Clement presents basic elements of rhetoric which are necessary for
Christians to be able to debate pagans. He stresses the importance of clear
definitions of words. He considers the confusion which might arise with
the question "Whether a dog were an animal?" "For I shall speak of the
land dog and the sea dog, and the constellation in heaven, and of Diogenes too, and all the other dogs in order."[45]

42. On dog = Cynic in collections of Cynic anecdotes, see for example D. L. 6.33, 40, 61,
77; *Gnomologium Vaticanum* 175, 194; Athenaeus, 5.216b; *Florilegium Monacense* 155 = Meinecke, 4.278; Stobaeus, 4.55.11; *Anth. Pal.* 7.63–68.

43. Κυνικός, in fact, looks like an adjectival form of κύων, and can also mean "doglike."
Cf. LSJ, s.v. On Cynics as dogs, see Ferrand Sayre, *Greek Cynicism and Sources of Cynicism* (Baltimore: Furst, 1948), pp. 4–5; see also Schulz-Falkenthal, "Kyniker—Zur inhaltlichen Deutung des Namens," *Wissenschaftliche Zeitschrift des Martin-Luther Universität Halle-Wittenberg*
(Gesellschaftsreihe) 26.2 (1977): 41–49.

44. Philo, *De plantatione* 151, *Philo*, ed. F. H. Colson and G. H. Whitaker, vol. 3 (London:
Heinemann, 1930), p. 290; my translation.

45. Clement, *Strom.* 8.12.4–7; trans. ANF 2:561. We should not think of Clement as dependent on Philo here; rather, it seems, the word *kuōn* was a stock example in rhetorical education. The "land-sea-and-heaven" trope is found in two scholia to Dionysius Thrax's treatise on grammar which date from the middle or late Byzantine periods, commenting in both
cases on the problem of homonyms. *Scholia in Dionysii Thracis Artem Grammaticum*, ed. A. Hil-

In fact, the multiple meanings of the word "dog" have a very long history in the educational tradition, as evidenced by the lexica which reflect the vocabulary taught by the grammar teachers.[46] Byzantine *grammatikoi* instructed by having their students give all the possible definitions of words which occurred in Homer and other school texts. Hesychius, a Christian and a *grammatikos* teaching in Alexandria in the late fifth or early sixth century, compiled a lexicon of these words which remained in use for some time. His list included under *kuōn*, among other things, "clearly then: the male member, and the barking animal, and the shameless one, and the star, and the sea animal."[47] That dogs were shameless animals was also a commonplace. John Chrysostom, for instance, in a list in the *Homilies Concerning the Statues* of the characters of various animals, tells us, "The dog is shameless [ἀναίσχυντος]."[48] But Hesychius clearly has something other than "the barking animal" in mind when he lists "the shameless one [ἀναιδής]" after the common definition of "dog." A later lexicon, known as the *Etymologikon Mega*, includes under *kuōn*: "Dog [is said] for the philosopher who does the same as dogs do."[49] "Shameless ones" is also offered as a definition here.[50] Manuel Moschopoulos's fourteenth-century compilation of earlier works, commonly known as the *Peri Schedōn*, defines *kuōn* thus:

> Animal barking, and of the sea, and a star in the heaven, from the dog who barks. Dogs, a class [γένος, perhaps "breed"] of philosophers, who have also been [called] "Cynics," on account of their jesting, and their biting just as if they were dogs.[51]

Throughout Late Antiquity, then (and beyond), "dog" meant, among other things, "Cynic philosopher."

---

gard (Leipzig: Teubner, 1901): Scholia Vaticana (cod. C) to Dionysius Thrax, p. 236; Scholia Marciana (VN), p. 389.

46. The lexica are very difficult to date and are remarkable for the high degree of continuity which they suggest in Greek education. On the grammarians generally, see Robert A. Kaster, *Guardians of Language: The Grammarian and Society in Late Antiquity* (Berkeley: University of California Press, 1988).

47. Hesychius of Alexandria, *Lexicon*, ed. Kurt Latte, vol. 2 (Copenhagen: Ejnar Munksgaard, 1953), p. 555, entry Kappa 1763. See Hesychius's prosopographical entry in Kaster, *Guardians of Language*, p. 292. Hesychius was a Christian.

48. John Chrysostom, *Ad populum Antiochenum de statuis* 12.2, PG 49.130; cf. English translation NPNF (first series) IX, p. 420. See also Aelian (*Varia Historia* 7.19, second or third century) who comments, "Dogs and flies are without shame," when he relates an incident of a dog committing adultery with a Roman woman.

49. *Etymologicum magnum*, ed. Frederic Sylburg (Leipzig: Wiegel, 1816), col. 498.

50. Cf. the *kuōn* entry of the Hellenistic *Homer Lexicon* of Apollonius Sophista (*Lexicon Homericum*, ed. J. C. Molini, vol. 2 [Paris, 1773], p. 510).

51. Manuel Moschopoulos, *De ratione examinandae orationibus libellus [Peri Schedōn]* (Paris: Stephanus, 1545), s.v. (p. 4). On the *Peri Schedōn*, see John J. Keaney, "Moschopulea," *BZ* 64 (1971): 303–21.

In addition, many Christian writers in Late Antiquity found the ties between "dog" and "Cynic" irresistible. Gregory of Nazianzus provides us with some particularly rich puns. When Gregory praised Maximus the Cynic he called him a "dog" and cited his "barking," "keeping watch," and "wagging [his] tail."[52] When he later condemned Maximus in his autobiographical *De vita sua*, Gregory described him as "a raging evil, a dog, a whelp [κυνίσκος], loitering on the streets."[53] Gregory puns on *kuōn* and *kunikos* throughout the section of the poem concerned with Maximus. He ridicules "our modern dogs" who do not compare with the great Cynics of the past, Diogenes, Antisthenes, and Crates.[54] In another poem he asks, "Who has not heard of the Sinopean dog?"[55] And Augustine, writing in Latin, referred to the Cynics as "canine philosophers" (*canini philosophi*).[56] The dog metaphors could be either positive or negative, a writer calling either on the watchdog's barking and biting to praise the Cynic's vigilant social criticism or on the canine's baser ways to attack a Cynic's inappropriate behavior.

In attaching Symeon to the dog, Leontius attaches Symeon to the Cynic tradition, both linguistically and metaphorically. Symeon brings this tradition back into the city, where he proceeds to imitate Diogenes, eating lupines, eating raw meat, and defecating in public.

Cynics and Madness

Each of these shameless activities is an example of Symeon's apparent madness, perhaps his most defining attribute. The accusation of madness also has parallels in anecdotes about Diogenes and in popular conceptions of Cynicism. Leontius explains that Symeon defecated in the agora, "wishing to persuade [others] by this that he did this because he had lost his natural sense" (p. 148). The phrase "having lost his natural sense" (or "having lost the sense in accord with nature") refers only secondarily to Symeon's feigned madness; it is primarily meant as a description of the sort of person who would defecate in public and claim to be living "in accord with nature," namely a Cynic.[57]

52. Greg. Naz., *Or.* 25.2.
53. Greg. Naz., *De vita sua*, ll. 751–52.
54. Greg. Naz., *De vita sua*, ll. 1030–33.
55. Greg. Naz., *Poems* 1.2.10, l. 218, PG 37.696.
56. Augustine, *Civ. Dei* 14.20.
57. Festugière, who appears to acknowledge the allusion to Diogenes here, remarks in a footnote that the last words of the passage, "having lost his senses," "show that it is not possible to confuse Symeon with the Cynics" (!) (my trans.). Festugière, *Vie de Syméon le Fou*, p. 21 n. 1.

It was a common notion that the Cynics, who behaved so strangely, were crazy. Diogenes Laertius's *Lives of the Philosophers* includes the following *chreia*: "When [Plato] was asked by someone, 'What sort of person does Diogenes seem to you to be?' 'A Socrates gone mad [μαινόμε-νος],' he answered."[58] The accusation that Diogenes was crazy also appears in John of Stobi's fifth-century *Florilegium*: "Someone said that Diogenes was out of his mind [ἀνόητος]. 'I'm not out of my mind,' he replied, 'but I don't have your mind [νοῦς].'"[59] The Hebrew word *kinukos* (*sic*)[60] appears in two passages in the Palestinian Talmud (yGittin 38a; yTerumoth 2a) in reference to "the signs of a madman."[61] Aëtius of Amida, physician to the Emperor Justinian, describes a form of madness known as *kunanthrōpia*.[62] And accounts of the "plague of madness" which fell upon Amida in 560 include descriptions of people barking like dogs.[63]

Symeon's social transgressions invited the accusation of madness. After Symeon entered the city gate with the dead dog, he passed a school full of children. Leontius writes, "When the children saw him, they began to cry, 'Hey, a crazy abba!' And they set about to run after him and box him on the ears" (p. 145). The cry *"abbas mōros"* recalls the statement attributed to Plato concerning Diogenes of Sinope. Like Diogenes, Symeon is accused incorrectly, but nevertheless understandably, of being mad. Diogenes had overstepped the boundaries of behavior appropriate to a philosopher into what appeared to be madness, while Symeon, in his pretense of madness, had overstepped the boundaries of behavior appropriate to the Christian religious (or anyone, for that matter) and appeared to be a mad monk.

58. D. L. 6.54. Cf. Aelian, *Var. Hist.* 14.33.
59. Stobaeus, 3.3.51.
60. Transliterated: qynwqws.
61. Luz, "A Description of the Greek Cynic in the Jerusalem Talmud," *JSJ* 20 (1989): 49–60. In yGittin, in a pericope which Luz dates to the mid-third century, a madman is defined as someone who sleeps in a graveyard, burns incense to demons, wears torn garments, and destroys his property. Such a madman is then called a Cynic. Luz correctly observes that these attributes do indeed identify a Cynic type. Such a type is distinguished in the passage from a *kanthropos* (spelled: qntrwpws) which Luz conjectures is a Hebrew version of the Greek κυνάνθρωπος "dog-man," a term with obvious Cynic overtones. Luz, "A Description of the Greek Cynic," p. 52 n. 14.
62. Aëtius of Amida, 6.11.1, 2. The condition is elsewhere referred to as *lukanthrōpia* (from λύκος, "wolf"). Cf. Giuseppe Roccatagliata, *A History of Ancient Psychiatry* (New York: Greenwood, 1986), pp. 155–56, 255; on Aëtius as a psychiatrist, see pp. 256–60.
63. Pseudo-Dionysius of Tell-Mahre, *Incerti auctoris chronicon* 3.7; Michael the Syrian, *Chronique* 9.32. On the "plague of madness" at Amida, see Susan Ashbrook Harvey, *Asceticism and Society in Crisis: John of Ephesus and* The Lives of the Eastern Saints (Berkeley: University of California Press, 1990), pp. 64–65.

Evaluating the Cynics

Here we have focused attention on individual instances of allusion to traditions about Cynics and Cynicism in the *Life of Symeon the Fool*. But the connection between Symeon and Diogenes is not merely embedded in individual episodes; rather, because of these allusions, Leontius sets up a parallel between Symeon and Diogenes which pervades the entire text. Despite denying a historical link between Symeon and the Cynics, Rydén and others have acknowledged that Symeon and the Cynics appear to be parallel phenomena. In light of the discussion here, we must concur that there indeed are cross-cultural parallels between Diogenes and Symeon, but this is because Leontius *constructs* Symeon and Diogenes as parallel phenomena. In short, Leontius portrays Symeon as a latter-day Cynic. Like Diogenes, Symeon comes to the city as an outsider. Once in town, Symeon wreaks havoc on the social order by challenging conventions, much as Diogenes does. He offends notions of common decency through obscene behavior. Like Diogenes, Symeon disrupts assemblies by eating in public.[64] Symeon disrupts a church service by throwing nuts at the women parishioners (pp. 145–46) and stops a theater performance by throwing a stone at a juggler (p. 150). Furthermore, just as Diogenes' apologists explain about him, Leontius argues that Symeon's behavior is calculated to instruct, although obscurely. It is claimed of both figures that they act in the name of an authority higher than human opinion.

Somehow, allusions to Diogenes render Symeon's behavior comprehensible. The precedent for tales of socially deviant behavior justifies Symeon, since as literary types, Cynics, namely Diogenes, were both intellectually and morally acceptable to educated Christians. Left with the problem of presenting the controversial subject matter which he desired, Leontius drew on Diogenes in order to legitimate Symeon. To the modern reader, it might seem that when Leontius alludes to Diogenes—that is, when Symeon seems most scandalous to us—Leontius most challenges his audience to condemn the saint. Ironically, what prevents the ancient reader from doing so, however, is the force of tradition. Diogenes, for all his profanity, was a familiar entity and was widely regarded as a figure worthy of praise. When Leontius informed his readers that Symeon defecated in public and ate lupines, he was placing Symeon on familiar ground. Like those who transmitted the anecdotes about the Cynics,

---

64. D. L. 6.57. Other anecdotes about Diogenes eating in public include D. L. 6.58 and 61, where Diogenes eats in the marketplace.

Leontius used obscene tales for moral instruction. Like Diogenes, the fool for Christ's sake was an instrument of cultural criticism. Through Symeon, Leontius was able to point out the hypocrisy and, therefore, the sinfulness of everyday urban life.

On the other hand, Leontius's employment of Cynic tropes is more complex than it might at first appear. Leontius's goals differed from those of the Cynic anecdotes, and his treatment is nuanced. In addition to the dog which Symeon drags through the gates of Emesa, there are two other dogs in the *Life of Symeon*. While these dogs do not suggest themselves as figures for Cynicism, they do expand an understanding of the cultural attitudes toward dogs in Leontius's world. These dogs represent the demonic. After Symeon exorcizes John the deacon's son of the demon who has caused him to fornicate with a married woman, the youth sees Symeon chasing a black dog, beating it with a wooden cross (p. 150). Elsewhere in the *Life of Symeon*, when a demon is haunting the market, Symeon throws stones in all directions to turn people back. When a dog passes by, the demon strikes it, causing it to foam (p. 157).[65] The association of dogs with demons was apparently commonplace, as was the association of dogs with madness.[66] Madness, moreover, was commonly regarded as a form of demonic possession, and Symeon, himself, pretends to be possessed by demons as part of his folly (p. 162; cf. p. 156).[67] While I believe we overread the text to assume that Leontius regarded the Cynics as demonic—not all dogs are demons—the generally negative attitude toward dogs betrays an ambivalence on Leontius's part toward Diogenes similar to that found in the writings of other Christians discussed in the previous chapter. By giving Symeon a *dead* dog, Leontius implies that Cynicism in itself is spiritually bankrupt.

For all the allusions and parallels to Diogenes, Leontius does not stop at showing Symeon to be like a Cynic; he goes on to show how Symeon surpasses the Cynics—but not merely in his capacity to violate human (and "natural") conventions. The church fathers were understandably concerned about Cynic obscenity. Leontius seems to have feared that his audience would have a similarly ambivalent attitude toward Symeon, and this explains Leontius's apologetics on Symeon's behalf. Leontius admits that there is some risk that Symeon's behavior could corrupt him,

65. The identification of a black dog as a demon is also found in the *Life of Theodore of Sykeon* where an innkeeper is afflicted with fever after such a dog yawns in front of him. Theodore explains that the dog was a demon; George of Sykeon, *Life of Theodore of Sykeon* 106.

66. See above.

67. On the relationship between madness and demonic possession see also Palladius, *LH* 34.

and so he explains that Symeon remained undefiled (pp. 148–49). Diogenes, as was well known, still had a sexual appetite. Once after masturbating in public he said, "Would that one could satisfy hunger by rubbing the belly."[68] Symeon, by contrast, had had a vision in which his genitals were sprinkled with holy water, thus purifying him and making him free of all sexual desire (p. 155).[69]

For Diogenes, the "life in accord with nature" was a life which indulged the body's basic needs, whether for food, sex, or relief of the bowels; Symeon on the other hand was, in Leontius's words, "entirely as if he had no body" (p. 148), that is, as if he were an angel. His behavior may have appeared like a Cynic's—in fact, Leontius suggests that Symeon wished to persuade people that he was a Cynic—but this was only a device to avoid recognition of his sanctity. He had transcended his body, and these were only appearances. Rather than living *kata phusin*, "in accord with nature," Symeon lives, as Leontius says, *kat' aretēn*, "in accord with virtue" (pp. 121, 127); or, even better, *kata theon*, "in accord with God" (pp. 128, 170). In his spiritual perfection, Symeon had transcended the very *phusis* to which Diogenes aspired.

68. D. L. 6.46.
69. See John Moschus, *Spiritual Meadow* 3 for a similar story.

SEVEN

SYMEON IN EMESA,
JESUS IN JERUSALEM

In the *Life of Symeon the Fool* Leontius of Neapolis is concerned to instill moral virtues in a lay audience through hagiographical narrative. He also invites his readers to engage in theological reflection. In pursuit of these goals, Leontius constructs Symeon to reenact the life of Jesus. The previous chapter demonstrated that Leontius makes allusion to traditions about Diogenes of Sinope, the Cynic philosopher. At the same time, in adherence to a pattern common in the composition of saints' lives, Leontius models his protagonist on the Christ. An exploration of Leontius's use of Jesus as a model for Symeon sheds light on various concerns which Leontius addresses in his work, particularly the moral problems raised by urban life and economic structures.

Students of hagiography have long recognized the use of biblical typology in the literary production of saints' lives, although the phenomenon as a whole has yet to receive a comprehensive treatment.[1] Late Antique authors employ what Patlagean has called the "scriptural model" in their compositions, such that the hagiographical narrative closely follows the characters and events of the Gospels. As she writes, "The scriptural

---

1. Réginald Grégoire's *Manuale di agiologia: introduzione alla letteratura agiographica* (Fabriano: Monastero San Silvestro Abate, 1987), with a subchapter entitled "L'itinerario delle tipologie" (pp. 249–303), provides a general overview of the subject. See also Henri Crouzel, "L'Imitation et la 'suite' de Dieu et du Christ dans les premiers siècles chrétiens ainsi que leurs sources gréco-romaines et hébraïques," *JAC* 21 (1978): 7–41.

model shows the similarity between the saint and Christ. . . . [T]he series of miraculous actions is chosen according to a rigorous criterion of scriptural reference."[2] In many *Lives,* the hagiographer uses Jesus or a figure in the Old Testament such as Moses or one of the prophets as a model for presenting the saint.

The invocation of Old Testament prophets can serve an apologetic function in hagiography. Perhaps the most striking instances of this are the various lives of Symeon the Stylite. In defense of his portrait of the man who stood for many years on a pillar, Theodoret of Cyrrhus invokes a number of Old Testament figures who behaved strangely. He mentions Isaiah walking naked (Is 20:2) and Jeremiah preaching first in a loincloth, then in a wooden collar, and finally in an iron one (Jer 13:1, 27:2, 28:13). He refers to Hosea's marriage with a harlot (Hos 1:2) and to the most peculiar details of Ezekiel's asceticism.[3] These biblical prototypes serve to place the stylite's outlandish behavior within a biblical pattern and thereby justify it in the face of critics. Theodoret's point is that holy people do the strangest things, that they are *sui generis.* In the *Life of Symeon the Fool,* the relationship between the saint and the Old Testament models for peculiar behavior remains implicit, although the biblical parallels are clearly in the air. One thinks not only of those types already mentioned but also of David dancing in the streets (2 Sm 6:20). More striking in the text, however, are the references to Jesus.

For early Christians, the use of Jesus as a prototype was a key to interpreting the experience of martyrdom and eventually ascetic practice.[4] Christian authors presented their subjects engaged in the "imitation of Christ." In the second-century *Martyrdom of Polycarp,* the protagonist is portrayed suffering and dying according to Christ's example. Depicting what he calls a "martyrdom in accord with the gospel," the anonymous author constructs his narrative to include many details which allude to

2. Evelyne Patlagean, "Ancient Byzantine Hagiography and Social History," in *Saints and Their Cults: Studies in Religious Sociology, Folklore, and History,* ed. S. Wilson (Cambridge: Cambridge University Press, 1983), pp. 105, 106–7.

3. Thdt., *HR* 26.12. The same figures are mentioned in the Syriac *Life of Symeon Stylite* 117. Cf. R. M. Price, trans., *A History of the Monks of Syria* (Kalamazoo: Cistercian, 1985), p. 174 n. 16. Cf. Susan Ashbrook Harvey, "The Sense of a Stylite: Perspectives on Symeon the Elder," *VC* 42 (1988): 376–94; and David T. M. Frankfurter, "Stylites and *Phallobates:* Pillar Religions in Late Antique Syria," *VC* 44 (1990): 188.

4. Hippolyte Delehaye, *Les Passions des martyrs et les genres littéraires* (Brussels: Société des Bollandistes, 1966), p. 19: "Le Christ est le modèle du chrétien; son parfait imitateur est le martyr qui suit dans la voie douloureuse. Cette idée était si familière aux premières générations chrétiennes que toute ressemblance plus étroite avec le Maître soutait immédiatement aux yeux et ne pouvait manquer d'être signalée." Cf. Etienne Leduer, "Imitation du Christ: II. Tradition Spirituelle," *DS,* esp. cols. 1563–67.

the life of Jesus: Polycarp has foreknowledge of his impending death; he is betrayed by a servant who is explicitly compared to Judas; he enjoys a last supper with his followers, after which he goes off to pray by himself for two hours; eventually, on the funeral pyre, where he is not burned, but appears "like bread that is baked," his side is pierced, and his blood flows forth.[5] Similarly, the rigorous life of the Christian ascetic was interpreted in literature as well as in practice as a daily reenactment either of Christ's temptation in the desert or of Christ's passion. Athanasius constructs his portrait of Antony, "the daily martyr," to depict the saint successfully battling demons and performing Christ-like miracles of healing.[6] The comparison of a saint to Christ, standard in Late Antique hagiography, was often achieved through literary allusion.[7] By fashioning his work in conformity with the gospel narrative, the author of a hagiographical text could attest to the saint's holiness and render the saint meaningful within a Christian framework. But this conscious modeling is more than a mere echoing of the life of Jesus in order to portray a saint. Modeling the saint on Jesus had several purposes. It allowed the hagiographer to highlight an aspect of the gospel which was particularly relevant to his audience. For instance, by identifying Polycarp with the Christ, the author implicitly interprets the Christ as a model martyr; by fashioning Antony in accord with the gospel, Athanasius presents Jesus as a healer and a resister of temptation. Thus, a saint's life is an implicit commentary on the Christ, a mode of exegesis by which an author addresses the significance of the Christ for his audience. Hagiography is, if you will, a Christological genre.[8]

5. *Martyrdom of Polycarp*, in *The Acts of the Christian Martyrs*, ed. Herbert Musurillo (Oxford: Clarendon, 1972), pp. 2–21.

6. Athanasius, *Life of Antony* 47. Shortly before Antony's death a military commander, recalling the Roman centurion at Jesus' crucifixion, exclaims, "Truly this was a servant of God" (85). In fact, Athanasius displays some discomfort with the degree to which the *Life of Antony* adheres to the patterns of the life of Jesus. He stresses that God performs the miracles, not Antony, and makes a point to inform his readers that Antony could not walk on water (59, 60). This form of "antitypology," of course, serves to highlight the degree to which Antony *is* modeled on Jesus.

7. Han Drijvers has pointed to the significance of the Syrian holy man, particularly the anonymous Man of God of Edessa, as an *alter Christus*. See Han J. W. Drijvers, "Hellenistic and Oriental Origins," in *The Byzantine Saint*, ed. Sergei Hackel (San Bernardino, Calif.: Borgo, 1983), pp. 26–28, and "Die Legende des heiligen Alexius und der Typus des Gottesmannes in syrischen Christentum," in *Typus, Symbol, Allegorie bei den östlichen Vätern und ihren Parallelen im Mittelalter*, ed. Margot Schmidt and Carl Friedrich Geyer (Regensburg: Pustet, 1982), pp. 187–217.

8. A similar point is made eloquently with regard to Athanasius's *Life of Antony* by Robert C. Gregg and Dennis E. Groh (*Early Arianism—A View of Salvation* [Philadelphia: Fortress, 1981], pp. 131–59).

Jesus as a Model for Symeon the Fool

In the *Life of Symeon*, in addition to his conventional Christological concerns with such issues as Origenism and Monophysitism, Leontius reflects on the meaning of the Christ for moral life through allusions to the gospel. In order to do this, Leontius uses the life of Jesus as a model for the composition of the *Life of Symeon the Fool*. Alexander Syrkin noted "a number of instances of parallelism (expressed either explicitly or more obliquely) between Symeon and Jesus." Symeon and Jesus both leave their "seclusion in the desert" and return to the world to save people; they both cast out the Devil, cure demoniacs, and inflict spells; they feed people miraculously; their burials involve Jews whom they have converted; and when their tombs are opened, their bodies are not found.⁹ Far from being accidental, these parallels are the result of Leontius's conscious efforts to draw parallels between Symeon and Jesus.¹⁰ In fact, Leontius's use of gospel material goes beyond loosely conceived, episodic allusions to Jesus; Leontius uses the narrative of the life of Jesus to shape the entire narrative of the *Life of Symeon*, such that the parallels to Jesus strongly influence his presentation of the fool for Christ's sake.

The Entry into Emesa

In order to illustrate Leontius's use of the gospel narrative, we turn to Symeon's first activities in Emesa (pp. 145–46). He enters the gate of the city dragging a dead dog. Schoolchildren see him and call out (κρά-ζειν), "Hey, a crazy abba." The next morning, a Sunday, he enters the church, puts out the lights, and throws nuts at the women. On the way out of the church, he overturns (ἔστρεψεν) the tables of the pastry chefs (πλακουντάριοι).

This sequence of events bears an obvious relationship to the Gospels' accounts of Jesus' entry into Jerusalem. According to the account in Matthew 21, Jesus enters Jerusalem on the backs of an ass and a colt.¹¹

---

9. Alexander Y. Syrkin, "On the Behavior of the 'Fool for Christ's Sake,'" *History of Religions* 22 (1982): 165. Such parallels are also noted by Lennart Rydén (*Bermerkungen zum Leben des heiligen Narren Symeon von Leontios von Neapolis* [Uppsala: Almquist and Wiksell, 1970], *passim*).

10. Syrkin does not discuss Leontius's intentions in constructing such parallels.

11. This impossible feat of riding two beasts at once is the result of the author's attempt to present Jesus' activities as a very literal fulfillment of Zechariah 9:9; in Mark 11 and Luke 19 he rides only a colt, while John 12 has him riding on an ass's colt.

Crowds follow Jesus shouting, "Hosanna to the Son of David," and so forth. Jesus then enters the temple, drives out those selling and buying there, and overturns (κατέστρεψεν; cf. Mk 11:15) the tables of the money changers. Jesus performs miracles, and children cry out (κράζοντας), "Hosanna to the Son of David." Thus Symeon's entry into Emesa echoes Jesus' entry into Jerusalem in several ways. Both enter the city with animals. Their identity is immediately proclaimed by onlookers. They proceed to the city's center of worship and disrupt its activities by overturning tables.[12] When the pieces of the entry into Emesa are placed together and the narrative pattern is seen as a whole, we observe that Leontius has structured this account to parallel the life of Jesus.

A slight divergence from the lectionary texts of the Gospels illuminates the way in which Leontius and his community received the gospel narrative in their lives and worship. The Gospel of Matthew does not mention the children the first time Jesus' identity is proclaimed by the crowd with the phrase "Hosanna to the Son of David"; instead, this phrase is uttered by children only after the events in the temple. However, liturgical texts for Palm Sunday used in Leontius's time presented the children as the ones who first proclaimed Jesus' identity as he entered Jerusalem.[13] Thus the gospel which Leontius follows is not the biblical text

12. Other scholars have noted some of these parallels in passing. Rydén (*Bemerkungen*, pp. 89–90) associated Symeon's entry with his dead dog with Jesus' riding on his ass. (Cf. Syrkin, "The 'Fool for Christ's Sake,'" p. 165; Ewald Kislinger, "Symeon Salos' Hund," *JÖB* 38 [1988]: 165.) Festugière briefly entertained the notion that Symeon was imitating Christ in overturning the tables, but rejected the possibility, arguing that Symeon acted in this way, "Plus probablement parce qu'on le bouscule" (*Vie de Syméon le Fou*, pp. 187–88). Of course, Festugière's observation (which is motivated by a desire to recover a historical Symeon) should hardly rule out the possibility that Leontius's Symeon is "imitating" Christ.

13. In the account of her travels, the Spanish pilgrim Egeria (*Itinerarium* 31.2; trans. John Wilkinson, *Egeria's Travels to the Holy Land* [London: S.P.C.K., 1971], p. 133), writing in the 380s, describes the celebration of Palm Sunday which she observed in Jerusalem. "At five o'clock the passage is read from the Gospel about the children who met the Lord with palm branches, saying, 'Blessed is he that cometh in the name of the Lord.'" A similar identification of the children as those who first proclaim Jesus' identity is found in the early-sixth-century *kontakion* of Romanus the Melodist, *Eis ta Baia*, written for Palm Sunday, still used today in the Orthodox Church:

In Heaven on Thy throne; on earth carried on an ass, O Christ, God,
Receive the praise of the angels and the song of the *children* crying out to Thee:
"Thou art the blessed One who comest to call up Adam."
. . . .
Since Thou hast conquered Hades and put to death Death, and resurrected the World,
The *children*, with palm branches shout aloud to Thee, Christ as victor,
And today, they are crying to Thee: "Hosannah to the Son of David."
                                        ll. 1–6, 7–10 (my emphasis)

The hymn is edited by Helle Kyriakaki in N. B. Tomadakis, *Rōmanou tou Melōdou Hymnoi*, vol. 3.2 (Athens: Typographeion Mēna Myrtidē, 1957), pp. 179–206; English translation by Marjorie Carpenter, *Kontakia of Romanos, Byzantine Melodist I: On the Person of Christ* (Colum-

itself but rather the biblical narrative as it was reenacted in the liturgical life of the Church. Symeon's entry into Emesa prompts the reader to draw parallels between the saint's activities and those of the Savior.

Implicit Christology

Symeon's entry into the city signals from the outset that his behavior is an "imitation of Christ." But what are the implications of such modeling? In addition to the similarities between the accounts of Jesus' entry into Jerusalem and Symeon's entry into Emesa, there are also striking inversions of the archetypal episode. Symeon's *adventus* is hardly triumphal. His dog is dead; he drags it rather than rides it. The children acclaim him not as the "Son of David," but as a mad monk; rather than spreading palms (a symbol of victory) before him, the children beat Symeon up. Far from cleansing the church, he merely disrupts the service in progress in a manner admittedly slapstick, pelting the parishioners with nuts. The tables of the Gospels' evil money changers have become trivialized as the tables of Symeon's pastry chefs. In short, Symeon does what Jesus did, but gets it all wrong. By employing a technique of narrative inversion at the beginning of Symeon's activity in Emesa, Leontius asks his readers to reflect on Symeon's relationship to Jesus, to consider whether Symeon's life is but a poor parody of Jesus'. Symeon's *adventus* appears the complete antithesis of Jesus'; his activity in Emesa, the life of Jesus turned upside down.

Leontius introduces similar inversions elsewhere in the text. Symeon's encounter with the man suffering from leucoma in both eyes reworks the account in the Gospel of John in which Jesus cures a blind man by placing saliva and clay on his eyes and telling him, "Go wash" ($\H{v}\pi\alpha\gamma\epsilon$ $\nu\H{\iota}\psi\alpha\iota$) in a pool (Jn 9:1–12; cf. Mk 8:22–26). When the man with leucoma approaches Symeon, the cure backfires. Symeon anoints the man's eyes with mustard, which burns him and aggravates his condition, making him completely blind (p. 161). Symeon then tells him to "Go wash" ($\H{v}\pi\alpha\gamma\epsilon$ $\nu\H{\iota}\psi\alpha\iota$) with vinegar and garlic, which finally cures him, restoring his sight.[14]

---

bia: University of Missouri Press, 1970), p. 159. For an excellent study of this kontakion see E. Catafygiotu-Topping, "Romanos, On the Entry into Jerusalem: A *Basilikos Logos*," *Byzantion* 47 (1977): 65–91. The children's acclamation of Jesus also figures prominently in the dramatic homily for Palm Sunday attributed to Eulogius (PG 86/2.2913–2937), Chalcedonian patriarch of Alexandria from 580 to 607.

14. Symeon appears to apply the wrong cure in the second instance as well, but the double attempt at healing mirrors the healing of the blind man of Bethsaida in Mark 8. In addition to the parallel to Jesus, the episode with the man with leucoma bears a resemblance to the story of how Elisha cured the leprosy of Naaman the Syrian (2 Kgs 5). In both stories when the victim is told to wash he becomes angry because he was not cured immediately. Only later does he wash as he had been instructed and become cured.

When performing "miraculous feedings," Symeon's excesses are comic. Symeon invites ten circus fans to lunch. Five of them follow Symeon, although they are skeptical about his ability to provide them anything other than grass to graze on. Symeon, an impoverished ascetic, then sets before them a lavish feast: "wheat bread, flat cakes, meat balls, fish, excellent wine, fried cakes, jam" (p. 164). The main features of the meal are the staples which Jesus feeds the multitudes in the various gospels—bread, fish, and wine—but the opulent menu of delicacies goes far beyond Jesus' humble provision of sustenance.[15] And while Jesus turns water to wine (Jn 2:1–11), Symeon turns wine to vinegar, a vinegar so foul "that a person might die smelling it" (pp. 164–65). So Leontius constructs Symeon by inverting his model.

Or does he? By parodying Jesus' activities, Leontius prompts his reader to reconsider the meaning of Jesus' actions. Symeon, who is only loosely modeled on Jesus, comes to Emesa to behave in a fashion which appears ridiculous to the majority of the city's inhabitants, and yet, as we shall see, reforms a great number of the inhabitants and prepares them for their salvation. In composing the *Life of Symeon* as he has, Leontius has, in fact, written a commentary on the life and meaning of the Christ. The *Life of Symeon* not only imitates the life of Jesus, it reinterprets it.

Through the fusion of the Christ and the Fool, Leontius shows that Jesus too came to the city and appeared ridiculous to the majority. Moreover, Symeon's presence in the city is an anomaly. The ascetic "belongs" in the desert. Symeon's shamelessness is also anomalous; holy people are supposed to behave in accord with a rigid set of norms which above all emphasize self-containment and self-control. Nevertheless, Leontius challenges his audience by mixing shamelessness and sanctity, and by placing holiness in the city. This sanctity where it does not belong, this "dislocation" of the holy, parallels the Orthodox teachings on the incarnation itself, in which the divine comes to dwell among a humanity deemed unworthy. The incarnate Christ himself is an anomaly which ennobles the creation, sanctifying it by the divine presence. Thus Symeon, dislocated from the desert, brings holiness to Emesa, just as God, dislocated from the divine realm, brings holiness to humanity.

15. Loaves and fishes: Mk 6:30–44 and parallels; Mk 8:10ff. and parallels; Jn 6:1–13. Wine: Jn 2:1–11. Like Jesus in the gospels, Symeon performs not one miraculous feeding but two. Leontius has mimicked the doublet of feedings in Matthew and Mark (Mt 14:13–21, 15:32–38; Mk 6:32–44, 8:1–10). The first instance of miraculous feeding is played straight enough. An Emesan merchant on pilgrimage to Jerusalem meets Symeon's companion, Abba John, in the desert and requests his blessing. Welcoming the merchant into his cave, John sets before him a table of fish, bread, and wine, the very things which Jesus feeds to the multitudes. When the merchant returns to Emesa, Symeon sets precisely the same table before him (p. 159).

The fact that the Emesans do not recognize the holiness that dwells among them is an extension of this incarnational theme. Symeon's concealed identity draws on the secrecy motif in the Gospel of Mark. As with Jesus, those who benefited from Symeon's actions knew him and eventually proclaimed his true identity, but most were mystified. Symeon and Jesus struggle to conceal their identity from those who witness their miracles and battles with demons. Jesus tells those whom he has cured not to tell others (Mk 1:44) and forbids the demons to speak because they know him (Mk 1:34). Similarly, Symeon forbids those whom he heals or reforms to reveal his identity: The deacon's son, out of whom Symeon casts the demon of fornication, is unable to speak the name of the one who cured him until after the saint's death (p. 150); the juggler whom Symeon convinces to give up the theater can say only that "[s]ome monk wearing a crown of palm branches" appeared to him in his sleep (p. 150); Symeon strikes dumb the Jewish artisan who sees him conversing with two angels at the baths (p. 154).[16] Like Mark's Jesus (cf. Mk 3:21–22), Symeon appears to others to be possessed by demons, although the demons themselves know better.[17] While under such a guise Symeon and Jesus bring salvation. Moreover, Symeon's secret work as a moral reformer is an imitation of Christ. By setting the confrontation with evils, both grave and petty, in the city of Emesa, Leontius explores the significance of the concealed Christ for an urban population.

Symeon in the City

In the *Life of Symeon,* Leontius implicitly locates the message of the gospel in the Christ's significance as a moral reformer, preparing the earthly city for the new Jerusalem. Leontius addresses the problem of living a holy life in an urban environment, an environment which was by its nature profane. This focus contrasts with the themes of many classic saints' lives. In many works composed between the fourth and the seventh centuries, the holy man lives outside the city, choosing to remain on the fringes of

16. These passages have a further biblical parallel in the account of Zachariah, the father of John the Baptist, who is struck dumb and is unable to speak about the things the angel has revealed to him concerning his son "until the day that these things come to pass" (Lk 1:20).

17. Leontius relates of Symeon, "Symeon had extraordinary compassion for those possessed by demons, so that from time to time he went off to make himself like one of them, and passed his time with them, healing many of them through his own prayer, and therefore some demoniacs cried out and said, "O violence, Fool, you jeer at the whole world. Have you also come near us to give us trouble? Retreat from here; you are not one of us" (p. 162; cf. pp. 152, 156. Cf. Mk 1:34, 3:11).

society. While it would be wrong to argue that these texts preclude the living of the holy life within the walls of the city, nevertheless, these texts surely problematize such an endeavor.[18] In Athanasius's *Life of Antony*, the anonymous text known to scholars as the *History of the Monks of Egypt*, Palladius's *Lausiac History*, and Theodoret of Cyrrhus's *Religious History*, the city is understood as a danger to the holy life, in opposition to the desert, where the holy man can achieve sanctity.[19] In the various lives of Symeon the Stylite the populace of Antioch pours into the countryside to see the saint high atop his pillar. And in the life of his follower, Daniel the Stylite, the saint situates himself up the Bosphorus from the imperial capital, entering Constantinople only to rally its inhabitants in defense of Orthodoxy. John Moschus's collection of saints' lives, the *Spiritual Meadow*, also carries an antiurban tone. Symeon, however, leaves the desert and goes to the city, and specifically to the market. What happens when the holy man goes to the center of the city, to the marketplace, which presents a feast for all the appetites, for gluttony, avarice, and lust? Perhaps the first impression which the *Life of Symeon* offers is that the only way to be holy in the city is to be crazy. But Leontius's message is more subtle than this.

Just as Symeon is a figure for Jesus, the Emesa which he visits is a figure for Jerusalem, which itself is already a figure for God's creation, a world which God is determined to save by sending messengers to instruct its inhabitants. When early in the *Life* Symeon and John pray for divine guidance to help them determine whether they should take the path toward the monastery, they invoke God "who would save the whole world" (p. 125). In a clever reversal, in leaving the desert, Symeon states his intention to "mock [ἐμπαίζω] the world" (p. 142), a world which had once

18. On the dichotomy between desert and city in ascetic literature see Peter Brown, *The Body and Society: Men, Women, and Sexual Renunciation in Early Christianity* (New York: Columbia University Press, 1988), pp. 213–24; James Goehring, "The Encroaching Desert: Literary Production and Ascetic Space in Early Christian Egypt," *JECS* 1 (1993): 281–96; Elizabeth A. Clark, *The Origenist Controversy: The Cultural Construction of an Early Christian Debate* (Princeton: Princeton University Press, 1992), p. 80. Nevertheless, much ascetic literature points out that the laity are as acceptable to God as monks. Cf. Price, *History of the Monks of Syria*, p. xxvi, and the story of Patermuthius in *HME* 10.

19. For specific statements in these texts see Athanasius, *Life of Antony* 8 and 14; Palladius, *LH* 66.2; *HME*, Prologue 2.10–11. Cf. Browning, "The 'Low Level' Saint's Life in the Early Byzantine World," in *The Byzantine Saint*, ed. Sergei Hackel (San Bernardino, Calif.: Borgo, 1983), p. 118; and Brown, "The Rise and Function of the Holy Man in Late Antiquity," *JRS* 61 (1971): 80–101. Robert Markus (*The End of Ancient Christianity* [Cambridge: Cambridge University Press, 1990], pp. 157–211) has suggested that in the West the initial fourth- and early-fifth-century movement away from the cities is reversed with an "ascetic invasion" of the city in subsequent decades. Such a trend is also observed in the East, although over a much longer period of time.

mocked Christ. And it is as part of God's plan of salvation that Symeon comes to Emesa to behave as he does.

Leontius is concerned with preparing his own city for the restoration of Jerusalem. At one point in the *Life of Symeon*, the saint encounters ten men washing their clothes outside the city (p. 163). This scenario recalls a passage in the Book of Revelation concerning those who will enter into the new Jerusalem:

> Blessed are those who wash their robes, that they may have the right to the tree of life and that they may enter the city by the gates. Outside are the dogs and sorcerers [φαρμακοί] and fornicators [πόρνοι] and murderers and idolaters, and every one who loves and practices falsehood. (Rv 22:14–15, trans. RSV)

This passage reads like a *dramatis personae* for the *Life of Symeon the Fool*, which includes a sorceress (p. 162), fornicators (pp. 149–50, 151), murderers (pp. 159–60), and even dogs. Through implicit comparison with the holy city, Leontius poses the question, Will the residents of Emesa ever be ready for the Kingdom of God?

Jerusalem, both heavenly and earthly, is never far from Leontius's mind. In addition to the events in the *Life of Symeon* modeled on Jesus' activities in and around the "holy city," Jerusalem itself figures twice in the narrative. Leontius opens the *Life* with Symeon and John's pilgrimage to Jerusalem to celebrate the Feast of the Exaltation of the Cross. Leontius tells how the "friends of Christ" come "eager to venerate Christ's holy places in the holy city" (p. 124). From the beginning, Leontius meditates on Jesus and Jerusalem: Jerusalem is the locus of Christ's sacred activities, activities which in turn impart holiness to the earthly city. Symeon and John's pilgrimage to Jerusalem is the catalyst for their conversion to the holy life.

Later in the narrative, Symeon travels again to Jerusalem. After twenty-nine years in the desert practicing the ascetic life (p. 142), the same length of time which preceded Jesus' own entry into Jerusalem, Symeon goes first to "the holy city of Christ our God."[20] He visits "Christ's holy and life-giving tomb, and the holy, saving, and victorious Golgotha" (p. 144). He remains in the city for a significantly numbered three days visiting "the Lord's all-holy places." Here it is that Symeon prays "that his works might be hidden" until his death so that he might "escape human glory [δόξα]" (p. 144). Symeon then travels to Emesa to begin his work.

---

20. Cf. Syrkin, "The 'Fool for Christ's Sake,'" p. 165. In Byzantium, Jesus was held to have died at thirty. Cf. Ephrem the Syrian, *Hymns on the Nativity* 4, l. 157; trans. Kathleen E. McVey (New York: Paulist, 1989), p. 101.

The contrast between the holiness of Jerusalem and the profanity of Emesa could not be starker, and it is further enhanced by Symeon's transgressive and defiling behavior. In Emesa, in order to prepare the inhabitants for salvation, Symeon pretends to be crazy.

> [Symeon] played all sorts of roles foolish and indecent, but language is not sufficient to paint a picture of his doings. For sometimes he pretended to have a limp, sometimes he jumped around, sometimes he dragged himself along on his buttocks, sometimes he stuck out his foot for someone running and tripped him. Other times when there was a new moon, he looked at the sky and fell down and thrashed about. (p. 155)

Symeon babbles in public, an activity which Leontius informs his reader is "most fitting and most useful to those who simulate folly for the sake of Christ" (pp. 155–56); he walks about naked (p. 149) and creates havoc in the marketplace by interfering with commerce (p. 157), eating freely without purchasing food (pp. 146, 158), giving some goods away (p. 146), and completely destroying others (pp. 146, 147, 163, 165). It is also here in the market that Symeon defecates (p. 148).

Leontius, we must remember, was an urban bishop. His tales of Symeon's activities reflect the role of the market in the Late Antique city. The market was the primary public space in the smaller cities of the Later Roman Empire. Such institutions as the theater and the hippodrome, which had been so important in the Eastern Mediterranean before the fourth century, became less important with the rise of Christianity, although they did not disappear. Urban planning in Late Antiquity tended to emphasize two main foci, the church and the marketplace. (Thus the Late Antique city has more in common with the early Islamic city, whose primary organization is based on the relationship between mosque and marketplace, than with the classical Greek *polis* organized around a large number of public institutions.) The markets of the East Roman Empire were not centers of production; the economy in the region remained overwhelmingly agricultural. The market, however, was an important structural element of Late Antique economic life and the center of urban activity.[21] Furthermore, in a society where a substantial portion of the population lived under constant threat of starvation,[22] the market came to embody,

---

21. On this point see John Haldon, "Some Considerations on Byzantine Society and Economy in the Seventh Century," *Byzantinische Forschungen* 10 (1985): 77–78.

22. Evelyne Patlagean, *Pauvreté économique et pauvreté sociale à Byzance 4ᵉ–7ᵉ siècles* (Paris: Mouton, 1977), pp. 36–53, 101–2; Aline Rousselle, *Porneia: On Desire and the Body in Antiquity*, trans. Felicia Pheasant (Oxford: Blackwell, 1988), pp. 160–64; cf. A. H. M. Jones, *The Later Roman Empire*, vol. 2 (Oxford: Oxford University Press, 1964), pp. 810–11; Brown,

at some times, wealth and prosperity; at other times, the prospects for survival.

Although some evidence suggests that by the late sixth century, both the agriculture and the cities of Syria and Egypt were in decline, scholarly debate on the topic has yet to reach a consensus.[23] A combination of plague, earthquake, and in the early seventh century invasion (both Persian and Arab), as well as an estrangement from imperial authority (in part a result of theological differences), left many cities beleaguered and vulnerable. The degree to which the cities of Cyprus were affected by these trends is uncertain. The evidence presented in chapter 1 suggests, on the contrary, that in the first half of the seventh century the Cypriot economy was relatively prosperous. The evidence of vibrant market life in the *Life of Symeon,* produced on Cyprus in the 640s, strengthens an argument for general economic health. Leontius wrote the *Life of Symeon the Fool* in the midst of the Arab conquest: Emesa had fallen in the previous decade, in 634; Alexandria, about which Leontius wrote in his only other extant biography, the *Life of John the Almsgiver,* had fallen in 641. Although one might expect that Leontius's vivid portrayal of flourishing urban life in these two cities was prompted by an element of nostalgia, neither text suggests that the economy which Leontius describes in his writings is different from the economy with which he was immediately familiar.

As we have seen, Symeon's activity in Emesa is modeled on Jesus' activities in Jerusalem. Just as Jesus enters the city to perform certain deeds which will lead to the salvation of the city's inhabitants, Leontius's Symeon enters Emesa to save souls (pp. 142, 157). Although, as Leontius informs his audience, some of Symeon's deeds were merely intended to conceal his sanctity, "Some of the deeds the righteous [Symeon] did out of compassion for the salvation of humans" (p. 149). Like Jesus in Jerusalem, Symeon in Emesa has a specific mission, preparing the inhabitants for salvation. But how is this salvation to be effected? What are the urban laity to

---

The World of Late Antiquity (New York: Norton, 1972), p. 12; Brown, "The Problem of Miraculous Feeding in the Graeco-Roman World," in *Center for Hermeneutical Studies: Colloquy 42* (Berkeley: Graduate Theological Union, 1982), pp. 16–24.

23. Haldon, "Some Considerations," p. 78; Hugh Kennedy, "The Last Century of Byzantine Syria: A Reinterpretation," *Byzantinische Forschungen* 10 (1985): 141–83. On the other hand see Mark Whittow, "Ruling the Late Roman and Early Byzantine City: A Continuous History," *Past and Present* 129 (November 1990): 24–25. Unfortunately Whittow's argument for economic prosperity in the sixth century depends on the evidence of hagiographical texts which he dates to the periods they purport to describe rather than the periods in which they were produced. For example, he uses the *Life of Symeon* to argue for the economic vibrance of Syria during the reign of Justinian rather than for Cyprus in the mid-seventh century.

do? Leontius's evocation of the city and Symeon's interactions with those who populate it focus on two themes: namely, concerns for the poor and for religious conformity.

Symeon and the Poor

On his way out of the churchyard and into the market, Symeon overturns the tables of the pastry chefs, a deed which recalls Jesus' activities in the temple. The casting out of those buying and selling and the overturning of the tables of the money changers were interpreted by some allegorizing biblical commentators, Origen among them, to refer not merely to trade in the temple but to Christians who, in Origen's words, were "inclined to merchandize," those whose business activities were considered unworthy of the Kingdom of God.[24] Leontius uses Symeon's overturning of tables full of pastry, slapstick though it is, to introduce his concerns about the place of commerce and the "love of money" in the Christian community.

Leontius sets much of Symeon's activity in the marketplace and in other venues where commercial activity takes place. Demons reside in Emesa's stores (pp. 147, 153–54) and in its market (p. 157); and these are among the demons which Leontius's Symeon seeks to drive out. Once in the market, Symeon is offered a job by the owner of a phouska-stand. Leontius writes, "When they set him up one day, Symeon began to give everything away to people and to eat, himself, insatiably" (p. 146). In fact, Symeon gives all the food away to the poor and to other monks, so that at the end of the day, the food is gone and the cash box is empty. The phouska-seller and his wife, who are (not incidently) Monophysite heretics, are furious; they beat Symeon and pull his beard. Symeon's behavior is both comic—the deeds of a madman—and saintly, since he feeds the hungry, donating to the poor food which the phouska-seller intends to sell at a profit to those who are able to pay.

As we saw above, on two other occasions, Symeon performs miraculous feedings, going far beyond Jesus' wine, loaves, and fishes (Mk 6:32–44 and parallels, Jn 2:1–11), adding jams, meatballs, and cakes for dessert (pp. 159, 163–64). He provides five former circus fans with a miraculously replenishing supply of bread (p. 164). In the world of Late Antiquity feeding the poor and hungry was a miracle in itself, a meritorious act of saintly compassion.

In Symeon's second job, he is employed carrying buckets of hot water in a tavern. But, as Leontius narrates,

24. Origen, *Commentary on John* 16; English trans. ANF 10.393–94.

> The tavern keeper was heartless, and he often gave Symeon no food at all, although he had great business, thanks to the Fool. For when the townspeople were ready for a diversion, they said to each other, "Let's go have a drink where the Fool is." (p. 147)

Symeon perceives that the Devil has come to reside in the heartless tavern keeper's shop and proceeds to smash all the jars of wine until the Devil is rooted out, at which point the tavern keeper is reformed, literally "edified" (οἰκοδομήθη). The tavern keeper's heartlessness is exemplified by the fact that he does not feed the poor monk; presumably the tavern keeper's edification involves learning to use his food and his profits to assist the poor.

Leontius is not opposed to commercial activity. Throughout the text, either through his folly or his miracles, Symeon brings prosperity to the citizens of Emesa. The tavern keeper's sales increase thanks to Symeon's presence (p. 147). Later Symeon advises a mule driver to open a tavern, which Symeon presages will turn a profit. Leontius says, "And when [the mule driver] opened it, God blessed him" (p. 165), that is, with good business. Symeon befriends the wealthy citizens of Emesa, whom he also reforms (pp. 151, 162–62). Leontius's point, however, is that those who benefit from commerce must support the poor.

Leontius's concern for the poor is made most explicit through Symeon's relationship with John, the deacon of the church in Emesa, the only person in Emesa with whom Symeon does not play the fool (cf. p. 160). At one point, Symeon saves John from execution when he has been framed for a murder and falsely convicted (pp. 159–60). Symeon explains to John the reason for his misfortune:

> The trial came to pass because yesterday two beggars came to you, and although you were quite able to give to them, you turned them away. The things which you give, are they yours, brother? Or do you not believe in Him who said that you will receive a hundredfold in this age and eternal life in the age to come? If you believe, give. And if you don't give, it will be manifest that you don't believe in the Lord. (p. 160)

Symeon expresses a similar message in the sermon he preaches to John shortly before his death.

> I beg you, never disregard a single soul, especially when it happens to be a monk or a beggar. For Your Charity knows that His place is among the beggars, especially among the blind, people made as pure as the sun through their patience and distress. . . . [S]how love of your neighbor through almsgiving. For this virtue, above all, will help us on [the Day of Judgment]. (pp. 166–67)

Here Symeon drops his persona of folly and obscurity and speaks plainly. Here too, we must imagine, Leontius momentarily abandons his role as a storyteller and speaks directly to his audience, an audience which must have had the means to donate to the poor. Here Leontius addresses the same concern he had addressed earlier and in more explicit detail in the *Life of John the Almsgiver:* the role of the poor in the salvation of the wealthy.

For Leontius, almsgiving, above all, will help on the Day of Judgment. While such an act does not overturn the social structure implied by the market, it does counteract some of its imbalances. At the same time, it allows those who benefit from the economic system to contribute to their own salvation. Complete detachment from the workings of the market, by leaving the city completely and retiring to the desert, was not an option for the urban laity. So Leontius instructs his congregants that concern for the poor is a crucial component in the Christian's effort to meet the challenge of living the moral life in an urban setting.

Symeon and Religious Conformity

Leontius's interest in religious uniformity echoes the imperial project which had been intensified during Heraclius's reign, calling for the holiness of Byzantine society in the face of external Persian and Arab threats. Many of the people whose conversion Symeon effects represent the intractable nonconformists of Leontius's early Byzantine world. Jews and heretics resisted joining the Orthodox community, and as such, Leontius's narrative represents a "wish fulfillment." Mid-seventh-century Cyprus had both Jewish and Monophysite populations,[25] who no doubt remained problematic in the eyes of a local bishop such as Leontius. Symeon achieves a degree of religious conformity in Emesa which Leontius could portray only as the work of a holy man. In fact, Symeon's successes in converting those generally regarded as intractable should be counted among the deeds attesting to his sanctity: for Leontius and his audience, such achievements were truly miraculous.

One of the artisans mentioned in the text is a Jewish glassblower (p. 163). Symeon breaks many of the drinking glasses in his shop by making the sign of the cross over them. He tells the glassblower that he will continue to break the glasses until the glassblower becomes a Christian. Eventually, in desperation, it would seem, the Jew makes the sign of the cross on his forehead and seeks baptism. This episode should surely be

25. On evidence for these communities, see chapter 1.

added to the collection of texts which suggest a rise in tensions between Jews and Christians during the first half of the seventh century.[26] Nevertheless, the episode is in keeping with Symeon's attempts to convert all non-Chalcedonian and immoral elements in the city. He converts the phouska-seller and his wife, both Acephalic Severian Monophysites, by sending a demon in the form of an Ethiopian to destroy their shop, "smash[ing] everything in sight" two days in a row until "in dire straits, they became Orthodox" (pp. 153–54). Another Jewish artisan, who has seen Symeon conversing with angels at the baths, is struck dumb and is threatened with being forced to beg until he is baptized together with his household (p. 154). Similarly Symeon reforms the sorceress who makes and sells amulets, since through her practices she was turning people away from God and toward herself (p. 163). In each case Symeon threatens the livelihood and economic status of those Emesans who are not members of the Chalcedonian Orthodox Christian community, conforming to the beliefs and practices which Leontius himself, as Chalcedonian bishop of Neapolis, represents.

Leontius does not limit Symeon's activities as a religious reformer to converting those who are not Orthodox in belief; he is also concerned with those Chalcedonians who do not conform to appropriate Christian practice. Symeon's success in reforming prostitutes belongs to the same class of miracles as his conversion of the non-Orthodox, since prostitutes were regarded as irredeemably drawn to immoral behavior.[27] Further-

26. See A. Sharf, "Byzantine Jewry in the Seventh Century," *BZ* 48 (1955): 103–15. Carl Laga ("Judaism and the Jews in Maximus Confessor's Works: Theoretical Controversy and Practical Attitude," *Byzantinoslavica* 51 [1990]: 178–183) has recently pointed out that this passage suggests that in the "social view of the common man," Jews were "simply part of the picture." Leontius neither concerns himself with the Jew's legal status, nor presents him in an "exclusive or specialized economic activity," nor characterizes him as dressed in any distinctive way. Laga, however, uses this episode to argue against an atmosphere of anti-Judaism during the reign of Justinian. Laga attempts to contrast the *Life of Symeon* with texts produced during the reign of Heraclius reflecting the legislation of forced baptism of Jews between 630 and 632, including the *Doctrina Jacobi*, written in 634. A correct dating of the evidence of the *Life of Symeon* to the 640s would require a modification in Laga's arguments.

27. The most striking example of this attitude is found in Procopius, *Anecdota* 17.5–6, where the prostitutes whom Theodora forces to live in a convent overlooking the Bosphorus hurl themselves over the cliff in order to escape the "unwilling transformation." In Leontius's *Life of John the Almsgiver,* Vitalius's ability to convert a prostitute also attests to his sanctity (*Life of John* 38). Consider also the story of Sarapion and the harlot in Anan-Isho, *Paradise of the Fathers* 31. In the same vein, stories which focus on the sanctity of the reformed harlot regard her abandoning of her sinful ways as a testimony to her holiness. Consider the legends of Thaïs, Mary of Egypt, and Pelagia recently discussed by Harvey in her essay "Women in Early Byzantine Hagiography: Reversing the Story," in *That Gentle Strength: Historical Perspectives on Women in Christianity,* ed. Lynda L. Coon, Katherine J. Haldane, and Elisabeth W. Sommer (Charlottesville: University Press of Virginia, 1990), pp. 46–48.

more Symeon reforms the tavern keeper's heartlessness (p. 147), curbs the deacon's son's urge to fornicate (pp. 149–50), and makes the juggler abandon performing in the theater (p. 150). He bribes five circus fans into abandoning their enthusiasm for the circus (p. 164). He chastises the goat thief (p. 161). He corrects one wealthy man who beats his slaves (p. 162) and another who cheats on his wife (pp. 165–66). He reforms not only prostitutes (pp. 155, 156) but ill-behaved schoolgirls (pp. 157–58). He even scolds his confidant, the Deacon John, for neglecting the poor (pp. 159–60).

In Leontius's narrative, Symeon achieves his goal of saving souls, a goal with obvious implications for the moral well-being of the city. Leontius writes:

> While the saint was there [in Emesa], he cried out against many because of the Holy Spirit and reproached thieves and fornicators. Some he faulted, crying that they had not taken communion often, and others he reproached for perjury, so that through his inventiveness he nearly put an end to sinning in the whole city. (p. 162)

In his native Neapolis, Leontius's flock of Chalcedonian Christians would have come into contact regularly with heretics and nonbelievers; there too his community of the faithful would have encountered sin. Purifying the city was one of Symeon's goals. Ridding the marketplace of unbelievers and profiteers lacking in compassion was part of this purification. Through his activities, Symeon attempts to make Emesa resemble the ideal Jerusalem, the heavenly city free from sin. We must conclude that Leontius's composition of such a narrative was intended to effect a similar change in his own community.

Symeon's work as a moral reformer is "Christomimetic"; Leontius locates the significance of the Christ for his urban audience in Jesus' preparation of the earthly city for salvation. It is perhaps surprising that the practical message of such a challenging work is so conventional: support the poor and live the morally upright life of a faithfully orthodox Christian. But this inverted Christ-figure is still a Christ-figure. In the end, the method of the tale may appear more remarkable than its moral. However, Symeon's resemblance to the Christ articulates an important theological question, namely, the nature of holiness. Averil Cameron has pointed to the importance of paradox in Late Ancient Christian literature.[28] The most important Christian paradox, of course, was the Orthodox teaching on the incarnation. In proclaiming "the Word made flesh," Orthodox theologians

---

28. Averil Cameron, *Christianity and the Rhetoric of Empire: The Development of a Christian Discourse* (Berkeley: University of California Press, 1991), pp. 155–70.

preached the joining of the divine to the human and, thus, the human to the divine.[29] This teaching blurred the distinction between the sacred and the profane, eradicating human convention through divine logic. The protagonist of the *Life of Symeon* embodies this paradox. The fool reenacts the work of the savior from triumphal entry to empty tomb. Through his strange tale, Leontius prompts his reader to reconsider the mystery of the Christ.

29. Cf. Athanasius, *Incarn.* 54.

· EIGHT ·

CONCLUSION:
CYNICS, CHRISTIANS,
AND HOLY FOOLS

The *Life of Symeon the Fool* is a complex and challenging work of Early Byzantine religious literature. That Leontius's readers were able to assimilate such a sophisticated narrative is a testament to the level of culture sustained on Cyprus into the middle of the seventh century. The *Life of Symeon* confirms that Late Ancient Christians indeed had a sense of humor. But in addition to being entertaining and witty, the *Life of Symeon* demonstrates that hagiography was for Leontius an intellectual project which allowed him to synthesize his cultural heritage and rework it for his specific context. Like Late Ancient architects who constructed buildings by making use of pediments, columns, and capitals quarried from abandoned classical structures, Leontius gathered the Cynic anecdotes, *spolia* of Greco-Roman culture, to use as the building blocks of Christian moral exhortation.

Thus, in Symeon, we find two prototypes, Diogenes and Christ. This double legacy of the "fool for Christ's sake" remains the most puzzling insight of our investigation. In his concern to rid urban life of vice and nonconformity, Leontius constructed a saint who in Emesa's public and commercial spaces performed his most unsaintly deeds. In front of the urban laity of Emesa, Symeon dances licentiously with whores (p. 156) and gorges himself on cakes in the middle of Holy Week (pp. 156–57). Here too, Symeon defecates and eats foods which will cause him to fart (pp. 148, 152–53). Obviously, in creating such episodes, Leontius has not modeled Symeon's actions on those of Jesus. Instead, in these episodes, as we have seen, Leontius models Symeon on the figure of Diogenes of Sinope. What then is the significance of Leontius's construction of Symeon as an *alter* Diogenes in addition to an *alter Christus*?

To answer this question, we must reconsider the significance of the anecdotal material about Diogenes of Sinope's shamelessness. Chapter 6 established that in the *Life of Symeon the Fool*, Leontius makes sustained allusion to anecdotes about Diogenes of Sinope. As a body, the Cynic *chreiai,* which were preserved in Late Antiquity and which were passed on to successive generations of elites through the schools of grammar and rhetoric, constitute a critique of urban life. This aspect of the traditions concerning the Cynics appealed to many of the church fathers because it was consonant with their own criticism of the city. As we have seen, much Cynic material was absorbed into the ascetic tradition. Despite the apparently radical content of many of these *chreiai*, the preservation of Cynic material was not intended to foster the rejection of the way of life of the educated urban elite, only to keep constant a moral perspective on that way of life. For some, then, the *chreiai* about Diogenes' shamelessness were an integral part of the elite's internal critique.[1] By its very nature, the school curriculum kept debate over the meaning and the social value of the activities attributed to Diogenes alive for Christian students of grammar and rhetoric.

Leontius's motives in modeling Symeon on Diogenes depend on the meaning Diogenes continued to embody in Late Antique culture, a meaning which had perhaps been best articulated by the Emperor Julian, some three centuries earlier. For Julian, Diogenes' behavior illustrated the difference between a life in accord with nature and one governed by social convention (*nomos*) and vain opinion (*doxa*), inherently devoid of moral reflection.[2] Diogenes' bodily functions served as the instruments for a critique of the way the majority of humans led their lives.[3] Julian recognized that "there is nothing strange in a wise man's jesting, since many of the philosophers appear to have done so."[4] Julian was concerned with the Cynic philosopher's role in the purification of the city, cities in which things "monstrous, disgusting, and sordid" were carried out in the "pub-

1. See my essay, "The Bawdy and Society: The Shamelessness of Diogenes in Roman Imperial Culture," in *The Cynics: The Movement in Antiquity and Its Legacy for Europe,* ed. R. Bracht Branham and Marie-Odile Goulet-Cazé (forthcoming).

2. Cf. Julian, *Or.* 6.188b, 193d, 196d.

3. Julian stresses the place of the body and its members in the philosophical enterprise; *Or.* 6.183a–84a, 189b–d.

4. Julian, *Or.* 6.186c.

lic baths, brothels, and retail shops."[5] Furthermore, Julian understood Cynic shamelessness as part of a moral philosophy—as a tactic designed not so much to illustrate, but rather to instruct others in appropriate moral behavior by raising questions about the moral content of everyday practices. For Julian the virtues expressed by the life of Diogenes were obvious: "freedom, self-governance, justice, prudence, caution, grace, and diligence."[6] And these virtues were indeed exemplified in the *chreiai* taught in the schools and cited repeatedly by Christian writers into the seventh century.

The moral lessons contained in these *chreiai* survived in the schools into periods when Cynicism, as such, had long ceased to be practiced. Leontius made allusions to *chreiai* about Diogenes because he too was convinced of the potential for moral instruction in the anecdotes of Cynic shamelessness. These anecdotes expressed moral concerns rooted in reflection upon urban experience in Late Antiquity, an urban experience which Christians interpreted through their classical traditions.

The Cynic references work for Leontius because the figure of Diogenes challenges human systems of categorization, revealing through his antics that distinctions which people make between polite and impolite, public and private, appropriate and inappropriate, and pure and impure are nothing more than human conventions. Like Diogenes', Symeon's profaning actions in the marketplace comment on society's hypocrisy, iniquity, and economic injustice. Moreover, Symeon's shamelessness participates in the same concerns Leontius expresses elsewhere in the *Life of Symeon,* in places where Symeon's activities are not directly modeled on Diogenes of Sinope. As we have seen, the allusions to Jesus also focus on the need for the city to clean up its act. Leontius constructs a convergence between the message implicit in Cynicism and the teachings of Christ.

There is perhaps here a sense of irony. Symeon's shamelessness is not presented as a model for Christian behavior. Despite the holy man's idiosyncrasy, the *Life of Symeon* does not advocate the expression of individuality. Rather Leontius is ultimately concerned with social and religious conformity. But this is true also of Cynic traditions on which it is modeled. The *chreiai* about Diogenes of Sinope were not presented to young men in Late Antiquity, whether pagan or Christian, in order that they might be encouraged to behave like the legendary Cynic, but rather that the example of the Cynic philosopher might assist them to discern the path to a life of virtue, simplicity, and civic responsibility.

5. Julian, *Or.* 6.186d.
6. Julian, *Or.* 6.202a. It is no accident that these virtues number seven.

In the end, of course, Symeon is not a Cynic, nor does Leontius present a Cynic interpretation of Jesus. The Cynic model is useful in Leontius's endeavor to instruct his audience, but it can only go so far. The story of Christ's fool uses only the methods of the Cynic anecdotes to tell a Christian story. Ultimately it is the life of Jesus which provides the guiding model both for Symeon, the fool for Christ's sake, and for the Christian life toward which Leontius directs his readers.

- APPENDIX -

THE LIFE OF SYMEON THE FOOL

by Leontius of Neapolis

[121]

The Life and Conduct[1] *of Abba Symeon Called the Fool for the Sake of Christ Written by Leontius, Most Pious Bishop of Neapolis on the Isle of Cyprus*

Those who are eager to pursue the worthy status which can be taught to others are obliged to demonstrate in their own life the teaching of still others and present themselves to all as a model of a way of living which is a virtue inspired by God, according to the divine word which says, "Let your light shine before men, that they may see your good works and give glory to your Father who is in heaven" [Mt 5:16], lest perhaps they are eager to chastise, reform, and guide others before they themselves are instructed and purified through working at the divine commandments, having failed to lament their own death, while concerning themselves with

---

This translation of the *Life of Symeon the Fool* by Leontius of Neapolis is based on the critical edition of the Greek text by Lennart Rydén in *Léontios de Néapolis: Vie de Syméon le Fou et Vie de Jean de Chypre*, ed. A. J. Festugière, in the series Bibliothèque archéologique et historique (Paris: Geuthner, 1974), pp. 55–104. The translator is indebted to the textual commentaries of Rydén (*Bemerkungen zum Leben des heiligen Narren Symeon von Leontius von Neapolis* [Uppsala: Almquist and Wiksell, 1970]) and Festugière (*Vie de Syméon le Fou*, pp. 161–222).

Numbers in square brackets refer to the pagination of the Greek text in *Das Leben des heiligen Narren Symeon*, ed. Lennart Rydén (Uppsala: Almquist and Wiksell, 1963), which is reproduced in the inner margins of Rydén's text in the volume edited by Festugière, *Vie de Syméon le Fou*. Biblical references also appear in brackets. Words supplied to clarify the sense of the Greek appear in parentheses.

1. πολιτεία. Lampe (s.v.) lists many instances where this word refers to Christian life and conduct. It may also refer to ascetic practice. I have translated it as "conduct" and as "way of life."

the death of another, and fulfill in themselves the truthful saying, so fitting to them, which says, "He who does not do and teach these things will be called least in the kingdom of heaven" [Mt 5:17], and again, "Hypocrite, first take the log out of your eye and then look to take out the speck in your brother's eye" [Mt 7:5]. For this reason also the wise author of the Acts of the Apostles says thus concerning our great and true God and teacher, "I have dealt with all that Jesus began to do and teach" [Acts 1:1]. For this also Paul, the great vessel of election, wrote rebuking the Romans, saying, "You then who teach others, will you not teach yourselves?" [Rom 2:21] and so forth.[2]

Since therefore I am unable to present instruction and the image and model of virtuous deeds from my own life, carrying with myself everywhere the mark of sin, come, and from the work of others and their sweaty toils, I shall today unveil for you a nourishment which does not perish but which leads our souls to life everlasting [cf. Jn 6:27]. For as bread strengthens the body, the word of God often awakens the soul to virtue in earnest, and especially the souls of those most slothful in the work of divine commandments and disposed to [122] carelessness. For the zealous, those whose intention is directed toward God, it is sufficient for their conscience to set them in the presence of instruction, recommending all good things and dissuading them from evil. Those more humble than these need to have the commandment of the written law set before them. But if someone escapes both from the first and from the second type of path which leads to virtue, it is necessary that from the zeal and concern of others, which he sees before his eyes, through his hearing, and through the stories which are told to him, a divine yearning be aroused in him to shake his soul from its sleep, that he may travel through the straight and narrow path and begin eternal life now. For it depends on us and lies within our power either to despise the desire for things which come in the present because they pass away, or, in the desire and longing for present things, to lose the unceasing good.

That what I have said is true is proven by all men who throughout the ages have been pleasing to God, and they themselves master our nature, especially those luminaries of our own generation who have shone forth. One of these was the very wise Symeon, who, indeed, is much more venerable than most because he rose to the most pure and impassible height, although to those more impassioned and more fleshly he seemed to be a defilement, a sort of poison, and an impediment to the virtuous life on ac-

2. Leontius's introduction focuses attention on the actions of holy persons as examples for others. This may seem particularly ironic, given the nature of the deeds to be described in the account which follows. By referring to Paul as a "vessel of election," Leontius suggests that Symeon also was the recipient of God's grace.

count of his appearance. Because of these things he was most pure, just as a pearl which has traveled through slime unsullied. Indeed, I say that through spending time in the city, hanging around with women, and the rest of the deception of his life, he truly sought to show a weakness in the virtuous life to the slothful and pretentious and the power granted by God to those who truly serve against the spirits of evil with all their souls.

I ask all who hear or read the narrative of his angelic conduct, which I have set down, to regard these writings with fear of the Lord and with the faith without doubt which is fitting to true Christians. For we know that to the most senseless and disdainful we seem to be relating something incredible and worthy of laughter. But if they had listened to the words, "If one wishes to be wise in this age, let him be a fool, that he may become wise" [1 Cor 3:18], and again, "We are fools for Christ's sake" [1 Cor 4:10], and again, [123] "For the foolishness of God is wiser than men" [1 Cor 1:25], they would not consider the achievements of this true athlete to be laughable; rather they would marvel again at those seeking the alternate ways[3] to virtue. For this was not someone undisciplined, still lacking a trainer, who has gone toward the world, but just as we see those arranged for battle, when the entire army stands with one intention: these men have confidence in themselves, or better yet, in the power of God, and in the soldiers' armor laid upon them, and in excellent skill at war and long-developed experience; and these alone tread forth from the ranks into single combat against the adversary—and this is what Symeon did. Because he was fighting the noble battle well and in accordance with the law, because he saw that he had been armed with the power of the spirit, because he had acquired the power to trample snakes and scorpions under foot [Lk 10:19], because he quenched the burning of the flesh with the dew of the Holy Spirit, because he spat upon all the softness and sentiment[4] of life as on a spider—what more can be said—and because he put impassivity[5] upon himself as a garment, both inside and outside, on account of his humility, and he was deemed worthy of adoption as a son according to the word in the Song of Songs concerning the purity and indifference of the soul, which says, "All fair," says Christ to the soul, "You are all fair, my love; there is no flaw in you" [Song 4:7]. Called by God, he went forth out of the desert and into the world, as into single combat against the Devil. For it was not thought just that the one thus honored by God and placed high should disdain the salvation of his fellow men, but remembering the one who said, "Love your neighbor as yourself" [Lk 10:27], who did not disdain to put on the form of a slave, although un-

3. πολιτεία.   4. δόξα.
5. ἀπάθεια.

changed, for the salvation of a slave [cf. Phil 2:6ff.], Symeon imitated his own master and truly used his own soul and body in order to save others.

But it is now time to relate to you, first of all, the manner of his coming from the desert into the world, and then of his strange[6] and marvelous deeds.

I

[124]
In the time of the reign of the Emperor Justinian, now faithfully departed, when the friends of Christ came, eager to venerate Christ's holy places in the holy city, according to the custom, on the Feast of the Exaltation of the honorable, life-giving, and venerable Cross[7] (all those who come there, as is the custom, to the holy and renowned festival know that crowds of cross-loving and Christ-bearing people from nearly every land gather together), at this celebrated festival it happened that two young men from Syria met each other according to God's plan. One was named John; the other Symeon. When they had spent a few days there and the holy festival of God was finished, the others returned home, each to his own city. But since the two young men had spent time together and had become friends, they would no longer part from each other. Therefore, on their return home they traveled together, along with their families. For John had an aging father, but no mother; and he had married a girl that year. He was about twenty-two years old. Symeon did not have a father, only a mother, a very old woman about eighty;[8] he had no one else. Therefore they formed one party. When they descended the slope to Jericho and passed through the city, John saw the monasteries all around the holy Jordan, and said in Syriac to Symeon, "Do you know the ones who dwell in these houses which are before us?" The other said to him, "Who are they?" And John said, "Angels of God." Symeon said to him in wonder, "Can we see them?" "If we will become like them, yes," said the other. However the two remounted their horses (for their families were very wealthy). Then straightaway they descended from their horses and

6. παράδοξα.

7. Celebrated on September 14. The celebration of the Exaltation of the Cross in Jerusalem was established in the sixth century, after which it spread to other parts of the empire. It was first celebrated at Constantinople in 614. Leontius's interest in the True Cross reflects an enthusiasm for the military successes of Heraclius. After the Cross had fallen into Persian hands, Heraclius restored the Cross to Jerusalem while on pilgrimage in 630. For bibliography see chapter 1.

8. This claim is problematic if Symeon is supposed to be 22 years old at the time.

handed them [125] to their slaves, saying, "Go on ahead," for they pretended to defecate there. By chance they found themselves on the wrong road, leading back into the holy Jordan. They both stopped, and John, pointing with his finger, said to Symeon, "Behold the road that leads to life!" and he showed him the road of the holy Jordan. "And behold the road which leads to death" [cf. Mt 7:13 ff], he said, showing him the main road, which their parents had preferred to take. "Come now, let us pray, and let each of us stand facing one of these roads and draw lots, and whichever is chosen, we shall convey ourselves on that path." They knelt down and said, moaning, "God, God, God who would save the whole world, reveal your will to your servants." And drawing their lots, ten more fell to Symeon than to John. But Symeon stood facing the road which leads to the holy Jordan. Then, overjoyed, forgetting all their property, wealth, and their parents, as in a dream, they embraced and kissed each other. They had been thoroughly instructed in Greek letters and endowed with much intellect.[9]

All this Symeon narrated in Emesa,[10] where he pretended to be a fool,[11] to a certain deacon of the holy cathedral church of the same city of Emesa, an excellent and virtuous man, who, by the divine grace which had come to him, understood the monk's work, and it was on his behalf that this most blessed Symeon performed a wonderful marvel, which we shall recall in its proper place. This aforementioned John, beloved of God, a virtuous deacon, narrated for us almost the entire life of that most wise one, calling on the Lord as witness to his story, that he had written nothing to add to the narrative, but rather that since that time he had forgotten most things.

Thereupon, he said,[12] they went down the path which would truly lead them to life. You can just see them overjoyed and running like Peter and John toward the Lord's life-giving tomb [cf. Jn 20:4]! And they aroused an eagerness in each other and made each other zealous. John was afraid that Symeon's sympathy [126] for his mother would stop him. On the other hand, Symeon wondered whether John's attachment to his newlywed wife would pull him back toward her like a magnet. So for this reason they addressed to each other admonishing and comforting words.

---

9. Symeon and John are native Syriac speakers. Presumably Greek was the dominant language in the monasteries of the Jordan in this period, despite the use of Palestinian Syriac by the native population. Cf. Sidney H. Griffith, "The Gospel in Arabic: An Inquiry into Its Appearance in the First Abbasid Century," *Oriens Christianus* 69 (1985): 161–63.

10. Modern Homs in Syria.   11. σαλός.

12. John the deacon.

And one said, "Be of good courage, brother Symeon. For we hope in God that this very day we are reborn. For how will these idle possessions of our life or our wealth have the power to help us on the Day of Judgment? Will they not harm us? Furthermore, the youth and the beauty which are joined to our body do not remain unfading up to the end, but are destroyed and extinguished either by old age in its time or by untimely death." And when John had said this and many other things to Symeon, then the other echoed back and remonstrated similarly, saying, "I have, brother John, neither a father, nor brothers, nor sisters, only that humble old mother who bore me. I do not consider this trouble for myself so much as I fear for your heart, lest your boiling for your newlywed wife drag you away from this good path."

After they had discussed this and many other things concerning one another, they arrived at a monastery named for Abba Gerasimos. For they had prayed, "Lord God, let us find open the door to the monastery where you command us to renounce the world." And this was where they had come. In this monastery there was an admirable man named Nikon, truly a person who achieved for himself a way of life according to his name.[13] For he was conquering[14] every demonic battalion, he shone in wonders and signs, and had been honored by God with the gift of prophecy. He had foreknowledge of the arrival of these blessed ones. For he said that on the day they arrived, he had seen in a dream someone who said to him, "Arise and open the flock's door, so that my sheep may enter." And he did so. Therefore, when they arrived they found the door open and the abba sitting and waiting for them. John said to Symeon, "It is a good sign, brother. Behold the door is open and the doorkeeper is sitting." When they approached, the superior[15] said to them, "Welcome, sheep of Christ." And he also said to Symeon, "Welcome fool,[16] truly you have (drawn) ten more (lots) than [127] Abba John. For the ten await you." He said this on account of his perfection in the virtuous life. Giving them a bite to eat he welcomed them as ones sent by God. And before they spoke to him, he spoke to them, in the following manner, as a prayer to the Lord. "Good, good and worthy is your love of God, but only as long as you do not weaken it so that it may be extinguished by our salvation's adversary. Your course is good, but do not give up running until you are crowned. Your resolve is good, but do not sleep, lest the fire burning your hearts today should cool. It is good that you prefer the permanent to that which passes away. Good are your parents according to the flesh, and it is good to serve them, but it is incomparably better to be well-pleasing to the

13. Nikon (Νίκων) means victorious.   14. νίκων.
15. Abba Nikon.   16. σαλός.

heavenly Father. Good are your fleshly brothers, but spiritual brothers are more useful. Good are the friends in Christ whom you have in the world, but better to have the saints for friends and intercessors before the Master. Good are the patrons whom you have, when you need them, against the powerful, but they are not necessary when we have holy angels interceding on our behalf. It is good and praiseworthy for the prosperous to give money and alms and charity to beggars, but God does not seek any offering from us, as long as we offer our souls. Sweet is the enjoyment of the good things in life, but they are not equal to the delight of paradise. Pleasant is wealth and desired by the majority of people, but it is not equal to that which 'No eye has seen, nor ear heard, nor the heart of man conceived' [1 Cor 2:9]. Pleasant is the beauty of youth, but it is nothing compared to that of Christ, the heavenly bridegroom. For David says, 'You are the fairest of the sons of men' [Ps 44:3, RSV 45:2]. It is a great thing to wage war for the earthly king, but such a campaign is temporary and dangerous."

He admonished them in this manner, and the devout man did not want to cease his admonition seeing the streams of tears pouring forth from their eyes. They paid attention to what was said, as if they had never heard the divine word. Then (Nikon) turned toward Symeon and said, "Do not worry; do not weep for the gray hair of the mistress, your mother, for God, persuaded by your combat, can console her much better than you. And if [128] you remained with her until her death, it is uncertain whether you would leave this life before her without having attained virtue, dying without having the power to protect yourself from the coming evils. Neither a mother's nor a father's love, nor a great number of brothers, neither wealth, nor glory,[17] nor marriage bonds, nor the sympathy of children could persuade the judge, nothing but virtuous conduct and toil and labors in accord with God." Then to John he said, "Lest, child, the enemy of our souls suggest to you, 'Who will feed my parents in old age? Who will console my spouse? Who will stop their tears?' For if you (pl.) had forsaken them for another god and left to serve him, then it would be well for you to be anxious whether he would care about them and console them or not. But now that you have run toward and consecrated yourselves to this one, for whom you have forsaken them, it is fitting to be confident and consider this, namely that if while we are in this world and serve life, God's goodness holds foreknowledge of all things, how much more does He care about your families, now that you have left them to serve and please Him? Therefore, O children, remember the word of the Lord to the one who said, 'Let me first go and bury my father.' (He

17. δόξα, possibly also "repute."

responded), 'Leave the dead to bury their own dead' [cf. Mt 8:21 ff.]. Run after Him with an unalterable mind and an unchanging heart. And why? If the earthly and mortal emperor, wanting you to gird up to be patricians or chamberlains, had persuaded you to rule his earthly palace, which appears and disappears as a shade in a dream, would you have despised all the advantages to yourselves, and wouldn't you rush up to him eagerly and unhindered, desiring to enjoy his honors, his perspective, and his license to speak, and preferring to survive all toil and suffering and death, only so that you would be judged worthy to see that day on which the emperor would doubtless receive you, and enlist you, and honor you with gifts before his entire senate?" When they said that they would, the great Nikon said, "How [129] much more, then, children, with more zeal and compunction, do we run to the immortal and eternal King of kings, being bound to follow Him as grateful slaves. We remember the love which God shows to us, such that, for our sake, He did not spare His only-begotten son, but He delivered him up for all of us. Therefore, even when we, who were ransomed from destruction and death by his precious blood, pour forth our own blood and are placed in the brigade of the legitimate sons, still we have not offered Him anything worth as much. For the shedding of royal blood and the shedding of slave's blood are not equal, my brothers."

All this and much else the God-bearing man counseled them, knowing already the contests and the course which had been set for them, having been assured by God. Indeed, I mean their life in the desert, absolutely homeless, as anchorites.[18] For he understood that this was neither a chance happening nor an everyday occurrence, but something righteous and brought about blamelessly, especially when he saw their delicate bodies, clothed in soft garments, and their youth, brought up on a luxurious life, accustomed to every comfort and delusion. Whence the wise doctor and teacher, by the divine knowledge and experience which was within him, having armed and prepared them with such precepts and instructions, said again to both of them, "Do you wish the hair on your head to be tonsured, or before this would you (rather) spend a little time today with your lay clothing on?" And just as from one consideration, or rather from one holy inspiration, both fell at the superior's feet beseeching him to tonsure them immediately and without delay. And Symeon said that unless Nikon did this with great haste, he would leave them immediately for another monastery. For Symeon was actually guileless and innocent. But John was wiser and had acquired greater knowledge. Therefore the pious Nikon took each one of them aside straightaway, wishing to test

18. Those who have withdrawn from the world—hermits.

[130] their hot renunciation for God, and said to Symeon certain things, trying to dissuade him from being tonsured on that day. But when Symeon would listen to absolutely none of it, he went to the other and said to him, "You see, I have prevailed upon your brother to remain for one year as he is, a layman." Immediately then John answered the one who had spoken thus, "If he wishes to remain so, let him. Truly, father, I cannot endure it." And Symeon said to him, when he spoke to him alone, "Quickly father, for the Lord's sake, for my heart trembles much for my brother John, because this year he was married to a very wealthy and beautiful woman, lest later his longing for her ravish him away and steal him from the longing for God." Then John said this alone to the virtuous man, with much supplication and tears—for they came to his eyes more naturally than to Symeon's—"Father, do not lose my brother by your error. For he has only a mother, and such is the extraordinary longing of each of them, that he cannot last two hours without her, but until today both slept together, his mother and he; they cannot be separated during the night. It is this above all which burns and gnaws at me until I see him tonsured and finally become free from anxiety about him."

The great one heard the concern that both had for the other, and being fully assured that God neither dishonored nor mistook their running to Him with whole hearts and without hesitation, he brought out a pair of scissors, and with the appropriate order, having placed the scissors upon the holy altar, he tonsured them. And stripping them of their garments, he dressed them in ones base, but nevertheless holy. The wise and most sympathetic man had pity on them because of the tenderness of their bodies, which were unaccustomed to suffering. When they were tonsured, John cried a lot, and Symeon nudged him to stop, not knowing exactly why he was crying. [131] For it seemed that he was crying because of distress about his parents and love for his wife. After they were tonsured and the superior had performed the Holy Eucharist, he sat down and advised them nearly the whole day. For he knew that they would not be with him for long, since God had planned it thus.

He wanted to give them their holy habit on the next day, since it was Sunday. Therefore certain brothers said to them, "Blessed are you, for tomorrow you will be reborn and become pure from all sin, as when you were born, as if on the day you were baptized." Both were astounded and ran to the divine Nikon late Saturday and fell at his feet, saying, "We beseech you, father, do not baptize us, for we are (already) Christians and born of Christian parents." But he did not know what they had heard from the fathers in the monastery, and he said to them, "My children, who wants to baptize you?" They said, "Our lords and masters the fathers of the monastery said to us, 'Tomorrow you will be rebaptized.'" Then the superior understood that the fathers had spoken concerning the holy habit, and he said to them, "They spoke well, my children. For with the Lord's consent, tomorrow we will clothe you in a holy and angelic habit." And when the innocent children of Christ understood that they did not lack anything except the monastic attire, they said to the abba, "What, father? Do we need anything else, in order to be dressed in this angelic habit, as you call it?" One week before, which was (the festival of) the Exaltation of the precious Cross, this great one had given the holy habit to a certain novice brother, and it was not yet seven full days since. He still wore the complete (habit), as is the rule. The great one commanded him to be brought into their midst immediately. When he came, both beheld him and immediately fell at the feet of the abba and said to him, "We beseech you, if you will clothe us and think us worthy of such honor and glory, do it this evening, lest perhaps, being human, during the night we die beforehand and miss such glory and joy, such an escort and crown." When the superior heard them, speaking of missing such an escort and crown, he understood that they had had a vision with regard to bearing the holy habit, and he commanded (the novice) to return to his cell, where he had been since he was clothed in the holy habit. When he had gone, the children of Christ were very distressed, and they said [132] to the superior, "For the Lord's sake, father, stand up, make us like that one, for there is not a man in your entire monastery who is so honored as he." The abbot said to them, "Honored in what way?" Then they said, "By Him who judges us worthy of (this monk's) habit and honor, father! We are blessed if we are escorted by such a crowd of monks with wax candles and carry on our heads such a brilliant crown." For they thought that the superior also saw what they saw. Wherefore, understanding this, he said nothing to them, because he had not seen. But he remained silent and amazed by their great innocence and purity, especially Symeon's. The great one said only this to them, most graciously, "Tomorrow we will also clothe you (in the habit), through the grace of the Holy Spirit." When the most pious deacon affirmed this, the truthful Symeon declared confidently, "We will see each other's faces tonight as in the day." And, each saw a crown on the head of the other, as they had seen (on the novice) before. "Our souls," said Symeon, "are in such joy, so that we can neither eat nor drink."

Two days after they received the holy garment, they saw the one who had received it seven days before, in regard to whom they had beheld the crown and the procession, and he wore a coarse cloak and was performing chores and no longer had either a crown around his head or monks processing with candles. And they were amazed. And Symeon said to John, "Believe me, my brother, if we also fulfill the same seven days, we will not have this fair appearance and grace." John said, "What do you want to happen, brother?" Then Symeon said to him, "Listen to me! Just as we renounced and set ourselves apart from worldly things, let us set ourselves apart completely from every person. For I behold another life and strange circumstances in this habit. For from the moment that this servant of God clothed us, my insides burn, I know not how, and my soul [133] seeks neither to see anyone nor speak to or hear anyone." John said to him, "What will we eat?" Symeon said to him, "What those called the Grazers [19] eat, of whom lord Nikon spoke yesterday. For perhaps it is because he wants us to lead such a life that he narrated to us how they live, how they sleep, and all about them." Thereupon John spoke, "And how (will we do this), since we have learned neither psalms nor rules?" Then God opened Abba Symeon's heart, and he said, "He who saved those who were well-pleasing to him before David [20] will also save us. If we are worthy, he will teach us as he taught David when he was with his flock in the desert. Therefore do not attempt to contain my zeal, brother. But henceforward, because we led ourselves to this deed, let us not suppress it." Then lord John said, "Let us do as you wish. But how will we leave, with the door closed at night?" Symeon said to him, "That which was open for us during the day is open for us at night."

After they had made their plan, as soon as night fell, the superior, in his sleep, saw someone opening the door of the monastery saying, "Come outside, O branded sheep of Christ, into your pasture." And waking immediately from his sleep, he went down to the gate and found it open, and believing that they had already left, he sat down gloomy, sighed deeply and said, "Hardened in sin, I was not judged worthy to receive the blessing of my fathers. Truly my fathers and masters and teachers were blessed and because of this I endeavored after their blessing. Heavens! Such precious stones,[21] as the scripture says, secretly rolling along the ground [cf. LXX Zec 9:16], seen by many, but discovered by few." While he pondered these things in his anguish, behold the pure bridegrooms of Christ came in order to go out. In front of them, the very pure superior, Nikon, saw some eunuchs carrying torches, while others held scepters in their hand. When he beheld them, he was overjoyed, because he had not lost his wish. Seeing him, the blessed ones wanted to turn back. They did not recognize him as the superior. Therefore the pious Nikon ran and called them to his side. When [134] they knew that he was the superior,

19. βοσκοί, hermits who ate grass in the desert.
20. I.e., before there were psalms to sing.
21. Symeon and John.

they were overjoyed, especially when they saw as well that the gate was open. For they understood that God had revealed this to him too. Therefore they wanted to make obeisance, but he stopped them, saying that it was not permitted for them to do such a thing on account of the honor of the angelic habit bestowed upon them. They said to him then, "We thank you, father, but we do not know what to bring to God and to your precious head. Who had hoped that we would be judged worthy of such gifts? What sort of king could honor us with such a status? What sort of earthly treasures made us so suddenly rich? What sort of baths so purified our soul? What sort of parents could so love and save us? What sort of presents and gifts are powerful enough to achieve for us the remission of our sins quickly, as you did, our dear father, beyond all our ancestors, and parents, you, our father and mother with Christ? You are our master, our helper, our leader, our guide, and all that language cannot express. Through you we obtain this inviolate treasure; through you we gain the much prized pearl; we truly learn the power of baptism, which the pious fathers proclaimed to us; we have understood the burning of our sins by the fire which inflames our hearts. Wherefore, lest we suffer it, thus burning our innards, we ask Your Beatitude to pray earnestly, father, and set your servants free to serve the God to whom we have consecrated ourselves, genuinely and with all our soul. O revered one, never forget the useless child at the time when you extend your precious hands; yes, yes, O one revered by us, your guests, pious one, remember how we are orphaned." And taking hold of the pious man's knees, they said again, "Remember, father, your humble sheep, whom you burnt as an offering to Christ. Remember the strange trees, whom you hastened to plant in the lovely garden of paradise. Do not forget the reluctant workers, whom you hired at the eleventh hour into Christ's vineyard" [cf. Mt 20:6–9]. And the pastor was astonished and amazed to see those who had two days before been laymen thus suddenly made wise through putting on the divine habit.

After they had both cried for a long time, the pious Nikon knelt down, placing Symeon on his right and John on his left. Then he stood up and stretching out his hands to heaven said, "God, just and praiseworthy; God, great and [135] mighty; God eternal: harken in this hour unto a sinful man. Hear me, God, hear me in your strength; during this my prayer, do not remember my constant disobediences with contempt. Hear me, Lord, hear my prayer from within the fire, as you heard your prophet [cf. Ex 3:2].[22] Yes, God of holy powers; yes, creator of the incorporeal;[23] yes,

22. Leontius refers to Moses and the burning bush.
23. The angels.

God who says, 'Ask, and you will receive' [Jn 16:24]. Do not despise me, clothed with impure lips and contained in sin. Hear me, you who promised to listen to those who call upon you in truth: guide the steps of your servants, and their feet to the path of peace. Have pity on your innocent children who are in a strange place; you who say, 'Be innocent as doves' [Mt 10:16]. I have cried out to you with my whole heart: God, God, hear me, the hope of all ends of the earth and all far off in strange lands [cf. LXX Ps 64:6, RSV Ps 65:5]. Banish all unclean spirits far from the face of your children. Take hold of your arms and your shield, and rise up for their help. Draw your sword and defend them against those who pursue [LXX Ps 34:2–3, RSV Ps 35:2–3]. Say, O Lord, Lord, to their soul, 'I am your salvation.' May the spirit of timidity withdraw slowly from their thought, and the spirit of despair, of arrogance, and of every evil, and may all their burning be quenched together with all motion created in their soul by diabolic energy. May their body, and their soul, and their spirit be enlightened with the light of your knowledge, so that, arriving at the unity of the faith and the full knowledge of the holy and venerable Trinity, attaining mature manhood, and the measure of the stature [Eph 4:13], they will extol forever and ever, together with the angels and all those well pleasing to you, O God, since eternity, your all-honorable and protecting name of the Father, the Son, and the Holy Spirit. Amen. Grant them, together with all the good people, O Lord, to have in their heart at all times the words of this my pitiable and unworthy prayer to you for glorification and praise of your goodness." [136] Again he said to them with many tears, "The God whom you have chosen, good children, and to whom you have run, sent out his angel before your face, and he will prepare your path in front of your feet. The angel, as the great Jacob says, 'who has delivered me from all opposing powers' [Gn 48:16], will lead you on your path. The one who delivered his prophet from the lions' mouth [cf. Dn 6:23] will deliver you from the lion's clutches. The God whom you have chosen will himself protect my bold offering." When he had prayed these things and more for them, the God-bearing man patted their backs and said, "Save, God, save those who love your name with their whole heart. For it would be unjust, Lord, if you overlooked or abandoned those who renounced the vain things in life." Thereupon again he said to them, "See, children, you have given yourselves into a frightful and invisible war. But do not fear; for God is mighty, and he will not let you be tempted beyond your strength to endure [1 Cor 10:13]. Struggle, my children, lest you be defeated by the Devil, but stand nobly, having the armor of the holy habit upon you. Remember the saying, 'No one who puts his hand to the plow and turns back is fit for the kingdom of heaven'" [Lk 9:62]. And again concerning the building of the tower:

"When you have begun this perfect and lofty building and way of life, do not slacken and fulfill in yourselves that, 'This man began to build and did not have the power and the zeal for the completion of the foundation' [cf. Lk 14:30]. Be on your guard, my children. The war is little; but great, the crown. Fleeting the labor; but eternal, the rest."

The hour was far advanced. As he was about to go out the gate, by which time the prayer bell had sounded, Symeon took the superior aside and said to him, "For God's sake, father, pray that God dissipate my brother John's memory of his wife, lest perchance because of evil he leave me by myself and I die grieving his loss and our separation. Pray, I ask for the sake of the Lord, that God console also his family, so that they are not anxious [137] about him." The old man was amazed at the affection which he held for his brother, and made no reply. Again in the same manner, Abba John took him and called him aside, for Symeon's sake, saying, "For God's sake, father, do not neglect my brother when you pray, so that he does not flee from me for his mother's sake, feeling for her, and is not found in the harbor suffering a shipwreck." As I said, he was astounded by the love of both for each other. He finally said to them, "Go, my children, for I have good news for you: He who opened (the door) for you here (on earth), has already opened (the door) for you there (in heaven)." And making the sign of the cross upon their breast and the whole of their body he left them in peace.

II

After they had departed, they said, "God of your great servant (Nikon), guide us to the strange and solitary place, because we know neither the place nor the country, but in going toward you, we committed ourselves to death in the open sea of this desert." Then John said to Symeon, "What now? Where do we go?" Symeon answered him, "Let us go to the right, because all on the right is good." And they went, arriving at the Dead Sea, at a place called Arnonas.[24] While God sustained them, never abandoning those who believed in him with their whole soul, they found a place where a monk who died a few days before had dwelt. Here, there were a few tools and tender plants for them to eat by which the monk who had lived here had sustained himself. Seeing the place our renowned ones rejoiced as if they had found a treasure; for they knew that it had been prepared and sent to them by God, and they began to thank God and the

24. The Arnon River (modern Mujib) flows through central Jordan into the Dead Sea.

great monk, Nikon. For they said, "Surely we have been well guided because of his prayers."

When they had stayed a few days, the Devil, the enemy of our souls, unable to bear the virtue of Christ's servants, began to war against them: against John concerning his wife, and against Symeon concerning his great love for his mother. When one of them saw himself afflicted, immediately he said to the other, "Get up, brother. Let us pray." And they prayed the prayer of [138] the monk who prayed, "Grant them, O Lord, in their hearts the words of this prayer." And immediately the two found that they knew it by heart. And they prayed it all the time in each temptation and in each of their requests to God. For it was the Devil who inflamed them, as the God-bearing Fool related, as he did when they ate meat and wine. And from the beginning, he suggested to them cowardice and despair concerning their asceticism, so that from time to time they sought to return from the desert to the monastery. And in their dreams, and sometimes in a delusion, the polymorphous snake made them see their own families weeping, driven mad, and many other things which it is not possible to narrate, unless someone has had the experience of such temptations. But as soon as they remembered the crowns which they had seen on one another and the teaching and tears of the old man (Nikon), their heart was soothed by them and encouraged, just as with holy oil.

Lord Nikon also appeared to them in a dream sometimes advising them, sometimes praying for them, and sometimes teaching them psalms, and they awoke repeating from memory that which he had taught them in their sleep, and they shared great joy. For they knew that he was anxious for their sake, and they assured him with their deeds. And before every request from God, both requested this above all: Symeon, that his mother's heart be encouraged and assured; John, that God take his wife in order to root out his affection for her from his thought. God, who said, "He fulfills the desire of those who fear him" [LXX Ps 144:19, RSV Ps 146:19], answered them both. After two years had passed, lord Symeon was assured by God that his mother was without grief concerning him, and he appeared to her during the night, and consoled her, and said to her in Syriac, "La dechre lich em," which is, "Do not grieve mother."[25] "For we are well, [139] lord John and I, and we are healthy, and we have entered service in the emperor's palace, and behold we wear crowns which the emperor placed upon us and glorious robes. Console the parents of my brother John, who is serving with me. But do not be grieved at all." And

---

25. This is a transliteration of the Syriac *l' tkr' lky 'my*, literally, "May it not grieve you, mother." Cf. R. P. Graffin's explanation quoted by Festugière, *Vie de Syméon le Fou*, p. 180.

Abba John saw someone wearing white who said to him, "Behold, I have made your father without grief; and your wife I have received this day."

They related to each other what both had seen, and they rejoiced and their heart was gladdened. And meanwhile from consideration for their parents God soon took them, and Symeon and John were henceforth at ease. They did not grieve at all for them, but untroubled and without fear, they continued their course of asceticism and silence all through the night and the day. They had no other work but undistracted preoccupation and untroubled concern. Indeed I speak of unceasing prayer, through which in a brief span the tireless workers progressed, so that after a few years they were judged worthy of divine visions, and God's assurances, and miracles. After a short time passed with both maintaining silence a stone's throw away from each other—for they had conceived this for themselves, that is, to withdraw from the world separately, because each one wished to pray alone, but when imaginings or weariness came to one of them, he would go to the other and together they would call on God to be delivered from temptation. On one day, Symeon, sitting in his accustomed place, saw himself in ecstasy, as if he was with his ailing mother in Edessa,[26] for he came from that place. And he said to her in Syriac, "How are you, mother?" She said, [140] "Well, my child." Again he said to her, "Go to the King, do not be afraid, because I have asked Him for help, and He has prepared for you a lovely place. And when He wishes, I will join you there."

When he came to himself, he knew in that hour that his mother had died, and he went running to his brother John, and said, "Arise, sir, let us pray." But John was troubled, for it seemed to him that some sort of temptation had fallen upon Symeon. Symeon said to him, "Do not be troubled, my brother, for nothing bad has happened to me, thanks be to God." Then John said to him, "But what is the cause of this running, Father Symeon?"—for he honored and reverenced him, as Symeon did John.[27] Then as his eyes poured forth with tears, and they began to flow onto his breast like pearls, he said to John, "Just now, the Lord took my good and blessed mother." And he told him of the vision. They knelt down and prayed, and one could hear Symeon speaking utterly wretched and imploring words to God. His insides twisted and churned, stirred up by nature, and he howled, "God, who accepted Abraham's sacrifice [Gn 22:1 ff.], who looked with favor upon Jephtha's holocaust [Jgs 11:30–39], who was not disgusted by Abel's gift [Gn 4:4], who, for the sake of

---

26. Modern Urfa in Turkey. Edessa was a major center for Christian learning in Mesopotamia.

27. The use of the title "Father" is the honor to which Leontius refers.

Samuel your child, declared Hannah your prophetess [1 Sm 2], You, my Lord, Lord, for my, your servant's sake, accept the soul of my good mother. Remember, God, the trouble and distress which she suffered on my account. Remember, Lord, her tears and moaning, which she poured forth because I fled to You from her. Remember, Lord, the breasts at which she suckled humble me, so that she might enjoy my youth, but she did not enjoy it. Do not forget, Master, that she could not be separated from me, even for an hour, and she was separated from me the whole time. Recall, Master who knows all, that although she wished to rejoice in me, I deprived her of myself for your name's sake. Do not forget, O righteous one, the rending of her innards, which she endured the day I fled to you. You understand, Lord, what sleeplessness she suffered every night [141] from the time when I abandoned her, when she remembered my youth. You know, Master, how many nights she was sleepless, while she sought the sheep who slept with her. Do not forget, lover of humanity, what sort of pain embraced her heart when she melted, seeing my habit, because her pearl no longer existed, being clothed thus. But recall, Master, that I robbed her of her consolation, joy, and exultation, so that I might serve you, my God and hers, and Master of all. Grant her angels who will keep her soul safe from the spirits and beasts of the air, evil and unmerciful beings who endeavor to swallow up everything which comes into their midst. Lord, Lord, send out to her mighty guards to rebuke every impure power molesting her, and, my God, command that her soul be separated from her body, without pain or torture. And if, being a woman, she sinned in word or deed in this life, forgive her soul on behalf of the sacrifice which she bore and offered to you, Master, namely me, your unworthy servant. Yes, Lord, Lord God, righteous judge and lover of humanity, do not carry her from oppression to oppression, from distress to distress, and from groanings to groanings, but instead of grief, which she suffered for the sake of her only child, (carry her) to joy, instead of tears, to the rejoicing prepared for your saints, God, my God, forever and ever. Amen."

When they got up from their prayer, brother John began to console him, and said, "Behold, brother Symeon, God has fulfilled your request and given heed to your prayer; He has received your mother. But now, toil together with me, and let us both pray for the Lord's sake, so that God has mercy also on her who, according to God's will was called my wife, so that God either brings her to consideration of the monastic habit or has mercy and takes her." And one night after they had prayed for a little while, [142] John saw Symeon's mother approaching, holding his wife's hand, saying to her, "Arise, my sister, come close to me, for the King who enlisted my son into his service has granted me a beautiful house. But change your garments and put on pure ones." And she got up, he saw, immediately and followed her, and he knew that she also had died and that the two were in a beautiful place, and he rejoiced in a very great joy.

III

After they had spent twenty-nine years in the desert practicing every asceticism and mortification, in cold and in heat, enduring many and unutterable temptations from the Devil and conquering them, and had arrived at a high level (of virtue)—especially Symeon, who, because of his being innocent and very pure on account of the power of the Holy Spirit dwelling within him, perceived himself fearing neither suffering, nor cold, nor hunger, nor burning heat, but rather nearly exceeded the limit of human nature—he said to John, "What more benefit do we derive, brother, from passing time in this desert? But if you hear me, get up, let us depart; let us save others. For as we are, we do not benefit anyone except ourselves, and have not brought anyone else to salvation." And he began to quote to him from the Holy Scripture such things as "Let no one seek his own good, but rather the good of his neighbor" [1 Cor 10:24], and again, "All things to all men, that I might save all" [1 Cor 9:22], and from the Gospel, "Let your light so shine before men, that they may see your good works and give glory to your Father who is in heaven" [Mt 5:16], and other such things. And lord John answered him, "I think, brother, that Satan is jealous of our silence and suggested this thought to you. On the contrary, sit down and let us complete our course in this desert, where we began and where we were called by God." Symeon said to him, "Believe (me), I won't stay, but I will go in the power of Christ; I will mock the world." Again his brother said to him, "No, good brother, please, for the Lord's sake, do not leave wretched me. For I have not yet reached this level, so that I can mock the world. Rather for the sake of Him who joined us, do not wish to be parted from your brother. [143] You know that, after God, I have no one except you, my brother, but I renounced all and was bound to you, and now you wish to leave me in the desert, as in an open sea. Remember that day when we drew lots and went down to lord Nikon, that we agreed not to be separated from each other. Remember the fearful hour when we were clothed in the holy habit, and we two were as one soul, so that all were astonished at our love. Don't forget the words of the great monk, with which he advised us on the night we left. Please don't, lest I die and God demands an account of my soul from you." Again Symeon said to him, "Think of me as dead. Wouldn't you have to think about being alone by yourself? Believe me, if you come, it would be well and good, since I myself am not staying." When brother John saw that he was persistent, he knew that he had been convinced by God to do this, since nothing would separate them except death, and perhaps not even that. For they had often prayed to God, that he would take the two of them together, and they knew that the Lord heard them in this as in all things.

Then John said to him, "Beware, Symeon, lest the Devil wishes to jest with you." Symeon said, "Only, do not forget me in your prayers, just as I won't forget you, and God and your prayers will save me." Again his brother began to admonish him and say, "Beware, be on your guard, brother Symeon, unless as the desert gathered together, the world disperses; and as silence helped, commotion hinders; and as much as keeping watch brought, you lose through sleep. Be on your guard, brother, lest the delusion of worldly things corrupt the prudence of the monastic life. Beware, lest the fruit from the privation of women, from whom God has saved you until today, be destroyed by spending time with them. Beware, lest the love of possessions carry off poverty, lest foods fatten the body, which fasting had melted away. Beware, brother, lest you lose your compunction through laughter and your prayer through your carelessness. Beware, please, lest when your face laughs, your mind be dissolved;[28] lest when your hands fondle,[29] your soul fondles as well; lest when your mouth eats, your heart eats as well; lest when your feet walk, your inner silence dances along recklessly; and to speak concisely, lest as much as the body does outwardly, the soul does inwardly. But if [144] you receive strength entirely from God, brother, so that whatever the forms, or words, or actions the body makes, your mind and your heart remain unmoved and untroubled and in no way are defiled or harmed by them, truly I rejoice in your salvation, if only you would pray to God, so that he won't separate us from each other in the world to come." Then Abba Symeon said to him, "Do not fear, brother John; for it is not by my own (will) that I wish to do this, but because God commands me. And you will know through His help that my work was well-pleasing to God by this: that before I die, I will come and call you and embrace you, and in a few days, you will join me. But get up, and let us pray." And after they had prayed for many hours and kissed each other's breast and drenched them with their tears, John let go of Symeon and traveled together with him a long

28. Or "melted at the same time."

29. ψηλαφάω, "to grope or stroke," probably has sexual connotations here. (In medicine it refers to uterine examinations [cf. LSJ, s.v.].) It is, however, unclear whether it refers here to sex with a partner or to masturbation.

distance. For his soul would not let him be separated from him, but whenever Abba Symeon said to him, "Turn back, brother," he heard the word as if a knife separated him from his body, and again he asked if he could accompany him a little further. Therefore, when Abba Symeon forced him, he turned back to his cell drenching the earth with tears.

Then straightaway Symeon ran ahead to the holy city of Christ our God. For during that time, he thirsted greatly and burned, as he said, yearning to savor Christ's holy places. And arriving at Christ's holy and life-giving tomb, and the holy, saving, and victorious Golgotha, he fulfilled his desire. He remained in the holy city for three days, visiting the Lord's all-holy places, worshipping and praying. And his every prayer was that his works might be hidden until his departure from life, so that he might escape human glory, through which human arrogance and conceit arises, and which also made the angels fall from heaven. For he had heard Him who said, "The righteous cry out, and the Lord hears them" [LXX Ps 33:18, RSV Ps 34:17]. For when he performed [145] such miracles and accomplished such unexpected things, as can be learned from what follows, the pious one's works were not manifest to people. For his request was that, until his death, it might be just as if there was a veil over the hearts of those who saw the things he did. For, I say, indeed, if God did not conceal the blessed one's virtue from people so that they might not glorify him, how was it that he was not manifest to all when he cured those possessed by demons, and again when he held live coals in his hand, (or) when often he predicted the future for some, while to others he announced what had been said about him far away, when in the desert he gathered up nourishment of all sorts miraculously from nowhere, (or) when also he converted Jews or heretics to the right belief or cured the sick, or rescued others from danger? Also he often brought some disreputable women and prostitutes to lawful marriage through his jesting; others he made chaste after captivating them with money; then he spurred them on to pursue the monastic life by means of the purity he had acquired. And I am not surprised, friends of Christ, that he remained unknown while he accomplished these things in God's (name). For He, who often makes the virtues which have been hidden from His servants manifest to all, by His plan also made manifest to all the virtues of this saint which were unknown.

IV

As was said above, after spending three days in the holy places, he arrived in the city of Emesa. The manner of his entry into the city was as fol-

lows: When the famous Symeon found a dead dog on a dunghill outside
the city, he loosened the rope belt he was wearing, and tied it to the dog's
foot. He dragged the dog as he ran and entered the gate, where there was
a children's school nearby. When the children saw him, they began to cry,
"Hey, a crazy abba!" And they set about to run after him and box him on
the ears.

On the next day, which was Sunday, he took nuts, and entering the
church at the beginning of the liturgy, he threw the nuts and put out the
candles. When they hurried [146] to run after him, he went up to the pul-
pit, and from there he pelted the women with nuts. With great trouble,
they chased after him, and while he was going out, he overturned the
tables of the pastry chefs,[30] who (nearly) beat him to death. Seeing himself
crushed by the blows, he said to himself, "Poor Symeon, if things like this
keep happening, you won't live for a week in these people's hands."

According to God's plan, a phouska-seller[31] saw him, who did not
know that he was playing the fool.[32] And he said to him (for he seemed to
be sane), "Would you like, my lord abba,[33] instead of wandering about, to
be set up to sell lupines?"[34] And he said, "Yes." When he set him up one
day, Symeon began to give everything away to people and to eat, himself,
insatiably, for he had not eaten the whole week. The phouska-seller's wife
said to her husband, "Where did you find us this abba? If he eats like this,
it's no use trying to sell anything! For while I observed him, he ate about a
pot full of lupines." But they did not know that he had given away all the
rest of the pots to fellow monks and others—the beans, the lentil soup, the
desert fruits, all of it. They thought that he had sold it. When they opened
the cash box and did not find a single cent, they beat him and fired him,
and pulled his beard. When evening fell he wanted to burn incense.[35]
Now he had not departed from them that evening, but slept there outside
their door. And not finding a shard of pottery, he put his hand in the oven
and filled it with live coals and burned incense. Because God wished to

30. Symeon's behavior recalls Jesus overturning the tables of the money changers in
the courtyard of the temple.

31. The φουσκάριος sold a soup called phouska, which was made with vinegar. (Cf.
Latin posca, a mixture of vinegar, hot water, and eggs.) He is not a "wine merchant" as others
have conjectured. On this point, cf. Rydén, "Style and Historical Fiction in the Life of St. Andreas Salos," DOP 32 (1978): 175–83. Leontius's phouskarios also sells baked beans and
boiled lentils in his stall in the market place. This should probably be understood as rather
humble fare.

32. σαλός.

33. The phouska-seller addresses him as mari abba, a transliteration of the Syriac mry
ab', "my lord abba."

34. θέρμια, a legume notorious for causing gas, and thus the rough equivalent of
"baked beans."

35. Presumably for evening prayer. Cf. Festugière, Vie de Syméon le Fou, pp. 190–91.

save the phouska-seller, for he was a heretic of the Acephalic Severian sect,[36] his wife saw Symeon burning incense in his hand and was very frightened and said, "Good God! Abba Symeon, are you burning incense in your hand?" And when the monk heard this, he pretended to be burned and was shaking the coals in his hand and threw them into the old cloak which he wore, and said to her, "And if you do not want it [147] in my hand, see I will burn incense in my cloak." And as in the presence of the Lord who preserved the bush [Ex 3:2] and the unburnt boys [Dn 3:19 ff.], neither the saint nor his cloak were burned by the coals. And the manner in which the phouska-seller and his wife were saved will be told in another chapter.

It was also the saint's practice, whenever he did something miraculous, to leave that neighborhood immediately, until the deed which he had done was forgotten. He hurried on immediately elsewhere to do something inappropriate, so that he might thereby hide his perfection.

Once he earned his food carrying hot water in a tavern. The tavern keeper was heartless, and he often gave Symeon no food at all, although he had great business, thanks to the Fool. For when the townspeople were ready for a diversion, they said to each other, "Let's go have a drink where the Fool is." One day a snake came in, drank from one of the jars of wine, vomited his venom in it and left. Abba Symeon was not inside; instead he was dancing outside with the members of a circus faction.[37] When the saint came into the tavern, he saw the wine jar, upon which "Death" had been written invisibly. Immediately he understood what had happened to it, and lifting up a piece of wood, he broke the jar in pieces, since it was full. His master took the wood out of his hand, beat him with it until he was exhausted, and chased him away. The next morning, Abba Symeon came and hid himself behind the tavern door. And behold! The snake came to drink again. And the tavern keeper saw it and took the same piece of wood in order to kill it. But his blow missed, and he broke all the

36. That is, he adhered to the theology of Severus of Antioch, a Monophysite who lived from about 465 to about 540. Severus rejected the notion that Christ had suffered hardship. He wrote in Greek, but his works are preserved only in Syriac. His teachings won wide currency in the Syrian churches in the sixth and seventh centuries. Cf. W. H. C. Frend, *The Rise of the Monophysite Movement* (Cambridge: Cambridge University Press, 1972), and John Meyendorff, *Imperial Unity and Christian Division* (Crestwood, N.Y.: St. Vladimir's Seminary, 1989), pp. 252 ff. For an extended discussion of Severus's theology see Roberta Chesnut, *Three Monophysite Christologies* (Oxford: Oxford University Press, 1976), esp. pp. 9–56.

37. δημόταες. Festugière translates "les habitués du cirque" (*Vie de Syméon le Fou*, p. 135) and justifies the translation at length (p. 194). Rydén, however, interpreted the term to mean a member of the crowd, an inhabitant of the city (*Bermerkungen*, pp. 94–96). I have adopted the translation "member of a circus faction" with some reservation. Circus factions were fans of various chariot-racing teams. Cf. Alan Cameron, *Circus Factions* (Oxford: Oxford University Press, 1976).

wine jars and cups. Then the Fool burst in and said to the tavern keeper, "What is it, stupid? See, I am not the only one who is clumsy."[38] Then the tavern keeper understood that Abba Symeon had broken the wine jar for the same reason. And he was edified and considered Symeon to be holy.

Thereupon the saint wanted to destroy his edification, so that the tavern keeper would not expose him. [148] One day when the tavern keeper's wife was asleep alone and the tavern keeper was selling wine, Abba Symeon approached her and pretended to undress. The woman screamed, and when her husband came in, she said to him, "Throw this thrice cursed man out! He wanted to rape me." And punching him with his fists, he carried him out of the shop and into the icy cold. Now there was a mighty storm and it was raining. And from that moment, not only did the tavern keeper think that he was beside himself, but if he heard someone else saying, "Perhaps Abba Symeon pretends to be like this," immediately he answered, "He is completely possessed. I know, and no one can persuade me otherwise. He tried to rape my wife. And he eats meat as if he's godless." For without tasting bread all week, the righteous one often ate meat. No one knew about his fasting, since he ate meat in front of everybody in order to deceive them.

It was entirely as if Symeon had no body, and he paid no attention to what might be judged disgraceful conduct either by human convention or by nature. Often, indeed, when his belly sought to do its private function, immediately, and without blushing, he squatted in the market place, wherever he found himself, in front of everyone, wishing to persuade (others) by this that he did this because he had lost his natural sense. For guarded, as I have often said, by the power of the Holy Spirit which dwelt within him, he was above the burning which is from the Devil and was not harmed by it at all. One day, when the aforementioned virtuous John, the friend of God who narrated this life for us, saw him mortified from his asceticism (for it was the time after Easter and he had passed all of Lent without food), he felt both pity and amazement at the indescribable austerity of Symeon's regimen, although he lived in the city and associated with women and men. And wanting him to refresh his body, John said to him playfully, "Come take a bath, Fool!" And Symeon said to him, laughing, "Yes, let's go, let's go!" And with these words, he stripped off his garment and placed it on his head, wrapping it around like a turban. And Deacon John said to him, "Put it back on, brother, [149] for truly if you are going to walk around naked, I won't go with you." Abba Symeon said to him, "Go away, idiot, I'm all ready. If you won't come, see, I'll go a little

---

38. The meaning of the word ἀπέργης is unclear. Lampe suggests "idle," but Festugière prefers "maladroit." This is the only known occurrence of the term.

ahead of you." And leaving him, he kept a little ahead. However, there were two baths next to each other, one for men and one for women. The Fool ignored the men's and rushed willingly into the women's. Deacon John cried out to him, "Where are you going, Fool? Wait, that's the women's!" The wonderful one turned and said to him, "Go away, you idiot, there's hot and cold water here, and there's hot and cold water there, and it doesn't matter at all whether (I use) this one or that." And he ran and entered into the midst of the women, as in the presence of the Lord of glory. The women rushed against him, beat him, and threw him out. The God-loving deacon (John) asked him, when he told him his whole life, "For God's sake, father, how did you feel when you entered into the women's bath?" He said, "Believe me, child, just as a piece of wood goes with other pieces of wood, thus was I there. For I felt neither that I had a body nor that I had entered among bodies, but the whole of my mind was on God's work, and I did not part from Him." Some of his deeds the righteous one did out of compassion for the salvation of humans, and others he did to hide his way of life.

Then one time (some youths) were outside the city playing lysoporta,[39] of whom one was the son of Symeon's friend, John the deacon, who a few days earlier had fornicated with a married woman. As he was leaving her house, he was possessed by a demon, although no one saw it happen. Therefore the saint wanted both to chasten him and heal him at the same time. And he said to the runners, "Truly, unless you let me play with you, I won't let you run." And they began to throw stones at him. They wanted to take him to the side where the one he wished to cure was running. Seeing this, Abba Symeon went off the opposite way instead. For he knew what he was going to do. And when they began to run, the saint rushed headlong toward the possessed boy and overtook him. When no one was looking, he punched him in the jaw, and said, "Commit adultery no more, wretch, and the Devil won't draw near you." And immediately [150] the demon threw the boy down, and everyone jumped on top of him. As he lay on the ground foaming, the afflicted one saw the Fool chasing a black dog away from him, beating it with a wooden cross. Many hours later, when the youth came to, they asked what happened to him. And he could not say anything except, "Someone said to me, 'Commit adultery no more.'" Only after Abba Symeon had died in peace, as if coming to his senses, the youth narrated the event carefully.

One day, some mimes were putting on a performance in the theater.

39. The game appears to be something like the American children's game red rover. Willem Aerts reports that a game similar to the one described here is still played on Cyprus; "Emesa in der Vita Symeonis Sali von Leontios von Neapolis," in *From Late Antiquity to Early Byzantium*, ed. Vladimír Vavrínek (Prague: Academia, 1985), pp. 114–15.

One of them was a juggler. The righteous one wanted to put a stop to such an evil thing—for the juggler mentioned had done some good deeds—he did not disdain to go, but went and sat below in the arena, where the mimes performed. And when he saw the juggler, he began to do wicked things: He threw a very small stone, after making the sign of the cross on it, and he hit the juggler's right hand, causing it to shrivel up. No one noticed who had thrown the stone. The saint appeared to the juggler that night in a dream and said to him, "Truly I hit the mark, and unless you swear that you will no longer do such things, you won't be healed." So the juggler swore to him by the Mother of God, "I will never again engage in such a game." And when he awoke, he found that his hand was healed. And he related all which he had seen, except that it was the Fool who spoke these things to him in his sleep. He could only say, "Some monk wearing a crown of palm branches said this to me."

Once when a large earthquake was about to seize the city, when Antioch fell, during the time of the faithfully departed Emperor Maurice[40]—for it was then that the saint came down from the desert into the inhabited world—he grabbed a whip from a school and began to strike the pillars and say to each one, "Your master says, 'Remain standing!'" And when the earthquake came, none of the pillars which he struck fell down. However he also went up to one pillar and said to it, "You neither fall nor stand!" And it was split from top to bottom and bent over a bit and stayed that way. No one figured out what the blessed one had done, but everyone said that he struck the pillars because he was out of his mind.

There was this for the glorification and admiration of God: The gestures which caused some to believe that Symeon led an [151] irredeemable life were often those through which he displayed his miracles. For once when a plague was about to come upon the city, he went around to all the schools and began to kiss the children, saying to each of them, as in jest, "Farewell, my dear." He did not kiss all of them, but only those whom the grace of God made known to him. And he said to the teacher at each school, "In God's name, idiot, do not thrash the children whom I kiss, for they have a long way to go." The teachers mocked him, sometimes giving him a whipping; sometimes also the teacher nodded to the children and they ridiculed him publicly. When the plague came, not one of the children whom Abba Symeon had kissed remained alive, but they all died.

It was the saint's habit to enter into the houses of the wealthy and

---

40. On chronology problems created by this passage, see chapter 2. Evagrius, *HE* includes accounts of numerous earthquakes in the eastern Mediterranean in the fifth and sixth centuries (1.17; 2.12, 14; 4.4, 8, 23; 5.17; 6.8). Agathias, *History* 2.15–17 includes a digression on earthquakes throughout the Eastern Mediterranean in the mid-sixth century as well as a discussion of various current theories of the causes of earthquakes.

clown around, often even pretending to fondle their female slaves. For example, one day a certain circus faction member had got a slave girl of one
of the notables pregnant. The slave girl did not want to expose the one
who had fornicated with her, and when her mistress asked her who had
seduced her, the slave girl said, "Symeon the Fool raped me." Therefore,
when he came into the house, according to his custom, the girl's mistress
said to him, "Well, Abba Symeon, so you seduced my slave and got her
pregnant." And immediately he laughed and hid his head in his right
hand and said to her, while at the same time squeezing his five fingers,
"Leave me alone, leave me alone, wretch, soon she will give birth for you,
and you will have a little Symeon!" Until her day arrived, Abba Symeon
kept bringing her wheat bread, meat, and pickled fish, and said, "Eat,
my wife." When the time and the hour for her to give birth came, she
struggled in child-birth for three days and almost died. Then her mistress
said to the Fool, "Pray, Abba Symeon, for your wife cannot give birth." He
said to her, dancing and clapping his hands, "By Jesus, by Jesus, wretch,
the child won't come out from there until [152] she says who its father is."
When the girl in danger heard this she said, "I slandered him. The child
belongs to so-and-so of the circus faction." Immediately then she gave
birth.[41] And while all were amazed, some in the house believed he was a
saint, while others said once again, "He prophesied this because of the
Devil, since he is a complete imbecile."

Two fathers then in a certain monastery near Emesa considered a
question among themselves and inquired why the heretic Origen had
fallen, although honored by God with such knowledge and wisdom.[42]
One said, "The knowledge which he had was not from God, but was a
natural advantage. Furthermore, he had a clever mind, and especially
when he devoted himself to his reading of the Holy Scriptures and to the
holy fathers, he sharpened his mind, and from this he wrote his books."
The other responded, "It is not possible for someone to say the things
which he put forth because of natural advantage (alone), especially the
statements in his Hexapla"—which is why even to this day the catholic
Church accepts them as indispensable. And the first answered again,
"Believe me, the pagans have acquired more wisdom than he and have
written more books than he. What then? Should we also approve them because of their wordy nonsense?" When they could not agree, thus standing their ground to the end, one said to the other, "I hear from those who
have come back from the Holy Places that the desert of the holy Jordan

41. A version of this story is one of the anecdotes about Symeon in Evagrius, *HE* 4.34.
42. One takes a pro-Origen position, the other an anti-Origen position. The anti-
Origenist classifies Origen's achievements with those of pagan wisemen.

has great monks. Let us go and learn from them." Thereupon they came to the Holy Places, and after they had prayed, they went also to the desert of the Dead Sea, in which John and Symeon of everlasting memory had been anchorites. God had not rendered their labors fruitless, for they found Abba John, who still remained there alone and had achieved an even higher level of virtue. When he saw them, he said, "Welcome, you who have left the sea and come to draw water at the dry pool." After having conversed for a long time together about things pleasing to God, they told him why they had made such a journey. And he said to them, "My fathers, I have not yet received the gift to discern God's judgments, but go to Symeon the Fool in your land, and he himself can explain both this and anything else that [153] you wish. Say to him, 'Pray also for John, so that a ten[43] might be cast for him.'" So they went to Emesa and asked where a fool named Symeon was. And everyone laughed at them and said, "What do you want from him, fathers? The man is beside himself, and he abuses and jeers at all of us, particularly monks." They sought him out and found him in the phouska-seller's shop, eating beans like a bear. Immediately one (of the fathers) was scandalized and said to himself, "Truly we have come to see a great sage;[44] this man has much to explain to us."[45] As they approached him, they said to him, "Bless us." He said to them, "You have come at a bad time, and the one who sent you is an idiot." Thereupon he grabbed the ear of the one who had been scandalized and gave him such a blow that (the bruise) could be seen for three days. And he said, "Have you found fault with my beans? They were soaked for forty days, but Origen would not eat them because he plunged into the sea and was not strong enough to get out, and he drowned in the deep." They were amazed that he said all this in advance—and also this, "Does the Fool want the ten? He's as much an idiot as you!—Do you want a kick on the shin?" he said. "Yes, yes, go away." And immediately lifting up a jug of hot wine he burned the two of them on their lips, so that they were unable to repeat what he had told them.

One day while he was in the phouska-seller's shop he picked up a pandora[46] and began to play in an alleyway, where there was an unclean spirit. He played and spoke the prayer of the great Nikon in order to chase the spirit away from the place, for it had abused many. When the spirit fled, it passed through the phouska-shop in the form of an Ethiopian and

43. Such as the lot cast by Symeon earlier in the narrative.
44. γνωστικός: i.e., enlightened one, the perfect monk. Cf. Lampe s.v.; consider the title of Evagrius Ponticus's Ὁ Γνωστικός. Here the term is obviously ironic.
45. ἐξαπλοῦν, perhaps a pun for Hexapla.
46. A stringed instrument much like a lute.

broke everything. The amazing Symeon, when he returned, said to his mistress, "Who [154] broke these things?" She said, "An accursed black man came and smashed everything." He said to her, laughing, "Too bad, too bad." She said, "Yes, indeed, Fool." He said to her, "Truly I sent him, so that he would break everything." When she heard this, she tried to beat him. But ducking down and scooping up a handful of dirt, he threw it in her eyes and blinded her. And the saint said, "Truly, you won't catch me, but either you will take communion in my church, or the black man will break everything every day." For they were members of the sect of Acephalic heretics. After he left her, behold the next day at the same hour, the black man came and again smashed everything in sight. In dire straits, they became Orthodox, taking Symeon to be a sorcerer. They did not dare to tell anyone about him, although every day the Fool came by and jeered at them.

One of the city's artisans wanted to unmask Symeon when he had perceived his virtue. For one time he saw Symeon at the baths conversing with two angels. Now the artisan was a Jew, and he blasphemed Christ all the time.[47] The saint appeared to him in his sleep and told him to say nothing about what he saw. That morning he wanted to expose him, and immediately the saint stood before him, touched his lips, and sealed up his mouth. He was silenced and unable to speak to anyone. He came up to the Fool and gestured to him with his hand to make it so he could speak. But Abba Symeon played the fool[48] and gestured back to him like an idiot. He gestured to him to make the sign of the cross. To see the two of them gesturing to each other was an impressive sight. Symeon appeared to him again in a dream and the monk said, "Either you get baptized, or you will go begging." At that time he refused to obey him, but after Abba Symeon died and the Jew saw the straits he was in, and especially after the (vision he had) at the transporting of the saint's remains,[49] then he was baptized together with his household. And as soon as he came up from the holy font, immediately he spoke. And every year he commemorated the Fool and he invited beggars (to join him).[50]

47. There was an increasing distrust of Jews among Syrian Christians during the early seventh century, presumably because they sympathized with the Persian invasion. For example, see Theophylact Simocatta, *History* 5.6.5–7. On Jews under Byzantine rule in this period see A. Sharf, "Byzantine Jewry in the Seventh Century," *BZ* 48 (1955): 103–15; also Vincent Déroche, "L'Authenticité de l' 'Apologie contre les Juifs' de Léontios de Néapolis," *Bulletin de correspondance hellénique* 110 (1986): 655–69.

48. σαλίζω, a verb derived from σαλός.

49. Leontius is recalling Joseph of Arimathea.

50. While this appears to be an explanation for a cult of Symeon, there is no evidence that such a cult existed.

The blessed one had advanced to such a level of purity and impassivity that often he skipped and danced, holding hands with one dancing-girl[51] [155] on this side and another on that, and he associated with them and played with them in the middle of the whole circus, so that the disreputable women threw their hands into his lap, fondled him, poked him, and pinched him. But the monk, like pure gold, was not defiled by them at all. For, as he said, when he had the burning desire[52] and the battle in the desert, he asked God and the great Nikon, so that they would lift him above the battle with unchastity. And one time he saw the celebrated Nikon coming to him and saying, "How are you, brother?" "And I said to him," Symeon reported, "'Badly, if you hadn't come. For my flesh troubles me, and I don't know why.'" The admirable Nikon, he reported, smiled and took some water from the holy Jordan and put it beneath Symeon's navel sealing the place with the sign of the precious cross. And he said to him, "Behold, you are healed." And from then on, so he swore, neither in his sleep, nor while awake, did he experience burning desire or bodily arousal. And because of this, and especially thus assured, the noble one returned to the world wishing to show compassion for those who were under siege and save them. For sometimes also he would say to one of the courtesans, "Do you want me to make you my girlfriend and give you a hundred gold pieces?" All excited, many were persuaded by him, for he also showed them the money. For he had as much as he wanted, because God supplied him invisibly for the sake of His inspired plan. And moreover he extracted a promise from the one receiving the money, that she would be faithful to him.

He played all sorts of roles foolish and indecent, but language is not sufficient to paint a portrait of his doings. For sometimes he pretended to have a limp, sometimes he jumped around, sometimes he dragged himself along on his buttocks, sometimes he stuck out his foot for someone running and tripped him. Other times when there was a new moon, he looked at the sky and fell down and thrashed about.[53] Sometimes also he pretended to babble, for he said that of all semblances, this one is most fitting and most useful to those who simulate folly[54] [156] for the sake of Christ. For this reason, often he reproved and restrained sins, and he sent divine wrath to someone to correct him, and he made predictions and did everything he wanted, only he changed his voice and (the position of) his limbs completely. And in all that he did, they believed that he was just like the many who babbled and prophesied because of demons. If one day one

---

51. Perhaps a "mime-actress."
52. πύρωσις, surely a euphemism for erection.
53. He behaves literally as a lunatic.   54. μωρία.

of the women whom he called his girlfriends betrayed him, he knew immediately by her spirit[55] whether she had fornicated, and he spoke to her, opening his mouth wide and screaming, "You have lapsed, you have lapsed! Holy Virgin, Holy Virgin, strike her!"[56] And either he prayed that a deadly disease would come to her, or often, if she continued in her unchastity, he would send her a demon. Because of this, henceforward, he got all those who promised him to remain chaste and not betray him.

There was a certain village headman living near Emesa, and when he heard about Symeon's way of life, he said, "Believe me, if I saw him, I would know if he's pretending or if he really is an idiot." Therefore, he came to the city and found Symeon by chance while one prostitute was carrying him and another was whipping him. Immediately the village headman was scandalized, and he reasoned with himself and said in Syriac, "Does Satan himself not believe that this false abba is fornicating with them?" At once, the Fool left the women and came toward the village headman, who was about a stone's throw away from him, and hit him. And stripping off his tunic, he danced naked and whistled. And he said to him, "Come here and play, wretch, there's no fraud here!" By this the man knew that Symeon had seen what was in his heart, and he was amazed. Every time he started to tell someone about this, his tongue was bound, and he was unable to utter a sound.[57]

Symeon possessed the gift of abstinence in a way not many of the saints do. For each time the sacred Lenten fasts came, he did not taste anything until Holy Thursday. From early on the morning of Holy Thursday he sat in the cake shop and gorged himself, so that those who saw him were scandalized since, as they said, "He doesn't fast on Holy Thursday." Now John [157] the deacon knew his behavior was (inspired by) God. When he saw him on Holy Thursday sitting in the cake shop having eaten since early morning, he said to him, "How much does it cost, Fool?" And he said to him, holding forty noumia in his hand, "Here's my follis, stupid," showing that he was eating after forty days (of fasting).[58]

55. Or, perhaps, "by *his* spirit."

56. ἁγία ἁγία. It is unclear who the holy woman called on is, but the Theotokos seems most likely. Cf. Rydén, *Bemerkungen*, p. 113. On the increasing importance of Mary in Late Antiquity and the Early Middle Ages, see Averil Cameron, "The Theotokos in Sixth Century Constantinople," *JThS* n.s. 29 (1978): 79–108, and "The Virgin's Robe: An Episode in the History of Early Seventh-Century Constantinople," *Byzantion* 49 (1979): 42–56.

57. The language here recalls binding spells. See H. J. Magoulias, "The Lives of Byzantine Saints as Sources of Data for the History of Magic in the Sixth and Seventh Centuries A.D.: Sorcery, Relics, and Icons," *Byzantion* 37 (1967): 228–69, and John G. Gager, ed., *Curse Tablets and Binding Spells from the Ancient World* (New York: Oxford University Press, 1992), esp. pp. 116–50.

58. One follis equals forty noumia. Symeon had not eaten for forty days.

Once again a demon was haunting another part of town. One day, while he was walking around, the saint saw it trying to strike one of the passersby. And taking stones from his pocket Symeon began to throw them every which way into the marketplace, and he turned back everyone who wanted to go across. At this moment, a dog passed by, and the demon struck it and (the dog) began to foam. Then the saint said to everyone, "Go on now, idiots!" For the all-wise one knew that if someone had gone across, the demon would have struck him instead of the dog. It was for this reason that he stopped them from crossing for a short while.

As I already said before, the all-wise Symeon's whole goal was this: first, to save souls, whether through afflictions which he sent them in ludicrous or methodical ways, or through miracles which he performed while seeming not to understand, or through maxims which he said to them while playing the fool; and second, that his virtue not be known, and he receive neither approval nor honor from men. For example, one day when some little girls were dancing and singing satiric songs,[59] he got the idea to pass through that street. When they saw him, they began to lampoon monks. The righteous one prayed, wishing to make them learn, and immediately God made all of them cross-eyed. And when they began to tell each other the bad thing which had happened to them, they knew that it was Symeon who had made them cross-eyed, and they ran after him, wailing behind him, and they cried, "Loose us, Fool, loose us!"[60] For they thought that he had made them squint with a spell. When they caught up to him, they seized him with force and they commanded the one who, they said, bound them to loose them. Then he said to them, joking, "You will be cured of such things; I will kiss your crossed eyes and heal them." Then all of them, said the saint, whom God wanted to be healed, consented, but the rest did not let him kiss them, and they stayed cross-eyed and wailed. Then a little while after [158] he left them, and the others began to run after him and cry, "Wait, Fool, wait! By God, wait! Kiss us too!" One can just see the monk running with the young girls behind him! And some people said that they were playing with him, while others thought that the girls too had been driven insane. Thus they remained permanently unhealed. For the saint said, "Unless God had made them cross-eyed, they would have exceeded all the women of Syria in debauchery. But through the disease of their eyes they gave up all their evil."

Once his friend, Deacon John, invited him to lunch, and they were hanging salted meats there. So Abba Symeon began to knock down the

59. Literally "dancing and making charges," but see Festugière, *Vie de Syméon le Fou*, p. 209.
60. The language again reflects that of binding spells.

raw meat and eat it. The all-wise John, not wanting to say anything to him with a loud voice, drew near his ear and said to him, "You really don't scandalize me, (even) if you eat raw camel. Do whatever you'd like with the rest." For he knew the Fool's virtue, because he also was a spiritual person.

Once some Emesans went to the holy city during Eastertide to celebrate the feast. One of them descended to the holy Jordan to pray. And when he visited the caves he gave gifts to the fathers. It happened that Abba John, Abba Symeon's brother, met the Emesan merchant in the desert by God's design. When the merchant saw him, he threw himself on the ground, begging for a blessing from him. Abba John said to him, "Where do you come from?" The merchant said to him, "From Emesa, father." Then he asked him, "And as long as you have Abba Symeon called the Fool there, what do you seek from wretched me? For I too have need of his prayers, as does the whole world." And Abba John took the merchant into his cave and set an abundant table before him. Everything he had was from God. For where in that parched desert can [159] white bread, hot fried fish, first-rate wine, and a full wine jar be found?[61] After they ate and had had their fill, John gave him a gift of three spiced fish,[62] which had also come from God, and said, "Give these to the Fool, and say to him for me, 'For the Lord's sake, pray for your brother John.'" Then the Lord's truth was confirmed: When the merchant came to Emesa, Abba Symeon met him at the city gate and said to him, "What is it, idiot? How is Abba John, who is a fool like you? Didn't you eat the gifts which he gave you? Really, really, if you ate all three, you have digested them badly." The merchant was astounded when he heard everything which he wanted to say coming out of Symeon's mouth. The Fool immediately took him into his hut, and the merchant affirmed confidently that "Everything he set before me was exactly the same as Abba John had," even the size of the wine jar, which he had seen in John's cave. "And after we ate, I gave him the three gifts and returned to my house, embarrassed to tell anyone anything about him, since everyone was convinced that he was an idiot."

I said before that he performed a miracle for the God-loving man who also narrated this life for us. The manner of the miracle was this: Some criminals committed a murder, and taking the corpse, they threw it through the window into the house of that most God-beloved man. This

61. Fish, bread, and wine, of course, are the things which Jesus feeds to the multitudes in unlimited supply.

62. Festugière translates ζεστά here not as "fish," but as "bread," although he translates it as "fish" in the line before. The point must be that the fish were well spiced, since they might give one indigestion.

caused not a little trouble: the matter came to the attention of the governor, and he decided that Deacon John should be hanged. When he went off to be executed, he said to himself nothing other than, "God of the Fool, help me, God of the Fool, stand beside me in this hour." Because the Lord wanted to save him from this false accusation, someone went and said to Abba Symeon, "You, wretched one, this friend of yours, Deacon John, is going to be hanged, and truly, if he dies, you will die of hunger, for no one looks out for you as he does." He also told him about the false charge of [160] murder. Then Abba Symeon, playing the idiot, according to his custom, left the man who had told him, and he retired to his hiding place, where he used to pray all the time, which no one knew about except his friend, God's beloved John. And on bended knee he beseeched God that his servant might be delivered from such danger. And when those who led him out to be hanged came to the place where they were going to erect his gallows, behold! the cavalrymen ran up and said that the man should be released because those who really committed the murder had been discovered. As soon as John was free he ran straight to the place where he knew Abba Symeon prayed all the time. And seeing him from afar stretching out his hands to heaven, he was afraid. For he swore that he saw balls of fire going up from him to heaven, "And round about him, like a baker's oven with him in the middle,[63] so that I did not dare to approach him, until he had finished his prayer. And he turned and saw me, and he immediately said to me, 'What is it, Deacon? By Jesus, by Jesus, you almost drank it.[64] But go and pray. This trial came to pass because yesterday two beggars came to you, and although you were quite able to give to them, you turned them away. The things which you give, are they yours, brother? Or do you not believe in Him who said that you will receive a hundredfold in this age and eternal life in the age to come [cf. Mt 19:29]? If you believe, give. And if you don't give, it will be manifest that you don't believe in the Lord.'" Behold the words of a fool, or rather of a holy wise man. For concerning this Deacon John, when the two found themselves alone together, the old man did not act like a fool at all, but he conversed with him so gracefully and with such compunction,[65] that often perfume came from his mouth,[66] as Deacon John maintained, "such that I almost doubted that he had been a fool only moments before."

63. Cf. *Martyrdom of Polycarp* 15.
64. Cf. Mt 26:42.
65. κατανενυγμένως. The word is found only in Leontius, and its meaning is unclear. I have followed Festugière (*Vie de Syméon le Fou*, p. 150) in translating it "with such compunction."
66. This is usually only the case with dead saints.

But he behaved otherwise before the crowd. For sometimes when Sunday came, he took a string of sausages and wore them as a (deacon's) stole. [161] In his left hand he held a pot of mustard, and he dipped (the sausages in the mustard) and ate them from morning on. And he smeared mustard on the mouths of some of those who came to joke with him. Wherefore also a certain rustic, who had leucoma in his two eyes, came to make fun of him. Symeon anointed his eyes with mustard. The man was nearly burned to death,[67] and Symeon said to him, "Go wash, idiot, with vinegar and garlic, and you will be healed immediately." As it seemed a better thing to do, he ran immediately to a doctor instead and was completely blinded. Finally, in a mad rage he swore in Syriac, "By the God of Heaven, even if my two eyes should suddenly leap (from their sockets), I will do whatever the Fool told me." And he washed himself as Symeon told him. Immediately his eyes were healed, clear as when he was born, so that he honored God.[68] Then the Fool came upon him and said to him, "Behold, you are healed, idiot! Never again steal your neighbor's goats."[69]

Someone in Emesa stole a sum of five hundred gold pieces, and when (the owner) looked for them, Abba Symeon came upon him, and the man, wishing to encourage himself, said to him, "Can you do something, idiot, so that the coins are found?" And Symeon said to him, "If you wish, yes." And he said to him, "Do it, and if they are found, I will give you ten." The Fool said to him, "Do everything I tell you, and you will find them in your money chest tonight." So he promised him with an oath that he would obey him in anything he might say, except if he told him to do something indecent. Symeon said again, "Go, the slave who is your cupbearer took your money. But behold, give me word that you won't thrash him nor anyone else in your house." For he thrashed them brutally. The other one thought that it was only in regard to the coins that he told him not to [162] thrash anyone. But Abba Symeon said this to him so that the man would *never* thrash his slaves. So the man gave Symeon his word with terrible oaths that he would not thrash anyone. And when he returned, he took his slave aside gently and got the money back from him. Then after this, sometimes he would be about to thrash someone and was not able to, but instantly his hand grew numb. And understanding why, he said, "Truly I

67. The meaning here is unclear. Literally, the man is "contracted to death"; however, this must not refer to his whole body but rather only to his eyes.

68. Cf. Jn 9:1–11.

69. αἰγίδια. This word usually means "goat kids," but it can also mean "eye salve," as it does in the writings of the sixth-century doctor, Aëtius of Amida (7.103) (cf. LSJ, s.v.). Consider also that αἰγίς, usually a "goatskin," refers to a "speck in the eye" in the Hippocratic corpus (cf. LSJ, s.v.). Given the context, this is probably meant as a pun.

have the Fool to thank for this." And he went to him and said, "Loose the oath, Fool." And immediately Symeon played the fool and pretended that he did not know what the man was saying to him. When the man continued to bother him, Symeon appeared to him in his sleep and said to him, "Truly, if I loose the oath, I will loose your money and disperse all of it. Would you disgrace yourself? Why do you want to thrash your fellow slaves who precede you in the age to come?" When he saw this, he ceased thrashing his slaves.

Symeon had extraordinary compassion for those possessed by demons, so that from time to time he went off to make himself like one of them, and passed his time with them, healing many of them through his own prayer, and therefore some daimoniacs cried out and said, "O violence, Fool, you jeer at the whole world. Have you also come by us to give us trouble? Retreat from here; you are not one of us. Why do you torture us all night long and burn us?" While the saint was there (in Emesa), he cried out against many because of the Holy Spirit and reproached thieves and fornicators. Some he faulted, crying that they had not taken communion often, and others he reproached for perjury, so that through his inventiveness he nearly put an end to sinning in the whole city.

During this time there was a woman clairvoyant and maker of amulets who performed incantations. The righteous one contrived to have her as a girlfriend and gave her things he had collected from those who gave him presents, whether coins or bread or even clothing. Then one day [163] he said to her, "Do you want me to make you an amulet so that you will never be touched by the evil eye?" And she said to him, "Yes, Fool," reasoning that although he was a fool, perhaps he would succeed. So he went off and wrote in Syriac on a tablet, "May God render you impotent and stop you from turning his people away from him and toward yourself." Then he gave it to her, and she wore it. And she was no longer able to make anyone either oracles or amulets.[70]

Another time he was sitting with his brothers (in poverty) and warming himself near a glassblower's furnace. The glassblower was Jewish. And Symeon said to the beggars, joking, "Do you want me to make you laugh? Behold, I will make the sign of the cross over the drinking glass which the craftsman is making, and it will break." When he had broken about seven, one after the other, the beggars began to laugh, and they told the glassblower about the matter, and he chased Symeon away, branding him. As he left, Symeon screamed at the glassblower, saying, "Truly, bas-

---

70. The amulet would have contained a piece of silver, gold, or papyrus with the text written on it.

tard,[71] until you make the sign of the cross on your forehead, all your glasses will be shattered." And again after the (glassblower) broke thirteen others, one after the other, he was shattered[72] and made the sign of the cross on his forehead. And nothing ever broke again. And because of this, he went out and became a Christian.

Once ten circus fans were washing their clothes outside the city. The blessed one came up to them and said, "Come here, idiots, and I will prepare a sumptuous lunch for you." The five of them said, "God knows! Let's go." But the rest prevented them, saying, "Sure, he's going to prepare us lunch from nothing.[73] This man begs from door to door, and where does he get anything? He only wants us to stop working." The five, however, believed and went off. And he said to them, "Wait here." And he left them alone and went about an arrow's flight away from them,[74] and hiding himself, prayed. Then they said among themselves, "Truly we have been tricked. For I think that Abba Symeon wants to bring us grass so that we may graze."[75] And behold, when [164] they said this, they saw him motioning them to come toward him. For he had prayed, as I said, and with God's help he had prepared everything. When they came to him they found, as before the Lord, lying in front of him wheat bread, flat cakes, meat balls, fish, excellent wine, fried cakes, jam, and simply everything tasty which life has (to offer). And while they ate, he said, "Wretches, take some also for your wives. And if you will stop being idiotic circus fans, truly this wheat bread will not be lacking in your houses until I die." They said to each other as they left, "Let us test it for a week and if the wheat bread does not stop, let us go no more with our companions to the circus." Then when they saw that the wheat bread did not stop even though they ate from it every day, they no longer took part in bad things, and three of them became monks, spurred on by the Fool's conduct.[76] But while the Fool lived in the flesh, they were unable to tell anyone anything about this.

It is worth relating in my writing about Symeon the thing he did for a certain wretched but worthy mule driver. For the mule driver was merci-

---

71. μάνζηρε = *mamzere*, a Hebrew word (cf. *mamzer* in Modern Hebrew) which does not appear in Syriac. Festugière (*Vie de Syméon le Fou*, p. 214) postulates that this word was still used as an insult among Jews. However, its occurrence in a Christian text suggests that it was known to Jews and Christians alike in seventh-century Cyprus.

72. Leontius identifies the Jew with the shattered glass.

73. Literally, "out of darkness."

74. Presumably more than a stone's throw.

75. A reference to the Grazers (βοσκοί) of the first half of the text.

76. It is unclear whether this means that they too became fools or merely became monks.

ful and through a series of accidents had bad luck in business. Then one day, when he had gone out to bring wine for his house and to sell, the blessed one met him and said to him, "Where are you going, idiot?" For he always had these words in the same way on his lips. Then the mule driver said to him, "For wine, Fool." Abba Symeon answered him, "Bring fleabane[77] too, when you come back." Regarding this as a bad omen, the mule driver then said to himself, as he went away, "What sort of Satan sent me this abba early in the morning saying to me, 'Bring me fleabane'? Truly this wine will spoil and either turn to vinegar or I don't know what." When he returned bringing very good wine, in his joy he forgot to bring the fleabane. Abba Symeon met him at the gate and said to him, "What is it, idiot? Did you bring the fleabane?" Again the mule driver said to him, "Truly, wretch, I forgot it." The Abba said to him smiling, [165] "Just go away, your matter is taken care of." Later, when he went to unload the wineskins, he discovered that they were (full of) vinegar so foul that a person might die smelling it. Then he understood that Abba Fool had done this, and he began to say, "Truly now, now let's go for the fleabane." Then he ran and went to the Fool and entreated—for he said that just as the juggler does an optical illusion, thus had Symeon done— "Unbind what you've done, Fool." He said to him, "What did I do?" He said, "I bought good wine, and after two hours it was found to be vinegar." And again Symeon said, "Go, go, it doesn't matter to you! Quickly, open a tavern and it will turn you profit." For the old man's aim and prayer was that the mule driver's toils might be blessed, because he was merciful. However, Symeon did not want to do anything in a clear manner; instead he always did things through clowning. Then the mule driver gave up and said, "Blessed be God, I will open a tavern." And when he opened it, God blessed him. And instead of thanking the Fool for these things, he was angry with him, for he did not know what Symeon had brought about for him. In this whole matter, God hid Abba Symeon's plan.

Once, one of the city's great men fell ill. The saint was in the habit of entering his house and clowning around. And when he was burdened (by illness) almost to death, he saw himself in his sleep playing dice with an Ethiopian, who was death. The sick man's turn came and, he said, he was about to roll the dice, and unless he threw a triple six, he would lose. Then Abba Symeon appeared to him in his sleep and said, "What is it, idiot? Truly this black man is about to beat you. But give me your word, that you will no longer soil your wife's bed,[78] and I will roll instead of you, and he

77. Or perhaps "pennyroyal."
78. It is unclear whether Symeon is demanding abstinence within marriage or merely marital fidelity.

won't beat you." "I swore," the one who saw this said, "and he took the dice from me, [166] rolled, and they fell triple six." The sick man woke up, and immediately the Fool went up and said to him, "You threw a beautiful triple six, stupid.[79] Believe me, if you transgress your oath, that black man will choke you." And after Symeon had insulted him and all those in his house, he left, running.

This wise man truly kept nothing in his hut—for he had a hut to sleep in, or rather in which to stay awake at night—except for one bundle of twigs. Often he passed the night without sleeping, praying until morning, drenching the ground with his tears. He went out in the early morning and cut branches either from an olive tree or shrub, and made himself a crown, and he wore it and held a branch in his hand and danced, crying, "Victory for the emperor and for the city!" But he said "the city" for the sake of the soul, and "the emperor" for the sake of the mind.

Also, the saint begged God that neither the hair on his head nor his beard should grow, lest in his having it cut, it become known that he was (only) playing the fool. Therefore, during all the time when he was continuing to behave this way, no one saw the hair on his head grow or saw him cut it.

He often carried on very helpful conversations with John the deacon alone, and threatened that if he unmasked him, he would meet with great torture in the coming age. Symeon said to the deacon, when he related his whole life to him just two days before he was translated from this life, "Today I went off to my brother John, and, thanks to God, I found him to have made great progress, and I was overjoyed. For I saw him wearing a crown upon which was written, 'Crown of patience in the desert.' And that blessed one said, 'I saw you, when you were coming, as someone who says to you, "Go away, go away, Fool," for you win not one crown, but the crowns of those souls whom you offer me.' But I maintain, Mister Archdeacon, that he saw nothing on me such as (I saw), but rather he was being gracious with me. For the Fool, who is an idiot, what sort of reward does he have to carry off?" And he spoke again, "I beg you, never disregard a single soul, [167] especially when it happens to be a monk or a beggar. For Your Charity knows that His place is among the beggars, especially among the blind, people made as pure as sun through their patience and distress. Such country peasants as I often saw in the city, coming in to receive communion,[80] are purer than gold on account of their innocence and simplicity, and by the sweat of their brow, they eat their bread [cf. Gn 3:19]. But do not blame me at all for what I say to you, master. For my

79. μάταιος.
80. There were few churches in the countryside, so peasants came to town on Sundays and festivals.

love for you compels me to relate to you also all the carelessness of my miserable life. Know that the Lord will soon receive you as well. But as long as you have the strength and the power, take thought for your own soul, so that you are able to pass by the worldly rulers of this airy darkness [cf. Eph 6:12]. For the Lord knows that I have much anxiety and fear until I am free from the cares which come from them. For that is the evil day about which the apostle and David spoke [cf. Eph 6:13; LXX Ps 40:2, RSV Ps 41:1]. For this reason I beg you, my child and brother John, with all your might, if possible beyond your might, show love for your neighbor through almsgiving. For this virtue, above all, will help us on that day. For it says, 'Blessed is he who meets with the poor, the Lord delivers him on the evil day' [LXX Ps 40:2, RSV Ps 41:1]. I ask this also of you: never approach the holy altar holding anything against someone else, lest your transgression make others also unworthy of the visitation of the Holy Spirit." These and many other things Symeon exhorted him; among them he begged for something which he never spoke to anyone, because not all received his words with faith: "Comfort yourself, for during these three days, the Lord will receive His most humble Fool and John, his brother. For I myself went to say to him, 'Brother, come, let us go, now is the time.' But after two days come to my hut and see what you find. For I want you to have a memento of the humble and sinful Fool." And when he had said these and many more things to him, he left and withdrew into his hut.

Now the time calls, O Friends, to narrate to you his marvelous death, [168] or rather sleep. For his death does not present ordinary edification, but it was more remarkable than everything I said before. It became both seal and guarantee of his triumph and confirmation that his behavior did not defile him. For when the great one perceived the profane hour, not wanting to obtain human honor after his death, what did he do? He went inside, lay down to sleep underneath the bundle of twigs in his sacred hut, and committed his spirit to the Lord in peace. When they had not seen him for two days, those who knew him said, "Let's go, let us visit the Fool in case he's ill." And they went and found him lying dead under his bundle of twigs. Then they said, "Now all will believe that he was beside himself. Behold his death is another idiocy."[81] And two of them lifted him up without washing him, and they went out without psalm singing, candles, or incense, and buried him in the place where strangers are buried.[82] Then when those who were bearing him and going out to bury

81. κατάσκαλμος. The meaning of this word is unclear. Cf. Festugière (*Vie de Syméon le Fou*, p. 221), who translates "enfouissement." I have chosen to follow Aerts, *Leven van Symeon de Dwaas* (Bonheiden, Belgium: Monastieke Cahiers, 1990), p. 87.

82. Symeon was a stranger in Emesa, not a resident, so this is perfectly sensible. Cf. *Life of the Man of God* where the Man of God is also buried in the strangers' cemetery.

him passed the house of the formerly Jewish glassblower, whom Symeon had made a Christian, as I said before, the aforementioned former Jew heard psalm singing,[83] music such as human lips could not sing, and a crowd such as all humanity could not gather. This man was astounded by the verse and the crowd. He glanced out and saw the saint carried out by the two men and them alone bearing his precious body. Then the one who heard the invisible music said, "Blessed are you, Fool, that while you do not have humans singing psalms for you, you have the heavenly powers honoring you with hymns." And immediately he went down and buried him with his own hands. And then he told everyone what he had heard in the angel's songs. John the deacon heard this and went running, with many others, to the place where he was buried, wishing to take up his precious remains in order to bury him honorably. But when they opened the grave, they did not find him. For the Lord had glorified him and translated him. Then all came to their senses,[84] as if from sleep, and told each other what miracles he had performed for each of them and that he had played the fool for God's sake.

[169] Such, O friend of Christ, was the life and conduct of this wondrous Symeon. Such were a few of his virtues collected from the many. Such truly was his hidden and heavenly course which no one saw, but which was suddenly found manifest to all. Such was the new Lot, just like the one in Sodom [cf. Gn 19:1 ff.] who thus went secretly in the world unseen. I was eager to commit his miracles and his praiseworthy victory-prize to writing, as far as it is possible for me in my worthlessness, even though I had already done another shorter one in addition to this, because detailed knowledge of this marvelous story had not yet come to me. Honoring him with encomia does not result from my knowledge, but from that of those to whom the power belongs also to compete with his virtue. For what language could praise one who is honored beyond language, or how can fleshly lips (praise) one who, while in the flesh, appeared plainly without flesh?[85] How can the wisdom of the tongue praise the one who obliterated all wisdom and prudence in the folly according to God? Truly human in face, but God in heart. Truly God will not see thus as a human sees. Truly no one knows a person's deeds without knowing the person's spirit. Truly we must not judge someone before the time, O friends of Christ, before the Lord comes and illuminates everything. Who knew, friends of Christ, that Judas who lived with the disciples in his body was

83. On the problem of which of the Jews mentioned earlier in the text is meant here, see chapter 2.

84. They were fools not to have seen Symeon's true nature.

85. I.e., free from carnal appetites.

with the Jews in his heart? Who in Jericho supposed that Rahab who was in a brothel in body was in the Lord in spirit [cf. Jos 2:1ff.]? Who had hoped that that beggar Lazarus who lived suffering such sores would be in such health in Abraham's bosom [cf. Lk 16:20ff.]? Knowing these things, beloved friends, let us also obey the one who counseled well, "Attend to yourself alone," neither to your family, nor those around you, but to yourself alone, because each carries his own [170] burden and will receive his own wages from the hand of Christ the heavenly king, to whom are glory and power with the Father and the All-holy Spirit forever and ever. Amen.

Having lived the angelic and most admirable life on earth, Symeon, who for Christ's sake was named Fool, died on July 21, having shone exceedingly in his achievements according to God and astounded even the supernatural powers of the angels with his virtues. And when he received confidence, he placed himself at the insufferable throne of God and Father of lights, and he honored Him in unceasing hymns along with all the heavenly powers. May the Lord grant us part and portion with this holy Symeon, and with all the saints in His eternal kingdom, for His is the glory forever and ever. Amen.

BIBLIOGRAPHY

Primary Sources

Note: Translations are cited below text editions.

Aelian. *Varia Historia*. Ed. Rudolph Hercher. Leipzig: Teubner, 1887.

Aëtius of Amida. *Libri Medicinales I–VIII*. 2 vols. Ed. Alexander Olivieri. Corpus Medicorum Graecorum 8. Leipzig: Teubner, 1950.

Agathias. *Agathiae Myrinaei historiarum libri quinque*. Ed. Rudolf Keydell. Corpus fontium bizantinae 2. Berlin: de Gruyter, 1967.

Anan-Isho. *The Paradise of the Fathers*. In *Book of Paradise, being the histories and sayings of the monks and ascetics of the Egyptian desert by Palladius, Hieronymus and others. The Syriac texts, according to the recension of Anân Ishô of Bêth Abhê . . . .* 2 vols. Ed. and trans. E. A. Wallis Budge. Lady Meux Manuscript 6. London: Drugulin, 1904. Translation republished as *The Paradise or Garden of the Holy Fathers . . .* , 2 vols. (London: Chatto and Windus, 1907).

Anastasius the Sinaite. "Le texte grec des récits utile à l'âme d'Anastase (le Sinaïte)." Ed. F. Nau. *Oriens Christianus* 3 (1903): 56–90.

Anthologia Palatina. In *The Greek Anthology*. 5 vols. Ed. W. R. Paton. LCL. London: Heinemann, 1927–60.

Apollonius Sophista. *Lexicon Homericum*. 2 vols. Ed. J. C. Molini. Paris, 1773.

Apophthegmata Patrum. PG 65.71–440.

———. *The Sayings of the Desert Fathers: The Alphabetical Collection*. Trans. Benedicta Ward. Kalamazoo: Cistercian, 1975.

Artemidorus. *Oneirocritica*. Ed. R. A. Pack. Leipzig: Teubner, 1963.

———. *The Interpretation of Dreams*. Trans. R. White. Park Ridge, N.J.: Noyes, 1975.

Athanasius. *Oratio de incarnatione Verbi*. PG 25.95–198.

————. *Life of Antony.* PG 26.835–976.

————. *The Life of Saint Antony.* Trans. Robert T. Meyer. ACW 10. New York: Newman, 1978.

Athenaeus. *The Deipnosophists.* 7 vols. Ed. Charles Burton Gulick. LCL. London: Heinemann, 1927–41.

Augustine. *De civitate dei.* PL 41.13–804.

————. *City of God.* Trans. John O'Meara. London: Penguin, 1984.

Aulus Gellius. *Attic Nights.* 3 vols. Ed. John C. Rolfe. LCL. London: Heinemann, 1927.

al-Balâdhuri, abu'l Abbâs Ahmad ibn-Jâbir [Ahmad ibn Yahya]. *The Origins of the Islamic State* (Kitâb futûh al-buldân). Trans. Philip K. Hitti. Studies in History, Economics, and Public Law 163. New York: Columbia University Press, 1916.

Basil of Caesarea. *Letters.* 4 vols. Ed. R. J. Deferrari and Martin R. P. McGuire. LCL. Cambridge: Harvard University Press, 1961–62.

————. *Ad adolescentes de legendis libris gentilium. Saint Basil on the Value of Greek Literature.* Ed. N. G. Wilson. London: Duckworth, 1975.

————. *Sermo asceticus.* PG 31.869–881.

Chronicon anoymum ad annum domini 819 pertinens. Trans. J.-B. Chabot. CSCO 109; Scriptores Syri 3.14. Louvain: Durbecq, 1937.

Cicero. *De divinatione. De senectute, De amicitia, De divinatione.* Ed. William Armstead Falconer. LCL. Cambridge: Harvard University Press, 1938.

Clement of Alexandria. *Opera.* Ed. O. Stählin. Die griechischen christlichen Schriftsteller der ersten drei Jahrhunderte, 12, 15, 17, 39. Leipzig: Hinrichs, 1905–9.

————. *Le Pédagogue.* 3 vols. Ed. M. Harl. SC 70, 108, 158. Paris: Cerf, 1960–70.

Damascius. *Damascii vitae Isidori reliquiae.* Ed. Clemens Zintzen. Hildesheim: Olms, 1967.

Daniel of Skete. *Vie (et récits) de l'Abbé Daniel le Scétiote.* Ed. Léon Clugnet. Paris: Picard et Fils, 1901.

Dio Chrysostom. *Discourses.* Ed. J. W. Cohoon. LCL. London: Heinemann, 1932.

Diogenes Laertius. *Lives of the Philosophers. Lives of Eminent Philosophers.* 2 vols. Ed. R. D. Hicks. LCL. London: Heinemann, 1925.

Pseudo-Dionysius of Tell-Mahre. *Incerti auctoris chronicon anonymum pseudo-Dionysianum vulgo dictum.* Ed. and trans. J.-B. Chabot. CSCO 91/43, 121/66, 104/53. Louvain: Durbecq, 1927–49.

Doctrina Jacobi nuper baptizati. Ed. F. Nau. PO 8 (1912): 711–80.

————. "Juifs et Chrétiens dans l'Orient du viie siècle." Ed. Gilbert Dagron and Vincent Déroche. *Travaux et mémoires* 11 (1991): 70–229.

Egeria. *Egeria's Travels to the Holy Land.* Trans. John Wilkinson. London: S.P.C.K., 1971.

Ephrem the Syrian. *Hymns.* Ed. and trans. Kathleen E. McVey. New York: Paulist, 1989.

Epictetus. *Discourses.* 2 vols. Ed. W. A. Oldfather. LCL. London: Heinemann, 1928–65.

Epistles of Diogenes. The Cynic Epistles: A Study Edition. Ed. Abraham J. Malherbe and trans. Benjamin Fiore. Atlanta: Scholars, 1977, pp. 92–183.

Etymologicum magnum. Ed. Frederic Sylburg. Leipzig: Wiegel, 1816.

Eulogius of Alexandria. *Eis ta Baia.* PG 86/2.2913–37.

Eunapius. *Lives of the Sophists.* In *Philostratus and Eunapius.* Ed. W. C. Wright. LCL. Cambridge: Harvard University Press, 1952.

Eusebius of Caesarea. *Preparatio Evangelica.* Ed. Karl Mras. Die griechischen christlichen Schriftsteller der ersten drei Jahrhunderte 43. Berlin: Akademie-Verlag, 1956.

Eutychius. *Annals.* PG 111.907–1156.

———. *Gli Annali.* Trans. Bartolomeo Pirone. Studia Orientalia Christiana Monographiae 1. Cairo: Franciscan Centre, 1987.

———. *Das Annalenwerk des Eutychios von Alexandrien.* Ed. Michael Breydy. CSCO 45. Louvain: Peeters, 1985.

Evagrius Ponticus. *The Praktikos and Chapters on Prayer.* Trans. John Eudes Bamberger. Spencer, Mass.: Cistercian, 1970.

———. *Traité pratique ou le moine.* Ed. and trans. A. and C. Guillaumont. SC 170, 171. Paris: Cerf, 1971.

Evagrius Scholasticus. *The Ecclesiastical History of Evagrius with the Scholia.* Ed. J. Bidez and L. Parmentier. 1898. Reprint, New York: AMS, 1979.

———. *Ecclesiastical History.* In *A History of the Church from A.D. 322 to the Death of Theodore of Mopsuestia, A.D. 427 by Theodoret, Bishop of Cyrus, and from A.D. 431 to A.D. 594 by Evagrius.* London: Bohn, 1854.

George of Pisidia. *Heraclias.* In *Poemi, I: Panegirici epici.* Ed. A. Pertusi. Studia patristica et byzantina 7. Ettal: Buch-Kunst Verlag, 1960.

George of Sykeon. *Vie de Théodore de Sykéon.* 2 vols. Ed. André-Jean Festugière. Subsidia Hagigraphica 48. Brussels: Société des Bollandistes, 1970.

———. *Life of Theodore of Sykeon.* In *Three Byzantine Saints.* Trans. Elizabeth Dawes and Norman H. Baynes. Crestwood, N.Y.: St. Vladimir's Seminary, 1977, pp. 88–192.

Gnomologium Vaticanum e Codice Vaticano Graeco. Ed. Leo Sternbach. Berlin: de Gruyter, 1963.

Gregory of Nazianzus. *Carmina.* PG 37.397–1600.

———. *De vita sua.* Ed. Christoph Jungck. Heidelberg: Winter, 1974.

———. *Three Poems.* Trans. Denis Malaise Meehan. FOTC 75. Washington, D.C.: Catholic University Press, 1987.

———. *Briefe.* Ed. Paul Gallay. Berlin: Akademie-Verlag, 1969.

———. *Briefe.* Trans. Michael Wittig. Bibliothek der griechischen Literatur 13. Stuttgart: Herisemann, 1981.

———. *Discours.* Ed. Justin Mossay et al. SC 284. Paris: Cerf, 1978.

Gregory of Nyssa. *Life of Macrina.* PG 46.960–1000.

———. *The Life of Saint Macrina.* Trans. Kevin Corringan. Toronto: Peregrina, 1987.

Hesychius of Alexandria. *Lexicon.* 2 vols. Ed. Kurt Latte. Copenhagen: Munksgaard, 1953.

Hippocrates. *Regimen*. In *Hippocrates*, vol. 4, ed. W. H. S. Jones. LCL. London: Heinemann, 1931.

———. *Regimen in Acute Diseases (Appendix)*. In *Hippocrates*, vol. 6, ed. Paul Potter. LCL. Cambridge: Harvard University Press, 1988.

"Histoire de Thaïs." Trans. F. Nau. *Annales du Musée Guimet* 30 (1903): 51–114.

Historia Monachorum in Aegypto. Ed. A.-J. Festugière. Subsidia Hagiographica 34. Brussels: Société des Bollandistes, 1961.

———. *The Lives of the Desert Fathers*. Trans. Norman Russell. London: Cistercian, 1980.

Iamblichus. *De vita Pythagorica*. Ed. Augustus Nauck. Amsterdam: Hakkert, 1965.

Isaac the Syrian. *The Ascetical Homilies of St. Isaac the Syrian*. Trans. the Holy Transfiguration Monastery [D. Miller]. Boston: Holy Transfiguration Monastery, 1984.

Ishodad of Merv. *The Commentaries*. Ed. Margaret Dunlop Gibson. Vol. 5. Horae Semiticae 9. Cambridge: Cambridge University Press, 1916.

Isidore of Pelusium. *Epistulae*. PG 78.177–1645.

Jacob of Serug. *Homily on Symeon the Stylite*. Trans. Susan Ashbrook Harvey. In *Ascetic Behavior in Greco-Roman Antiquity: A Sourcebook*. Ed. Vincent Winbush. Minneapolis: Fortress, 1990, pp. 15–28.

———. "Jacob of Serugh's Homilies on the Spectacles of the Theatre." Ed. C. Moss. *Muséon* 48 (1935): 87–112.

John Chrysostom. *Ad populum Antiochenum de statuis*. PG 49.15–222.

———. *Adversus oppugnatores vitae monasticae*. PG 47.319–386.

———. *Ad viduam juniorem*. PG 48.599–610.

———. *De sanctum Babyla contra Julianum et Gentiles*. PG 50.571–8.

———. *Saint John Chrysostom, Apologist*. Trans. Margaret A. Shatkin. FOTC 73. Washington, D.C.: Catholic University Press, 1985.

———. *Homilia in Matt*. 70. PG 58.665–662.

———. *Homiliae in 1 Cor*. PG 61.9–382.

John Malalas. *Chronicle*. Trans. Elizabeth Jeffreys et al. Byzantina Australiensia 4. Melbourne: Australian Association for Byzantine Studies, 1986.

John Moschus. *Pratum Spirituale*. PG 87/3.2851–3112.

———. *Le Pré spirituel*. Trans. M.-J. Rouët de Journel. SC 12. Paris: Cerf, 1946.

———. *The Spiritual Meadow*. Trans. John Wortley. Kalamazoo: Cistercian, 1992.

John of Damascus. *On the Divine Images*. PG 94.1231–420.

———. *On the Divine Images: Three Apologies against Those Who Attack the Divine Images*. Trans. David Anderson. Crestwood, N.Y.: St. Vladimir's Seminary, 1980.

———. *Sacra Parallela*. PG 95.1040–1588, 96.9–442.

John of Ephesus. *Ioannis Ephesini historiae ecclesiasticae pars tertia*. Ed. and trans. E. W. Brooks. CSCO 105/54, 106/55. Paris: e Typographeo Reipublica, 1935–36.

———. *Lives of the Eastern Saints*. Ed. and trans. E. W. Brooks. PO 17 (1923): 1–307; 18 (1924): 513–698; 19 (1925): 153–285.

John of Nikiu. *The Chronicle of John, Bishop of Nikiu*. Trans. R. H. Charles. London: Williams and Norgate, 1916.

John of Stobi. *Anthologium*. 5 vols. 2nd ed. Ed. C. Wachsmuth and O. Hense. Berlin: Weidmann, 1958. (First edition, 1884–1923)

———. *Florilegium*. 4 vols. Ed. Augustus Meinecke. Leipzig: Teubner, 1855–57.

John Rufus. *Plerophoriae*. Ed. F. Nau. *PO* 8 (1912): 1–208.

Julian. *Orations. The Works of the Emperor Julian*. 3 vols. Ed. Wilmer Cave Wright. LCL. London: Heinemann, 1913–30.

La légende de S. Spyridon, évêque de Trimithonte. Trans. P. van den Ven. Bibliothèque du Muséon 33. Louvain: Publications universitaires, 1953, pp. 104–28.

La légende Syriac de Saint Alexis, l'homme de Dieu. Ed. and trans. Arthur Amiaud. Paris: Vieweg, 1889.

Leontius of Neapolis. *Opera*. PG 93.1565–748.

———. *Life of John the Almsgiver*. [Editions and translations:]

———. ———. *Leben des heiligen Iohannes des Barmherzigen*. Ed. H. Gelzer. Freiburg: Mohr, 1893.

———. ———. In *Vie de Syméon le Fou et Vie de Jean de Chypre*. Ed. and trans. A. J. Festugière. Bibliothèque archéologique et historique 95. Paris: Geuthner, 1974, pp. 257–637.

———. ———. In *Three Byzantine Saints*. Trans. Elizabeth Dawes and Norman H. Baynes. Crestwood, N.Y.: Saint Vladimir's Seminary, 1977, pp. 199–262.

———. *Life of Symeon the Fool*. [Editions and translations:]

———. ———. *Das Leben des heiligen Narren Symeon von Leontios von Neapolis*. Ed. Lennart Rydén. Studia Graeca Upsaliensia 4. Uppsala: Almquist and Wiksell, 1963.

———. ———. In *Vie de Syméon le Fou et Vie de Jean de Chypre*. Ed. with trans. and commentary by A. J. Festugière. (Greek text of the *Life of Symeon* edited by Lennart Rydén.) Bibliothèque archéologique et historique 95. Paris: Geuthner, 1974, pp. 1–222.

———. ———. *O agios Symeōn o dia Christon salos*. Trans. G. Boudarēs and P. Giachanatzēs. Thessalonica: To Periboli tēs Panagias, 1984.

———. ———. *Byzantinische Legenden*. Trans. Hans Lietzmann. Jena: Diederichs, 1911.

———. ———. *Byzantské legendy: Vyber textu že IV.–XII. stoleti*. Prague: Vyšehrad, 1980, pp. 73–110.

———. ———. *Leven van Symeon de Dwass*. Trans. W. J. Aerts. Bonheiden, Belgium: Monastieke Cahiers, 1990.

———. ———. *I Santi folli di Bisanzio*. Trans. P. Cesaretti. Milan: Mondadori, 1990.

———. ———. *Vizantijskie legendy*. Ed. and trans. S. V. Poljakova. Leningrad: Nauka, 1972.

Liber Graduum. Ed. Michael Kmosko. Patrologia Syriaca 3. Paris: Firmin-Didot, 1926.

Life of Andrew the Fool. PG 111.628–888.

Life of Daniel the Stylite. Les saints stylites, ed. H. Delehaye. Subsidia Hagiographica 14. Brussels: Société des Bollandistes, 1923, pp. 1–94.

———. In *Three Byzantine Saints*. Trans. Elizabeth Dawes and Norman H. Baynes. Crestwood, N.Y.: St. Vladimir's Seminary, 1977, pp. 1–71.

Life of Epiphanius of Salamis. PG 41.23–116.

Life of Melania the Younger. Trans. Elizabeth A. Clark. Studies in Women and Religion 14. Lewiston: Mellen, 1984.

Life of Nicholas of Sion. Ed. and trans. Ihor Ševčenko and Nancy Patterson Ševčenko. Brookline, Mass.: Hellenic College, 1984.

Lucian. *Demonax*. In *Lucian*, vol. 1, ed. A. M. Harmon. LCL. London: Heinemann, 1927.

———. *The Passing of Peregrinus*. In *Lucian*, vol. 5, ed. A. M. Harmon. LCL. Cambridge: Harvard University Press, 1936.

———. *Philosophies for Sale*. In *Lucian*, vol. 2, ed. A. M. Harmon. LCL. London: Heinemann, 1929.

Pseudo-Macarius. *Die 50 geistlichen Homilien des Makarios*. Ed. Hermann Dörries et al. Berlin: de Gruyter, 1964.

———. *Intoxicated with God: Fifty Spiritual Homilies of Macarius*. Trans. George A. Maloney. Denville, N.J.: Dimension Books, 1978.

Mansi, G. D. *Sacrorum conciliorum nova et amplissima collectio*. 53 vols. Paris: Weller, 1901–27.

Manuel Moschopoulus. *De ratione examinandae orationibus libellus [Peri Schedōn]*. Paris: Stephanus, 1545.

Martyrdom of Polycarp. In *The Acts of the Christian Martyrs*. Ed. Herbert Musurillo. Oxford: Clarendon, 1972, pp. 2–21.

Maximus the Confessor. *Ambigua*. PG 91.1032–417.

———. *Epistulae*. PG 91.364–649.

———. *Relatio motionis*. PG 90.109–29.

Menologii anonymi byzantini saeculi X. Ed. Basilius Latyšev. St. Petersburg, 1912.

Menologium of Basil II. PG 117.9–614.

Michael Psellus. "Encomium on Symeon Metaphrastes." *Scripta minora*. Ed. Edward Kurtz. Vol. 1. Milan: Società editrice "vita e pensiero," 1936, pp. 94–107.

Michael the Syrian. *Chronique*. 3 vols. Ed. and trans. J.-B. Chabot. Paris: Leroux, 1899–1905.

Nicephorus. *Short History*. Ed. and trans. Cyril Mango. Dumbarton Oaks Texts 10. Washington, D.C.: Dumbarton Oaks, 1990.

Origen. *Contra Celsum*. PG 11.641–1632.

———. *Contra Celsum*. Trans. Henry Chadwick. Cambridge: Cambridge University Press, 1953.

———. *In Iohannem*. PG 14.21–830.

Palladius. *Lausiac History*. 2 vols. Ed. C. Butler. Text and Studies: Contributions to Biblical and Patristic Literature 6. Cambridge: Cambridge University Press, 1898–1904.

———. *The Lausiac History*. Trans. Robert T. Meyer. ACW 34. New York: Newman, 1964.

Pélagie la Pénitente: Metamorphoses d'une légende. Vol. 1, *Les textes et leur histoire*. Séminar d'Histoire des Textes. Paris: Études Augustiniennes, 1981.

Philo. *De plantatione.* In *Philo,* vol. 3, ed. F. H. Colson and G. H. Whitaker. LCL. London: Heinemann, 1930.

———. *Quod omnis probus liber sit.* In *Philo,* vol. 9, ed. F. H. Colson. LCL. London: Heinemann, 1939.

Photius. *Bibliothèque.* 8 vols. Ed. and trans. R. Henry. Paris: Les Belles Lettres, 1959–77.

Pliny the Elder. *Natural History.* 9 vols. Ed. H. Rackham and W. H. S. Jones. LCL. London: Heinemann, 1938–63.

Plutarch. *Moralia.* 15 vols. Ed. F. C. Babbitt et al. LCL. Cambridge: Harvard University Press, 1927–76.

Porphyry. *Vita Pythagorae.* Ed. A. Nauck. Leipzig: Teubner, 1886.

Procopius. *Anecdota.* Ed. H. B. Dewing. LCL. Cambridge: Harvard University Press, 1969.

Romanus. *Rōmanou tou Melōdou Hymnoi.* Vol. 3.2. Ed. N. B. Thomadakis et al. Athens: Typographeion Mēna Myrtidē, 1957.

———. *Kontakia of Romanos, Byzantine Melodist I: On the Person of Christ.* Trans. Marjorie Carpenter. Columbia: University of Missouri Press, 1970.

Scholia in Dionysii Thracis Artem Grammaticum. Ed. A. Hilgard. Grammatici graeci 3. Leipzig: Teubner, 1901.

Simplicius. *Commentary on the Enchiridion of Epictetus.* In *Theophrasti Characteres, Marci Antonii Commentarii Epicteti . . . et Enchiridion cum Commentario Simplicii.* Ed. F. Dübner. Paris: Firmin-Didot, 1872.

Sozomen. *Historia ecclesiastica.* Ed. J. Bidez and G. C. Hansen. Die griechischen christlichen Schriftsteller der ersten drei Jahrhundert 50. Berlin: Akademie-Verlag, 1960.

Le Synaxaire arménien de Ter Israel (XII. mois de Hrotits). Ed. and trans. G. Bayan. PO 21 (1930): 681–838.

Synaxarium ecclesiae Constantinopolitanae e codice Sirmondiano nunc Berolinensi adiectis synaxariis selectis. Ed. Hippolyte Delehaye. Propylaeum ad *Acta Sanctorum Novembris.* Brussels: Société des Bollandistes, 1902.

Theodoret of Cyrrhus. *De providentia.* PG 83.556–773.

———. *Discours sur la providence.* Trans. Yvan Azéma. Paris: Les Belles Lettres, 1954.

———. *Graecarum affectionum curatio.* 2 vols. Ed. and trans. Pierre Canivet. SC 57. Paris: Cerf, 1958.

———. *Historia ecclesiastica.* PG 82.881–1280.

———. *L'histoire des moines de Syrie.* 2 vols. Ed. P. Canivet and A. Leroy-Molinghen, SC 234. Paris: Cerf, 1977.

———. *A History of the Monks of Syria.* Trans. R. M. Price. Kalamazoo: Cistercian, 1985.

Theophanes. *The Chronicle.* Trans. Harry Turtledove. Philadelphia: University of Pennsylvania Press, 1982.

Theophylact Simocatta. *Epistulae.* Ed. Joseph Zanetto. Leipzig: Teubner, 1985.

La vie ancienne de S. Syméon Stylite le jeune (521–592). 2 vols. Ed. P. van den Ven. Subsidia Hagiographica 32. Brussels: Société des Bollandistes, 1962–70.

"La Vision de Kaioumos et le sort éternel de Philentolos Olympiou." Ed. F. Halkin.
    AB 63 (1945): 56–64.

Secondary Sources

Abrahamse, Dorothy Zani de Ferranti. "Hagiographic Sources for Byzantine
    Cities, 500–900 A.D." Ph.D. diss., University of Michigan, 1967.
Adams, J. N. *The Latin Sexual Vocabulary*. Baltimore: Johns Hopkins University
    Press, 1982.
Aerts, Willem. "Emesa in der Vita Symeonis Sali von Leontios von Neapolis." In
    From Late Antiquity to Early Byzantium. Ed. Vladimír Vavrínek. Prague: Aca-
    demia, 1985, pp. 113–16.
———. "Leontios of Neapolis and Cypriot Dialect Genesis." *Praktika B' diethnous
    Kypriologikou Synedriou*. Vol. 2. Nicosia: Etaireia Kypriakōn Spoudōn, 1986,
    pp. 379–89.
Allen, Pauline. *Evagrius Scholasticus the Church Historian*. Études et Documents 41.
    Louvain: Spicilegium Sacrum Lovaniense, 1981.
———. "The 'Justinianic' Plague." *Byzantion* 49 (1979): 5–20.
Asmus, Rudolf. "Der Kyniker Sallustius bei Damascius." *Neue Jahrbücher für das
    klassisch altertum Geschichte und deutsche Literatur* 25 (1910): 504–22.
Athanassiadi-Fowden, Polymnia. *Julian and Hellenism: An Intellectual Biography*.
    Oxford: Clarendon, 1981.
Attridge, Harold W. *First Century Cynicism in the Epistles of Heraclitus*. Missoula,
    Mont.: Scholars, 1976.
———. "The Philosophical Critique of Religion." In *Aufstieg und Niedergang*
    II.16.1. Berlin: de Gruyter, 1978, pp. 45–78.
Barns, J. "A New Gnomologium." *Classical Quarterly* 44 (1950): 126–37; 45 (1951):
    1–19.
Benz, Ernst. "Christus und Sokrates in der alten Kirche." *ZNTW* 24 (1950/51):
    195–224.
———. "Heilige Narrheit." *Kyrios* 3 (1938): 1–55.
Billerbeck, Margarethe. *Epiktet, Vom Kynismus: Herausgegeben und Übersetzung mit
    einem Kommentar*. Philosophia Antiqua 34. Leiden: Brill, 1978.
———. *Der Kyniker Demetrius*. Leiden: Brill, 1979.
Bowersock, G. W. *Julian the Apostate*. Cambridge: Harvard University Press, 1978.
Brancacci, Aldo. *Rhetorike philosophousa: Dione Crisostomo nella cultura antica e bi-
    zantina*. Rome: Bibliopolis, 1986.
Brock, Sebastian. "An Early Syriac Life of Maximus the Confessor." *AB* 91 (1973):
    299–346.
Brock, Sebastian, and Susan Ashbrook Harvey. *Holy Women of the Syrian Orient*.
    Berkeley: University of California Press, 1987.
Brown, Peter. *The Body and Society: Men, Women, and Sexual Renunciation in Early
    Christianity*. New York: Columbia University Press, 1988.

———. "The Problem of Miraculous Feeding in the Graeco-Roman World." In *Center for Hermeneutical Studies: Colloquy 42.* Berkeley: Graduate Theological Union, 1982, pp. 16–24.

———. "The Rise and Function of the Holy Man in Late Antiquity." *JRS* 61 (1971): 80–101. Reprinted in *Society and the Holy in Late Antiquity* (Berkeley: University of California Press, 1982), pp. 103–52.

———. "The Saint as Exemplar in Late Antiquity." *Representations* 1.2 (1983): 1–25. Reprinted in *Saints and Virtues,* ed. J. S. Hawley (Berkeley: University of California Press, 1987), pp. 1–23.

———. *The World of Late Antiquity.* New York: Norton, 1972.

Browning, Robert. "Byzantium and Islam in Cyprus in the Early Middle Ages." *Epeteris tou Kentrou Epistemonikon Spoudon* 9 (1977/79): 101–16. Reprinted in *History, Language, and Literacy in the Byzantine World* (London: Variorum, 1989), III.

———. "The 'Low Level' Saint's Life in the Early Byzantine World." In *The Byzantine Saint.* Ed. Sergei Hackel. University of Birmingham, 14th Spring Symposium of Byzantine Studies. Studies Supplementary to *Sobornost* 5. San Bernardino, Calif.: Borgo, 1983, pp. 117–27. Reprinted in *History, Language, and Literacy in the Byzantine World* (London: Variorum 1989), VIII.

Bultmann, Rudolf. *Der Stil der paulinischen Predigt und die kynisch-stoische Diatribe.* Göttingen: Vandenhoeck und Ruprecht, 1910.

Cameron, Alan. *Circus Factions.* Oxford: Oxford University Press, 1976.

———. "The Last Days of the Academy at Athens." *Proceedings of the Cambridge Philological Society* 195; n.s. 15 (1969): 7–30.

Cameron, Averil. *Christianity and the Rhetoric of Empire: The Development of a Christian Discourse.* Berkeley: University of California Press, 1991.

———. "Cyprus at the Time of the Arab Conquests." *Epetiris tis Kypriakis Etaireias Istorikōn Spoudōn 1989.* Nicosia, 1992, pp. 27–50.

———. *The Mediterranean World in Late Antiquity, AD 395–600.* London: Routledge, 1993.

———. "The Theotokos in Sixth Century Constantinople." *JThS* n.s. 29 (1978): 79–108. Reprinted in *Continuity and Change in Sixth-Century Byzantium* (London: Variorum, 1981), XVI.

———. "The Virgin's Robe: An Episode in the History of Early Seventh-Century Constantinople." *Byzantion* 49 (1979): 42–56. Reprinted in *Continuity and Change in Sixth-Century Byzantium* (London: Variorum, 1981), XVII.

Canivet, P. *Histoire d'une enterprise apologétique au ve siècle.* Paris: Bloud et Gay, 1957.

Catafygiotu-Topping, E. "Romanos, On the Entry into Jerusalem: A *Basilikos Logos.*" *Byzantion* 47 (1977): 65–91.

Certeau, Michel de. *La Fable mystique: XVIe–XVIIe siècle.* Paris: Gallimard, 1982.

Chadwick, Henry. "John Moschus and His Friend Sophronius the Sophist." *JThS* 25 (1974): 41–74.

Challis, Natalie, and Horace W. Dewey. "Byzantine Models for Russia's Literature of Divine Folly (*Jurodstvo*)." In *Papers in Slavic Philology in Honor of James Ferrell*. Vol. 1. Ed. Benjamin Stolz. Ann Arbor: University of Michigan, Department of Slavic Languages and Literatures, 1977, pp. 36–48.

Chesnut, Roberta. *Three Monophysite Christologies*. Oxford: Oxford University Press, 1976.

Chitty, Derwas J. *The Desert a City*. Oxford: Blackwell, 1966.

Clark, Donald Lemen. *Rhetoric in Greco-Roman Education*. New York: Columbia University Press, 1957.

Clark, Elizabeth A. "Ascetic Renunciation and Feminine Advancement: A Paradox of Late Ancient Christianity." *Anglican Theological Review* 63 (1981): 240–57.

———. "New Perspectives on the Origenist Controversy: Human Embodiment and Ascetic Strategies." *Church History* 59 (1990): 145–62.

———. *The Origenist Controversy: The Cultural Construction of an Early Christian Debate*. Princeton: Princeton University Press, 1992.

Claude, Dietrich. *Die byzantinische Stadt im 6. Jahrhundert*. Byzantinisches Archiv 13. Munich: Beck, 1969.

Cobham, Claude Delaval. *Excerpta Cypria: Materials for a History of Cyprus*. Cambridge: Cambridge University Press, 1908.

Coleman-Norton, P. R. "St. Chrysostom and the Greek Philosophers." *Classical Philology* 25 (1930): 305–17.

Colish, Marcia L. *The Stoic Traditions from Antiquity to the Early Middle Ages*. Vol. 1, *Stoicism in Classical Latin Literature*. Leiden: Brill, 1985.

Conca, Fabrizio. "La narrazione nell'agiografia tardo greca." In *Le trasformazioni della cultura nella tarda antichità*. Ed. Claudia Giuffrida and Mario Mazza. Atti del Convegno tenuto a Catania Università degli Studi, 27 sett.–2 ott. 1982. Rome: Jouvence, 1985, pp. 647–61.

Coulie, Bernard. *Les Richesses dans l'oeuvre de Saint Grégoire de Nazianze*. Louvain: Institut Orientaliste, 1985.

Crouzel, Henri. "L'Imitation et la 'suite' de Dieu et du Christ dans les premiers siècles chrétiens ainsi que leurs sources gréco-romaines et hébraïques." *JAC* 21 (1978): 7–41.

Dagron, Gilbert. "L'Homme sans honneur ou le saint scandaleux." *Annales* 45 (1990): 929–39.

Dagron, Gilbert, and Vincent Déroche. "Juifs et Chrétiens dans l'orient du viie siècle." *Travaux et mémoires* 11 (1991): 17–273.

Dalton, O. M. "A Byzantine Silver Treasure from the District of Kerynia, Cyprus, Now Preserved in the British Museum." *Archaeologia* 57 (1900): 159–74.

———. "A Second Silver Treasure from Cyprus." *Archaeologia* 60 (1906): 1–24.

Delehaye, Hippolyte. *Les Passions des martyrs et les genres littéraires*. Subsidia Hagiographica 13B. Brussels: Société des Bollandistes, 1966.

———. "Saints de Chypre." *AB* 26 (1907): 161–301.

———. *Les saints stylites*. Subsidia Hagiographica 14. Brussels: Société des Bollandistes, 1923.

————. *Synaxaires byzantins, ménologes, typica*. London: Variorum, 1977.

Dembińska, Maria. "Diet: A Comparison of Food Consumption between Some Eastern and Western Monasteries in the 4th–12th Centuries." *Byzantion* 55 (1985): 431–62.

Déroche, Vincent. "L'Authenticité de l' 'Apologie contre les Juifs' de Léontios de Néapolis." *Bulletin de corrrespondance hellénique* 110 (1986): 655–69.

————. "La polémique anti-Judaïque au vi^e et au viie siècle: un mémento inédit, les Képhalaia." *Travaux et mémoires* 11 (1991): 275–311.

Dieten, Jan Louis van. *Geschichte der Patriarchen von Sergios I. bis Johannes VI. (610–715)*. Enzyklopädie der Byzantinistik 24. Amsterdam: Hakkert, 1972.

Dikigoropoulos, A. I. "The Political Status of Cyprus A.D. 648–965." In *Report of the Department of Antiquities, Cyprus, 1940–1948*. Nicosia: Government Printing Office, 1958, pp. 94–114.

Dölger, F. *Regesten der Kaiserurkunden des oströmischen Reiches von 565–1453*. Munich: Oldenbourg, 1924–65.

Dols, Michael. "Insanity in Byzantine and Islamic Medicine." *DOP* 38 (1984): 135–48.

Döring, Klaus. *Exemplum Socrates: Studien zur Sokrates Nachwirkung in der kynisch-stoischen Popularphilosophie der frühen Kaiserzeit und im frühen Christentum*. Hermes Einzelschriften 42. Wiesbaden: Steiner, 1974.

Douglas, Mary. "Jokes." *Implicit Meanings: Essays in Anthropology*. London: Routledge and Kegan Paul, 1975, pp. 90–114.

————. *Natural Symbols: Explorations in Cosmology*. 2nd ed. New York: Pantheon, 1982. (First edition, 1970)

————. "Social Preconditions of Enthusiasm and Heterodoxy." In *Forms of Symbolic Action: Proceedings of the 1969 Annual Spring Meeting of the American Ethnological Society*. Ed. Robert F. Spencer. Seattle: University of Washington Press, 1969, pp. 69–80.

Downing, F. Gerald. "A Bas les Aristos: The Relevance of Higher Literature for the Understanding of the Earliest Christian Writings." *NovTest* 30 (1988): 212–30.

————. *Christ and the Cynics*. Sheffield: Sheffield Academic, 1988.

————. "Compositional Conventions and the Synoptic Problem." *JBL* 107 (1988): 68–85.

————. "Cynics and Christians." *NTSt* 30 (1984): 584–93.

————. *Cynics and Christian Origins*. Edinburgh: T. & T. Clark, 1992.

————. "Quite like Q: A Genre for 'Q': The 'Lives' of the Cynic Philosophers." *Biblica* 69 (1988): 196–225.

————. "The Social Contexts of Jesus the Teacher." *NTSt* 33 (1987): 439–51.

Drijvers, Han J. W. "Hellenistic and Oriental Origins." In *The Byzantine Saint*. University of Birmingham, 14th Spring Symposium of Byzantine Studies. Studies Supplementary to *Sobernost* 5. Ed. Sergei Hackel. San Bernardino, Calif.: Borgo, 1983, pp. 25–33.

————. "Die Legende des heiligen Alexius und der Typus des Gottesmannes im syrischen Christentum." In *Typus, Symbol, Allegorie bei den östlichen Vätern und ihren Parallelen im Mittelalter*. Ed. Margot Schmidt and Carl Friedrich Geyer. Eichstätter Beiträge 4. Regensburg: Pustet, 1982, pp. 187–217.

Dudley, Donald R. *A History of Cynicism from Diogenes to the Sixth Century A.D.* London: Methuen, 1937.

Ehrhard, A. "Zu den 'Sacra Parallela' des Johannes Damascenus und dem Florilegium des 'Maximus.'" *BZ* 10 (1901): 394–415.

Elisséeff, N. "Ḥimṣ." *Encyclopedia of Islam*. New edition.

Elliot, Alison Goddard. *Roads to Paradise: Reading the Lives of the Early Saints*. Hanover, N.H.: University Press of New England, 1987.

Estienne, H. *Thesaurus Linguae Graecae*. Vol. 7. 1572. Ed. A. Firmin-Didot. Paris: F. Didot frères, 1865.

Fedetov, George P. *The Russian Religious Mind II: The Middle Ages, the 13th to the 15th Centuries*. Ed. with a foreword by John Meyendorff. Belmont, Mass.: Nordland, 1975.

Fischel, Henry A. *Rabbinic Literature and Greco-Roman Philosophy*. Leiden: Brill, 1973.

————. "Studies in Cynicism and the Ancient Near East: The Transformation of a *Chria*." In *Religions in Antiquity: Essays in Memory of Erwin Ramsdell Goodenough*. Ed. J. Neusner. Leiden: Brill, 1968, pp. 372–411.

Flusin, Bernard. *Vie et miracle dans l'oeuvre de Cyrille de Scythopolis*. Paris: Études Augustiniennes, 1983.

Foucault, Michel. *The Care of the Self*. Vol. 3 of *The History of Sexuality*. Trans. Robert Hurley. New York: Vintage, 1986.

Frankfurter, David T. M. "Stylites and *Phallobates*: Pillar Religions in Late Ancient Syria." *VC* 44 (1990): 168–98.

Frend, W. H. C. *The Rise of the Monophysite Movement*. Cambridge: Cambridge University Press, 1972.

Frendo, D. F. "Classical and Christian Influences in the *Heracliad* of George of Pisidia." *Classical Bulletin* 64.2 (1986): 53–62.

Frey, R. P. Jean-Baptiste. *Corpus inscriptionum judaicarum*. Vol. 2. Vatican: Pontificio instituto di archeologia christiana, 1952.

Fritz, K. von. *Quellenuntersuchung zu Leben und Philosophie des Diogenes von Sinope*. Philologos Suppl. 18.2. Leipzig: Dietrich, 1926.

Frolow, A. "La Vraie Croix et les expéditions d'Héraclius en Perse." *REB* 11 (1953): 88–105.

Gager, John G., ed. *Curse Tablets and Binding Spells from the Ancient World*. New York: Oxford University Press, 1992.

Gagniers, Jean des, and Tran Tam Tinh. *Soloi: Dix campagnes de fouilles (1964–1974)*. Vol. 1. Récherches archéologique de l'Université Laval. Sainte-Foy, Québec: Université Laval, 1985.

Geffcken, Johannes. *Kynika und Verwandtes*. Heidelberg: C. Winter, 1909.

————. *The Last Days of Greco-Roman Paganism*. 1929. Trans. Sabine MacCormack. Amsterdam: North Holland, 1978.

————. *Sokrates und das alte Christentum*. Heidelberg: C. Winter, 1908.

Gelzer, Heinrich. "Ein griechischer Volksschriftsteller des 7. Jahrhunderts." In *Ausgewählte Kleine Schriften*. Leipzig: Teubner, 1907, pp. 1–56.

Gerhard, G. A. "Zur Legende von Kyniker Diogenes." *Archiv für Religionswissenschaft* 15 (1912): 388–408.

Goehring, James. "The Encroaching Desert: Literary Production and Ascetic Space in Early Christian Egypt." *JECS* 1 (1993): 281–96.

Goraïnoff, Irina. *Les Fols en Christ dans la tradition orthodoxe*. [Paris]: Desclée de Brouwer, 1983.

Gouillard, Jean. "Quatre procès de mystiques à Byzance (vers 960–1143): Inspiration et autorité." *REB* 36 (1978): 5–81.

Goulet-Cazé, Marie-Odile. *L'Ascèse Cynique: Un Commentaire de Diogène Laërce VI 70–71*. Paris: Vrin, 1986.

Grant, Robert M. "Charges of 'Immorality' against Various Religious Groups in Antiquity." In *Studies in Gnosticism and Hellenistic Religions Presented to Gilles Quispel*. Ed. R. van den Broek and M. J. Vermaseren. Leiden: Brill, 1981, pp. 161–70.

————. *Christian Beginnings: Apocalypse to History*. London: Variorum, 1983.

Gregg, Robert C., and Dennis E. Groh. *Early Arianism—A View of Salvation*. Philadelphia: Fortress, 1981.

Grégoire, Réginald. *Manuale di agiologia: introduzione alla letteratura agiographica*. Bibliotheca Montisfani 12. Fabriano: Monastero San Silvestro Abate, 1987.

Grierson, Philip. *Byzantine Coins*. London: Methuen, 1982.

Griffith, Sidney H. "The Gospel in Arabic: An Inquiry into Its Appearance in the First Abbasid Century." *Oriens Christianus* 69 (1985): 127–67.

Grmek, Mirko D. *Diseases of the Ancient Greek World*. Trans. Mireille Muellner and Leonard Muellner. Baltimore: Johns Hopkins University Press, 1989.

Grosdidier de Matons, José. "Les Thèmes d'édification dans la Vie d'André Salos." *Travaux et mémoires* 4 (1970): 277–329.

Grumel, V. "Recherches sur l'histoire du monothélisme." *Echos d'Orient* 27 (1928): 16–28.

Guidorizzi, Giulio. "Motivi fabieschi nell'agiographica bizantina." In *Studi bizantini e neogreci: Atti del IV congresso nazionale di studi bizantini*. Ed. Pietro Luigi Leone. Galatina: Congedo, 1983, pp. 457–67.

Guillaumont, Antoine. "Le Dépaysement comme forme d'ascèse dans le monachisme ancien." *Annuaire de l'École Practique des Hautes Études, Section des Sciences Religieuses* 76 (1968/9): 31–58.

————. *Les "Képhalaia Gnostica" d'Évagre le Pontique et l'histoire de l'origénisme chez les grecs et chez les syriens*. Patristica Sorbonensia 5. Paris: du Seuil, 1962.

Hackett, J. *A History of the Orthodox Church of Cyprus*. London: Methuen, 1901.

Hadot, Ilsetraut. "La vie et l'oeuvre de Simplicius." In *Simplicius: Sa vie, son oeuvre, sa survie: Actes du colloque international de Paris (28 Sept.–1 Oct. 1985)*. Ed. Ilsetraut Hadot. Berlin: de Gruyter, 1987, pp. 3–39.

Haldon, John F. *Byzantium in the Seventh Century*. Cambridge: Cambridge University Press, 1990.

———. "Some Considerations on Byzantine Society and Economy in the Seventh Century." *Byzantinische Forschungen* 10 (1985): 75–112.

Halkin, F. "La Vision de Kaioumos et le sort éternal de Philentolos Olympiou." *AB* 63 (1945): 56–64.

Hargar, F. P. "Natur." *Historisches Wörterbuch der Philosophie*. Basel: Schwebe, 1971–.

Harnack, Adolf von. "Socrates in die alten Kirche." In *Reden und Aufsätze*. Vol. 1. Giessen: J. Ricker, 1904, pp. 27–48.

Harvey, Susan Ashbrook. *Asceticism and Society in Crisis: John of Ephesus and* The Lives of the Eastern Saints. Berkeley: University of California Press, 1990.

———. "The Sense of a Stylite: Perspectives on Symeon the Elder." *VC* 42 (1988): 376–94.

———. "Women in Early Byzantine Hagiography: Reversing the Story." In *That Gentle Strength: Historical Perspectives on Women in Christianity*. Ed. Lynda L. Coon, Katherine J. Haldane, and Elisabeth W. Sommer. Charlottesville: University Press of Virginia, 1990, pp. 36–59.

Hauptmann, Peter. "Die 'Narren um Christi Willen' in der Ostkirche." *Kirche im Osten* 2 (1959): 27–49.

Henderson, Jeffrey. *The Maculate Muse: Obscene Language in Attic Comedy*. New Haven: Yale University Press, 1975.

Hendy, Michael. *Studies in the Byzantine Monetary Economy, 300–1450*. Cambridge: Cambridge University Press, 1985.

Herrin, Judith. *The Formation of Christendom*. Princeton: Princeton University Press, 1987.

Hill, George. *A History of Cyprus*. Vol. 1. Cambridge: Cambridge University Press, 1940.

Hitti, Philip K. *History of the Arabs: From the Earliest Times to the Present*. 10th ed. New York: St. Martin's, 1970.

Hock, Ronald F., and Edward N. O'Neil. *The Chreia in Ancient Rhetoric*. Vol. 1, *The Progymnasmata*. Graeco-Roman Religion Series 9. Atlanta: Scholars, 1986.

Hofstra, J. "Leontius van Neapolis als Hagiograaf." In *De heiligenverering in de eerste eeuwen van het christendom*. Ed. A. Hilhorst. Nijmegen: Dekker en van de Vegt, 1988, pp. 186–92.

Hoïstad, Ragnar. *Cynic Hero and Cynic King*. Uppsala: Gleerup, 1948.

Holl, Karl. "Die *Sacra Parallela* des Johannes Damascenus." *Texte und Untersuchungen* 16 (1897): 1–392.

Hope, Richard. *The Book of Diogenes Laertius*. New York: Columbia University Press, 1930.

Jaeger, Werner. *Early Christianity and Greek Paideia*. Cambridge, Mass.: Belknap, 1961.

Jones, A. H. M. *The Later Roman Empire*. 2 vols. Oxford: Oxford University Press, 1964.

Jones, Christopher P. *The Roman World of Dio Chrysostom*. Cambridge: Harvard University Press, 1978.

Kaegi, Walter. *Byzantium and the Early Islamic Conquests*. Cambridge: Cambridge University Press, 1992.

———. "The Disputed Muslim Negotiations with Cyprus in 649." *Fourteenth Annual Byzantine Studies Conference (1988): Abstracts of Papers*. Houston: Byzantine Studies Conference, 1988, pp. 5–6.

Kaster, Robert A. *Guardians of Language: The Grammarian and Society in Late Antiquity*. Berkeley: University of California Press, 1988.

Keaney, John J. "Moschopulea." *BZ* 64 (1971): 303–21.

Kennedy, Hugh. "The Last Century of Byzantine Syria: A Reinterpretation." *Byzantinische Forschungen* 10 (1985): 141–83.

Kislinger, Ewald. "Symeon Salos' Hund." *JÖB* 38 (1988): 165–70.

Kloppenborg, J. S. *The Formation of Q*. Philadelphia: Fortress, 1987.

Kotter, B. "John Damascene, St." *New Catholic Encyclopedia*. 1967 ed.

Kowalski, Aleksander. *Perfezione e giustizia di Adamo nel Liber Graduum*. Orientalia christiana analecta 232. Rome: Pontificum Institutum Orientale, 1989.

Kresten, Otto. "Leontios von Neapolis als Tachygraph? Hagiographische Texte als Quellen zu Schriftlichkeit und Buchkultur im 6. und 7. Jahrhundert." *Scrittura e civiltà* 1 (1977): 155–75.

Krueger, Derek. "The Bawdy and Society: The Shamelessness of Diogenes in Roman Imperial Culture." In *The Cynics: The Movement in Antiquity and Its Legacy for Europe*. Ed. R. Bracht Branham and Marie-Odile Goulet-Cazé. Forthcoming.

———. "Diogenes the Cynic among the Fourth-Century Fathers." *VC* 47 (1993): 29–49.

———. "The *Life of Symeon the Fool* and the Cynic Tradition." *JECS* 1 (1993): 423–42.

Krumbacher, Karl. *Geschichte der Byzantinischen Literatur von Justinian bis zum Ende des oströmischen Reiches (527–1453)*. Munich: Beck, 1897.

Kyrris, Costas P. "The Admission of the Souls of Immoral but Humane People into the '*Limbus Puerorum*,' According to the Cypriot Abbot Kaïoumos (VIIth Century A.D.) Compared to the Quran's *al 'Araf* (Suras 7:44–46, 57:13ff.)." *Revue des études sud-est européennes* 9 (1971): 461–77.

———. "Cypriot Ascetics and the Christian Orient." *Vyzantinos Domos* 1 (1987): 95–108.

———. *History of Cyprus: With an Introduction to the Geography of Cyprus*. Nicosia: Nicocles, 1985.

Laga, Carl. "Judaism and the Jews in Maximus Confessor's Works: Theoretical Controversy and Practical Attitude." *Byzantinoslavica* 51 (1990): 178–83.

Leduer, Etienne. "Imitation du Christ: II. Tradition Spirituelle." *DS*.

Lifshitz, Baruch. *Donateurs et fondateurs dans les synagogues juives*. Cahiers de la revue biblique 7. Paris: Gabalda, 1967.

Luz, M. "A Description of the Greek Cynic in the Jerusalem Talmud." *JSJ* 20 (1989): 49–60.

Mack, Burton. *The Myth of Innocence*. Philadelphia: Fortress, 1988.

Magoulias, H. J. "The Lives of Byzantine Saints as Sources of Data for the History of Magic in the Sixth and Seventh Centuries A.D.: Sorcery, Relics, and Icons." *Byzantion* 37 (1967): 228–69.

Maisano, Riccardo. "Tradizione orale e sviluppi narrativi nel 'Prato' di Giovanni Mosco." In *Le trasformazioni della cultura nella tarda antichità*. Ed. Claudia Giuffrida and Mario Mazza. Atti del Convegno tenuto a Catania Università degli Studi, 27 sett.–2 ott. 1982. Rome: Jouvence, 1985, pp. 663–77.

Malherbe, Abraham J. "Antisthenes and Odysseus, and Paul at War." *HTR* 76 (1983): 143–73.

———. *The Cynic Epistles: A Study Edition*. Missoula, Mont.: Scholars, 1977.

———. "Exhortation in First Thessalonians." *NovTest* 25 (1983): 238–56.

———. "'Gentle as a Nurse': The Cynic Background to 1 Thess 2." *Novum Testamentum* 12 (1970): 203–17.

———. "'In Season and Out of Season': 2 Timothy 4:2." *JBL* 103 (1984): 235–43.

———. *Paul and the Popular Philosophers*. Minneapolis: Fortress, 1989.

———. *Paul and the Thessalonians*. Philadelphia: Fortress, 1987.

———. "Ps.-Heraclitus, Ep. 4: The Divinization of the Wise Man." *JAC* 21 (1978): 42–64.

———. "Self-Definition Among Epicureans and Cynics." In *Jewish and Christian Self-Definition in the Greco-Roman World*. Vol. 3. Ed. B. F. Meyer and E. P. Sanders. Philadelphia: Fortress, 1983, pp. 46–59.

Mango, Cyril. "A Byzantine Hagiographer at Work: Leontios of Neapolis." In *Byzanz und der Westen: Studien zur Kunst des europäischen Mittelalters*. Ed. Irmgard Hutter. Vienna: Österreichischen Akademie der Wissenschaften, 1984, pp. 25–41.

———. "Chypre: Carrefour du monde byzantin." *XVᵉ Congrès international d'études byzantines: rapports et co-rapports* 5.5. Athens, 1976.

———. "The Life of Saint Andrew the Fool Reconsidered." *Rivista di studi bizantini e slavi* 2 (1982): 297–313.

Markus, Robert. *The End of Ancient Christianity*. Cambridge: Cambridge University Press, 1990.

Marrou, H. I. *A History of Education in Antiquity*. Trans. George Lamb. 1956. Reprint, Madison: University of Wisconsin Press, 1982.

Martindale, J. R. *The Prosopography of the Later Roman Empire*. Vol. 3, A.D. 527–641. 2 bks. Cambridge: Cambridge University Press, 1992.

Meeks, Wayne A. *The Moral World of the First Christians*. Philadelphia: Westminster, 1986.

Meillard, Jean-Marie. "L'Anti-intellectuelisme de Diogène le Cynique." *RevThPh* 115 (1983): 233–46.

Mejer, Jorgen. *Diogenes Laertius and His Hellenistic Background*. Wiesbaden: Steiner, 1978.

Meyendorff, John. *Imperial Unity and Christian Division*. The Church in History 2. Crestwood, N.Y.: St. Vladimir's Seminary, 1989.

Mitford, T. B. "Some New Inscriptions from Early Christian Cyprus." *Byzantion* 20 (1950): 105–75.

Moorhead, John. "Iconoclasm, the Cross, and the Imperial Image." *Byzantion* 55 (1985): 165–79.

Murray, S. *A Study of the Life of Andreas*. Borna-Leipzig: Noske, 1910.

Nachov, I. "Der Mensch in der Philosophie der Kyniker." In *Der Mensch als Mass der Dinge*. Ed. R. Müller. Berlin: Akademie-Verlag, 1976, pp. 361–98.

Nasrallah, J. "Survie de Saint Siméon Stylite l'alépin dans les gaules." *Syria* 51 (1974): 171–97.

Nau, F. "Histoire de Thaïs." *Annales du Musée Guimet* 30 (1903): 51–114.

Nau, F., and L. Clugnet. "Vies et récits d'anacorètes (IVᵉ–VIIᵉ siècles)." *Revue de l'Orient Chrétien* 8 (1903): 91–100.

Niehues-Pröbsting, Heinrich. *Der Kynismus des Diogenes und der Begriff des Zynismus*. Munich: Funk, 1979.

O'Laughlin, Michael Wallace. "Origenism in the Desert: Anthropology and Integration in Evagrius Ponticus." Th.D. diss., Harvard University, 1987.

Ortiz de Urbina, Ignatius. *Patrologia Syriaca*. Rome: Pontifical Institute, 1958.

Ostrogorsky, George. *History of the Byzantine State*. Trans. Joan Hussey. New Brunswick, N.J.: Rutgers University Press, 1969.

Packmohr, Augustinus. *De Diogenes Sinopensis Apothegmatis Questiones Selectae*. Diss. Muenster, 1913.

Paquet, Léonce. *Les Cyniques grecs*. Ottawa: Éditions de L'Université d'Ottawa, 1975.

Patlagean, Evelyne. "Ancient Byzantine Hagiography and Social History." In *Saints and Their Cults: Studies in Religious Sociology, Folklore, and History*. Ed. S. Wilson. Cambridge: Cambridge University Press, 1983, pp. 101–21.

———. *Pauvreté économique et pauvreté sociale à Byzance 4ᵉ–7ᵉ siècles*. Civilisations et Société 48. Paris: Mouton, 1977.

Praechter, K. "Richtungen und Schulen im Neuplatonismus." In *Genethliakon für Carl Robert*. Berlin: Weidmann, 1910, pp. 105–56.

Radermacher, Ludwig. "*Pordē*." In *RE*. Vol. 22.

Rahn, H. "Die Frömmigkeit der Kyniker." *Paideuma* 7 (1960): 280–90.

Ratcliff, Robert Arden. "Steps along the Way of Perfection: The *Liber Graduum* and Early Syrian Monasticism." Ph.D. diss., Emory University, 1988.

Reitzenstein, Richard. *Hellenistische Wundererzählungen*. Leipzig: Teubner, 1906.

Richard, Marcel. "Florilèges spirituels grecs." *DS*.

Riedinger, Rudolf. "Die Lateransynode von 649 und Maximos der Bekenner." In *Maximus Confessor: Actes du Symposium pour Maxime le confesseur (Fribourg, 2–5 Sept. 1980)*. Ed. F. Heinzer and C. Schönborn. Fribourg: Éditions Universitaires, 1982, pp. 111–21.

———, ed. *Concilium Lateranense a. 649 celebratum*. Acta Conciliorum Oecumenicorum, 2nd ser. Vol. 1. Berlin, 1984.

Roccatagliata, Guiseppe. *A History of Ancient Psychiatry*. Contributions in Medical Studies 16. New York: Greenwood, 1986.

Rousselle, Aline. *Porneia: On Desire and the Body in Antiquity*. Trans. Felicia Pheasant. Oxford: Blackwell, 1988.

Rudberg, Gunnar. "Zur Diogenes Tradition." *Symbolae Osloenses* 14 (1935): 22–43.

———. "Zum Diogenes Typus." *Symbolae Osloenses* 15 (1936): 1–18.

Rydén, Lennart. *Bemerkungen zum Leben des heiligen Narren Symeon von Leontios von Neapolis.* Studia Graeca Upsaliensia 6. Uppsala: Almquist and Wiksell, 1970.

———. "The Date of the *Life of Andreas Salos*." *DOP* 32 (1978): 129–55.

———. "The Holy Fool." In *The Byzantine Saint.* Ed. Sergei Hackel. University of Birmingham, 14th Spring Symposium of Byzantine Studies. Studies Supplementary to *Sobornost* 5. San Bernardino, Calif.: Borgo, 1983, pp. 106–13.

———. "Style and Historical Fiction in the Life of St. Andreas Salos." *JÖB* 32 (1982): 175–83.

Sacopoulo, Marina. *La Theotokos à la mandorle de Lythrankomi.* Paris: Maisonneuve et Larose, 1975.

Sansterre, Jean-Marie. *Les Moines grecs et orientaux à Rome aux époques byzantine et carolingienne (milieu du vi^e s.–fin du ixe s.).* 2 vols. Brussels: Palais des académies, 1980.

Saward, John. *Perfect Fools: Folly for Christ's Sake in Catholic and Orthodox Spirituality.* Oxford: Oxford University Press, 1980.

Sayre, Ferrand. *Greek Cynicism and Sources of Cynicism.* Baltimore: Furst, 1948.

Schulz-Falkenthal, Heinz. "Kyniker—Zur inhaltlichen Deutung des Namens." *Wissenschaftliche Zeitschrift des Martin-Luther Universität, Halle-Wittenberg (Gesellschaftsreihe)* 26.2 (1977): 41–49.

Sharf, A. "Byzantine Jewry in the Seventh Century." *BZ* 48 (1955): 103–15.

Sherwood, Polycarp. *An Annotated Date-List of the Works of Maximus the Confessor.* Studia Anselmiana 30. Rome: Pontifical Institute, 1952.

———. *The Earlier Ambigua of Saint Maximus the Confessor and His Refutation of Origenism.* Studia Anselmiana 36. Rome: Pontifical Institute, 1955.

Spanneut, Michel. *Permanence du Stoïcisme: de Zénon à Malraux.* Genbloux, Belgium: Duculot, 1973.

———. *Le Stoïcisme des pères de l'église: de Clément de Rome à Clément d'Alexandrie.* 2nd ed. Paris: du Seuil, 1969.

Speck, Paul. "Zu dem Dialog mit einem Juden des Leontios von Neapolis." *Poikila Byzantina* 4 (1984): 242–49.

Speyer, Wolfgang. *Die Literarische Fälschung im heidnischen und christlischen Altertum: Ein Versuch ihrer Deutung.* Handbuch der Altertumswissenschaft 1.2. Munich: Beck, 1971.

Spidlík, Thomas. "Fous pour le Christ en Orient." *DS.*

Starr, Joshua. "Byzantine Jewry on the Eve of the Arab Conquest (565–638)." *Journal of the Palestine Oriental Society* 15 (1935): 280–93.

———. *The Jews of the Byzantine Empire (641–1204).* Athens: Verlag der "Byzantinisch-Neugriechischen Jahrbucher," 1939.

Stratos, Andreas N. *Byzantium in the Seventh Century.* 5 vols. Trans. Harry T. Hionides. Amsterdam: Hakkert, 1968–80.

Stylianou, A., and J. Stylianou. *The Treasures of Lambousa.* Vasilia, Cyprus, 1969.

Swain, Joseph Ward. *The Hellenistic Origins of Christian Asceticism.* New York, 1916.

Syrkin, Alexander Y. "On the Behavior of the 'Fool for Christ's Sake.'" *History of Religions* 22 (1982): 150–71.

Tardieu, Michel. "Les Calendrier en usage à Harran d'après les source arabes et le commentaire de Simplicius à la Physique d'Aristote." In *Simplicius: Sa vie, son oeuvre, sa survie: Actes du colloque international de Paris (28 Sept.–1 Oct. 1985)*. Ed. Ilsetraut Hadot. Berlin: de Gruyter, 1987, pp. 40–57.

Thesaurus Linguae Graecae: Pilot CD ROM #C (1987).

Thompson, Ewa. *Understanding Russia: The Holy Fool in Russian Culture*. Lanham, Md.: University Press of America, 1987.

Trombley, Frank R. "The Decline of the Seventh-Century Town: The Exception of Euchaita." In *Byzantine Studies in Honor of Milton V. Anastos*. Ed. Speros Vryonis, Jr. Byzantina kai Metabyzantina 4. Malibu: Undena, 1985, pp. 65–90.

Tuckett, C. M. "A Cynic Q?" *Biblica* 70 (1989): 349–76.

Usener, Hermann. *Der Heilige Tychon*. Leipzig: Teubner, 1907.

Vandenbroucke, François. "Fous pour le Christ en Occident." *DS*.

Verghese, P. "The Monothelite Controversy—A Historical Survey." *Greek Orthodox Theological Review* 13 (1968): 196–211.

Vogt, Kari. "La Moniale folle du monastère des Tabbenésiotes: Une interprétation du chapitre 34 de l'Historia Lausiaca de Pallade." *Symbolae Osloenses* 62 (1987): 95–108.

Vööbus, Arthur. *History of Asceticism in the Syrian Orient: A Contribution to the History of Culture in the Near East*. Vol. 3. CSCO Subsidia 81. Louvain: Peeters, 1988.

Ward, Benedicta. *Harlots of the Desert: A Study of Repentence in Early Monastic Sources*. Kalamazoo: Cistercian, 1987.

Warkotsch, Albert. *Antike Philosophie in Urtiel der Kirchenväter: Christlichen Glaube im Widerstreit der Philosophien: Texte und Übersetzungen*. Munich: Schöningh, 1973.

Wessely, C. "Neues über Diogenes den Kyniker." In *Festschrift für Theodor Gomperz*. Vienna, 1902, pp. 67–74.

Whitby, Michael, and Mary Whitby. *The History of Theophylact Simocatta*. Oxford: Clarendon, 1986.

Whittow, Mark. "Ruling the Late Roman and Early Byzantine City: A Continuous History." *Past and Present* 129 (November 1990): 3–29.

Wilson, N. G. *Saint Basil on the Value of Greek Literature*. London: Duckworth, 1975.

———. *Scholars of Byzantium*. Baltimore: Johns Hopkins University Press, 1983.

Wortley, John. "The Political Significance of the Andreas-Salos Apocalypse." *Byzantion* 43 (1973): 248–63.

———. "The *Vita Sancti Andreae Sali* as a Source of Byzantine Social History." *Societas* 4 (1974): 1–20.

Wright, William. *Catalogue of Syriac Manuscripts in the British Museum*. London, 1871.

———. *A Short History of Syriac Literature*. London: Black, 1894.

INDEX

Composition:	G & S Typesetters, Inc.
Text:	10/13 Palatino
Display:	Palatino
Printing and binding:	Thomson-Shore, Inc.